MW01034544

HOW TO COOK AND EAT IN CHINESE

How to Cook
and Eat
in Chinese

BUWEI YANG CHAO

THIRD EDITION
REVISED AND ENLARGED

ECHO POINT BOOKS & MEDIA, LLC
Brattleboro, Vermont

Published by Echo Point Books & Media
Brattleboro, Vermont
www.EchoPointBooks.com

How to Cook and Eat in Chinese
ISBN: 978-1-64837-094-6 (casebound)
          978-1-64837-095-3 (paperback)

Cover design by Kaitlyn Whitaker

Cover image: *Asian Food Frame* by DiViArt, courtesy of
Shutterstock

TO AGNES HOCKING

who told me to write this book

NOTE TO THIRD, REVISED EDITION

"Mrs. Chao, why don't you include some of the more fancy dishes in the next edition of your cookbook? Stewed snakes, monkey's brain, honeyed mice, shark's fin in silver netting—dishes one sometimes hears about and rarely has an opportunity to taste."

My answer is, as many users of the book will confirm, that my purpose in writing such a book was in the first place to instruct and not to impress. Everybody has to cook and eat. If you live where you can get special Chinese materials, well and good. If not, you can always cook in Chinese with American materials, although, since the last edition came out, more and more vegetables and fruits formerly regarded as exotic have appeared in the general markets in some of the larger cities in America. Peas in the pod, bock choy (Chinese green), soybean, tangerine—the newlyweds of today will hardly recall that not so long ago tangerine growers in Florida had to get live pollen from China to make the fruit grow sweet.

My main point of view will then continue to be from the housewife's kitchen, modernized to be sure, with new gadgets with which to demonstrate new things Chinese. Not secret recipes secretly passed along, but general and open principles openly arrived at. Not sliced snails from Foochow or goat's cheese from Kunming, but Louisiana soybean curd made in Long Island or San Francisco. In other words, nothing fancy, but everything folksy, things for folks like you and me.[1]

One of the modern features in household gadgetry that has become common since the last edition of this book is the wide use of freezers or freezing compartments in refrigerators. This has made it possible to do many things with Chinese foods which were formerly not possible. In ordinary refrigerators, fish and fowl rarely keep their fresh flavor if stored for several days, at least not fresh

[1] You mean "folks as you and I"?—Y. R. C.

enough for certain Chinese dishes. But with the advent of deep freezing, I found to my pleasant surprise that deep-frozen food material thawed for immediate use tasted just as fresh as fresh. Different things will keep in deep freeze for different lengths of time, to be sure, but I have found that the times for various categories of food listed in the instruction booklet of your refrigerator (with freezing compartment) are on the whole also applicable to Chinese cooking. The experienced reader and housewife will of course know that it is not good to have something frozen and thawed out and frozen and thawed out again, especially with meat, which loses all flavor this way. The thing to do is that once you have thawed a piece, it should be used and if it cannot be used at one meal, the leftovers can be frozen, which is a different story from re-freezing raw material. Another way I often adopt is to divide a large piece— a ten-pound chuck roast from a sale, a 15-pound striped bass a friend gave me from a fishing trip, or what have you—into portions, each small enough to be used once, and wrap and freeze them separately. If you ever stuff ground meat into the space where the ice tray is supposed to be, as I have often had to, be sure not to make the package bulge too big, or you would never get it out again without thawing out the whole compartment! An obvious advantage of small packaging is of course that you can cook some of a large piece one way one day and another piece another way another day.

Since the last edition of this book, I have eaten a few Chinese meals in homes and restaurants in a few countries, including those in China, I was going to say—but since all provinces from mainland China are well represented in Taiwan in the culinary, as well as many other aspects, it was a kind of epitome of mainland China that I revisited in 1959. Knowing that I had written a cookbook that was circulating in America and Europe, and knowing that I appreciated good and original ideas in cooking, my friends and relatives in Taiwan one after another invited me to their homes (some with name cooks) or their favorite restaurants to show me what's good over cups of warm (literally warm), mellow "Shaohsing" rice wine fermented in Taipei. Some of them warned the restaurants ahead who was going to be among their guests and be sure to keep up their reputation. Thus, at the end of three months I ate more than two hundred dinners. That I did not get sick or gain weight speaks pretty well of the state of the ration in Taiwan.

As in the metropolitan cities in China, the restaurants in Taipei represent the styles of all the provinces famous for their cooking: Shantung, Szechwan, Fukien, Canton, and others. For similar reasons, none of the provincial restaurants keep to their pure original style. Eaters from Shanghai will tell a Hunan or Szechwan restaurant to please go easy on red pepper. Eaters from Canton will tell the waiter in a Yangchow restaurant to be sparing on oil. Thus, there has grown a tendency to converge toward less extreme localisms. This does not mean, however, that you are approaching a melting-pot future in Chinese cooking. More often than not, the following is rather typical of what happens: For example, a shiny Peking roast duck sometimes alights on the platter of a Yangchow restaurant. Yangchow sizzling fried rice-toast may drop in and steam up a soup of Szechwan in a Cantonese restaurant. Such things even happen in the American Chinatowns, as they happen in Shanghai and Taipei. On the whole, the restaurants in Taipei keep their provincial flavors pretty faithfully. And I am going to include here some of their recipes in this new edition. You tell the waiter to tell the cook not to use so much grease and the cook tells the waiter to tell the customer, Who are you to tell me how to cook? And if I had dared to say I am Mrs. Chao, he would probably have said, Who is Mrs. Chao? Now that this cookbook has been pirated in Taipei, I am no longer only known to the limited academic and medical circles there.

Two other things I have noticed about restaurant practices. One is the use of oil on top of dishes. Many Chinese dishes are not good without enough oil. But there is a difference how it is used. If the cook in a restaurant or at home does not have to use his own oil, he does it the proper way: use adequate amounts, especially in stir-frying, and drain and pour off extra oil after frying. The dish tastes rich but not greasy, not so fattening. But if you board with your cook, he uses too little oil in actual cooking, but pours oil over the finished dish. That costs him less oil. The dish looks rich but tastes greasy. That is one of the differences between home cooking and ordinary restaurant cooking. The other thing is the growing excessive use of soy sauce and taste powder. As you see from the book, there is in Chinese cooking red cooking and there is white cooking. Nothing is so detrimental to a discriminating use of different Chinese dishes as the indiscriminant use of soy sauce. Needless to say, the all too common practice of pouring soy sauce over one's white boiled rice never fails to make a Chinese laugh. It is however permissible to dip white boiled meat in soy sauce (*sheng-ch'ou,* or first grade sauce), and it has a quite different flavor from red-cooked meat. Excessive use of taste powder, which is monosodium glutamate under many trade names, is a common practice among restaurants, especially the cheaper ones, since it is easier and cheaper to give dishes as much taste that way than to depend upon the excellence and individuality of the material—mushrooms, Virginia ham being expensive—why not put a pinch of taste powder in all dishes? So that is what they do. Taste powder has its place as one among many tastes. But when used excessively in all dishes, it obliterates the identity of the different flavors and even obliterates the sensitivity of the tongue, which is what happens after eating too often in medium-grade restaurants.[1]

To continue with my recent impressions of Chinese restaurants in various corners of the world, I find that in England they are mostly run by people from Szechwan and Shantung, provinces famous for their cooking. Unfortunately, the price for an adequate meal in a Chinese restaurant in England is usually too high for the average person to go very often. In France, however, there are numerous small Chinese restaurants run by people from various parts of China. As the basic materials and even the methods in French cooking are often similar to those of the Chinese, it makes the problem easier. In Germany the people who open Chinese restaurants often come from Ningpo and parts further north. As in

[1] Medium-grade as to quality, not as to size and price. Some small restaurants with reasonable prices in the Chinatowns serve first-rate food, while some large and expensive restaurants serve medium-grade food.

England the prices are higher than what one is willing to pay for casual meals.

Japan presents a rich fare of Chinese foods. There is now much more eating in Chinese in Japan than in my student days there. There are not only many Chinese restaurants, but Chinese dishes get into Japanese menus. Practically every restaurant, including the lunchrooms in the department stores, will have *chūka soba*, i.e. Chinese noodles. Szechwan, Shantung, and Canton are well represented in the larger cities. Quality and price are sometimes very high, even by New York standards. As to the materials used for Chinese cooking, they are not only easy to get there, but even exported to America for use in the Chinese restaurants.

To finish my trip, back in America, good Chinese restaurants are increasing in number in the last decade, notably in the larger cities like New York, Washington, Boston, and San Francisco. As usual, the price for a meal beyond a certain level is all for style and it is worth it if you have a good appetite for eating style. Otherwise it is a question whether the place is lucky enough to have a good cook. The difficulty is that nowadays restaurants grow faster than cooks can be trained or immigrated under the quota of technical personnel. The situation is still fluid and different restaurants bid for the same chefs harder than universities bid for professors. Add to this the fact that many cooks are temperamental and not to be had for money. In one well-known restaurant in San Francisco a cook was imported from Hong Kong at a fabulous salary and after a couple of months he resigned and went back because he could not stand the tempo of life in America.

I am often asked what are the good Chinese restaurants to go to in various cities. My usual recommendation is: Go where there are mostly Chinese customers and few or no Caucasians. I used to be afraid that the result of following my advice would be that as more and more Caucasians go to the place the management will feel obliged to give the Americans what it thinks they like and that the style would then slide back into the conventional type of fare. But I have been pleasantly surprised that this has not always been the case in recent years. In one instance I noted an increase from

25 per cent to 75 per cent patronage by Caucasians, with only slight changes in the manner of serving and hardly any change in the methods of cooking, which is all to the good.

But I forget that this is a cookbook and not a tourist guide. I started to tell you what's new in this Third Edition. I have not yet mentioned the two principal additions, as can be seen from the Table of Contents. One is a whole new chapter on the soybean family of foods, which are important from the point of view of both nutrition and cuisine. The other is a chapter on Chinese diet as diet. I have often noticed that dining out in American makes me gain weight and eating at home in Chinese keeps my weight down. As I have said, the Chinese apparently don't need to diet, because the Chinese diet is already practically diet. However, it is not quite that simple and sometimes people do get fat on Chinese food. Hence the new chapter to explain the how and why.

Additions and changes have been made in the recipes in various parts of the book, so as to make use of recent developments, both in the Chinese pantry and in American gadgetry.

Buwei Yang Chao

Berkeley, California
April, 1963

NOTE TO SECOND, REVISED EDITION

The warm reception this book has enjoyed from the cooking and eating public has made it both a duty and a pleasure to bring out a revised edition. A duty, because I must not let little errors of detail[1] go uncorrected in printing after printing. A pleasure, because in the few years since the publication of this book, there has already been a noticeable increase in things Chinese at American markets. (No cause and effect implied!) Fava or horse beans are no longer limited to Italian vegetable stands. Tender peas eaten with the pod have appeared in some general markets. Fresh ginger, though still limited to Chinese stores, is more available, as there is a constant supply of Mexican-grown ginger to answer the needs of Chinatowns. It is therefore a pleasure to be able to revise the book by allowing for a greater range of possibilities.

It is also a pleasure to be able to answer in this new edition questions or requests from correspondents which I have been unable to answer one by one adequately. Some of the most frequent questions, such as the use of the pressure cooker and the Chinese way of preparing crabs have now been answered.

But the greatest pleasure of all is to be able to add several major recipes (Nos. 2.10, 5.11, 8.22, 8.23, 8.24, 8.25, 9.9, 12.14, 14.34, 20.10) and a number of new variations on original recipes. I had not dared to invade the field of American cookery by Sinicizing some American dishes, and even if I had, I was never sure how literally Americans were going to follow my recipes. But both the way my American guests have approved my Chinese-style roast turkey, Chinese-style roast chicken, etc. and the way they have themselves

[1] Shortly after the publication of my wife's book, my teacher of philosophy, whose attention had been called to the problem in mathematical logic in Recipe No. 13.1, called me up and said: "Chao, isn't it awful? One of the cross references in your wife's cookbook doesn't refer!"—Y. R. C.

It does now.—B. Y. C.

turned out 100-per-cent Chinese dishes from close reading of my Chinese recipes have encouraged me to expect more of them. When an American member of a Cambridge, Mass., eating club, who had never seen a Chinese recipe before buying this book, surprised a Chinese fellow member with an authentic full-course Chinese dinner with Red-Cooked Meat, Mushrooms Stir Shrimps, Steamed Rice, Changsha style, and stir-fried vegetable dishes, I felt that my unseen pupils have really graduated with high honors. But you must never let the students graduate with the idea that they know everything. So here is a new edition with some brand-new recipes.

Buwei Yang Chao

Berkeley, California
September 1, 1949

TABLE OF CONTENTS

CONTENTS

FOREWORD

Long, long ago, Confucius made this observation: "There is no one who does not eat and drink. But few there are who can appreciate taste."

This observation is all the more remarkable because it came from a man who elsewhere declared that he could enjoy life even though he had only coarse food to eat and water to drink and his own bended arm to pillow.

The essence of Chinese cooking lies in the traditional insistence that food must have taste or flavor even though the materials used may be the most common and inexpensive kind of fish or vegetable. It is taste which gives joy in eating. And it is the art of the housewife, the cook, or the gourmet to work out the ways and means to give taste to food.

A Chinese gourmet of the eighth century A.D., has left us this dictum: "Every eating material can be made palatable provided that it is given the proper cooking-time (*huo-hou*, literally, 'fire-timing')." Please note that this expert did not say that palatability depended upon the use of the right kind of seasoning or flavoring materials. It is the proper "fire-timing" which really counts in all good cooking.

"Good cooking," says Mrs. Chao, "consists in making the best use of the eating material. The cooking materials should only enhance the natural taste of the eating material and not take its place." In these words, our author has summed up the art and the philosophy of Chinese cooking. All the "twenty and one" principal methods of cooking described in this book—from the slow and time-consuming "red-cooking" and "clear-simmering" to the quick and impressionistic "stir-frying" and "plunging"—are in reality gradations in "fire-timing."

Mrs. Buwei Yang Chao has prepared a really wonderful book

on Chinese cooking. Her chapters on Cooking Materials and Methods of Cooking are masterpieces of analysis and synthesis. With the help of her daughter and her husband, who is an artist with the written word, she has created a new terminology, a new vocabulary, without which the art of Chinese cooking cannot be adequately introduced to the Western world. Some of the new terms like "Defishers," "Stir-frying," "Meeting," "Plunging," and a host of others, I venture to predict, will come to stay as the Chaos' contributions to the English language.

Of course I am not qualified to pass judgment on her recipes, not even to praise them. But I must tell a story to testify to the accuracy of her descriptions. I happened to be at Mrs. Chao's house just before she returned the galley proofs of her book to the publisher. I picked up one sheet at random and read the tail end of a recipe. "Why," I exclaimed, "this must be the Huichou Pot!" When I found the preceding page, there it was, the title "Huichou Pot," which, I believe, Mrs. Chao had learned from my wife and which was nostalgically familiar to me.

Twenty-three years ago, I was one of the two friends who had the honor to serve as witnesses at the wedding of Dr. and Mrs. Yuen-ren Chao. The unconventional bride cooked the dinner for the four of us. Since that memorable evening, I must have partaken at least a hundred meals prepared by Mrs. Chao. She has become not only a truly excellent cook, but, as this book testifies, an analytical and scientific teacher of Chinese cooking. It is, therefore, as a family friend and an appreciative "taster" of her food that I now have the pleasure of presenting her book to the English-speaking world.

Chinese cooking, as Mrs. Chao tells us in the introduction, is not difficult to learn. A little thinking and a little willingness to experiment will go very far. Here is what our author has to say about roasting chestnuts:

Roast chestnuts are never good in America. They crack and stay raw because of uneven and interrupted heating. In China chestnuts are roasted in sand. The hot sand, stirred all the time, surrounds the chestnuts on all sides with medium heat. In the course of time, the meat becomes soft and fragrant like well-baked sweet potatoes.

All of her hundreds of recipes, like this one on roasting chestnuts in hot sand, represent the successful results of thinking and experimentation on the part of numberless frugal and ingenious men and women. They are now precisely recorded for the benefit and enjoyment of all those who would approach them in the spirit of willingness to think and experiment.

Hu Shih

PREFACE

I am trying to write this preface as an American housewife who is daily responsible for the meals of a large family and for occasional guests as well. Before I can establish the point of view I must confess that the first time I read this cookbook, which was in manuscript, I put it down, although it was in the middle of my work day, and rushed to the kitchen, unable to keep from cooking a large Chinese meal. It turned out perfectly. I say this without pride, although I am a fair Chinese cook, because the perfection of the meal was due entirely to Mrs. Chao's cookbook.

Now I have just completed a second reading of the cookbook, and this time I have not allowed myself, as I did the first time, to yield to its evocations of wonderful meals I have eaten since childhood in China. I have steadily remembered that I now live in the United States and that I am limited to American meats and vegetables, fats and fruits. It is as an American woman therefore that I should like to say that it seems to me this is a perfect cookbook. There is not a dish in its pages which an American housewife cannot produce, without qualms over its difficulty. But good as this is, even this is not the best thing about the book. So few cookbooks really tell one what to do or how to do it. Mrs. Chao, out of her long knowledge of American women and American food markets, knows what to tell us and how to tell us about Chinese cooking. As a Chinese, she knows exactly what Americans don't know. It is worth this book's weight in gold and diamonds if American women will learn how to cook vegetables as the Chinese cook them, quickly and lightly, without water and waste. It is worth jade and rubies if they will abandon the horrid American custom of putting cooked rice under the cold water faucet and washing out all its flavor. It is of inestimable value to the war effort and also to the economy of peace if they will learn to use meat for its taste in a dish of something else, instead of using it chiefly for its substance. It is well to remember that upon Chinese diet of the simplest kind men and women work incredible hours and perform stupendous tasks of endurance and strength. Their food nourishes the human frame.

In short, I wholeheartedly endorse this cookbook for Americans. I wish I could put a copy of it, as a Christmas gift, into the hands of every woman and every man who has any share in the feeding of our nation.

As for Mrs. Chao, I would like to nominate her for the Nobel Peace Prize. For what better road to universal peace is there than to gather around the table where new and delicious dishes are set forth, dishes which, though yet untasted by us, we are destined to enjoy and love? What better road to friendship, upon which alone the peace can stand? I consider this cookbook a contribution to international understanding. We have known, abstractly, that the Chinese people is one of the oldest and most civilized on earth. But this book proves it. Only the profoundly civilized can feed upon such food.

Pearl S. Buck

AUTHOR'S NOTE

I am ashamed to have written this book. First, because I am a doctor and ought to be practicing instead of cooking. Secondly, because I didn't write the book. The way I didn't was like this. You know I speak little English and write less. So I cooked my dishes in Chinese, my daughter Rulan put my Chinese into English, and my husband, finding the English dull, put much of it back into Chinese again. Thus, when I call a dish "Mushrooms Stir Shrimps," Rulan says that that's not English and that it ought to be "Shrimps Fried with Mushrooms." But Yuen Ren argues that if Mr. Smith can Go to Town in a movie, why can't Mushrooms Stir Shrimps in a dish? So Mushrooms Stir Shrimps you shall have, or what have you?

I never stirred an egg until I went to college—the Tokyo Women's Medical College. I found Japanese food so uneatable that I had to cook my own meals. I had always looked down upon food and things, but I hated to look down upon a Japanese dinner under my nose. So by the time I became a doctor, I also became something of a cook. On my return to China, I surprised my old friends and relatives when I prepared a complete dinner of sixteen dishes to celebrate the opening of my hospital.

How did I learn to cook so many things? My answer is: with an open mind and an open mouth. I grew up with the idea that nice ladies should not be in a kitchen, but as I told you, necessity opened my mind first. Then being often left to my own devices under all sorts of conditions has made me feel most conventions of cooking, serving, and eating to be a little silly. It is well to know the exact practice in China, in America, and in dietetics, but nothing takes the place of a little thinking. If you cannot get beef, get pork. If you cannot find an egg-beater, use your head.

An open mouth is important because you ought to be willing to try anything at least once. I usually scold my children by saying,

How do you know you don't like it before you have tasted it? I often boast that anything I have eaten I can cook, if you give me long enough to try. Since I know what it ought to taste like, I can be my own judge as to whether I am getting nearer or farther from the right taste after each try, and that's the way to learn.

Another use of keeping your mouth open is that you can ask information by it. "Not ashamed to ask," was Confucius' good word for one of his pupils. I learned about many of the local customs and recipes in this way. In recent years, I often accompanied my husband on his trips to make surveys of the dialects. While he was asking how this word or that phrase was pronounced by his language informants, I had my informants tell me how this dish or that pastry was prepared and where the materials came from. As his informants and hosts often represent quite varied classes of people, we had a chance to eat a great variety of food from each locality.

It was far enough from my thoughts to get interested in cooking. It was even farther from my idea to write about it. My purpose was not scientific. I got those new ideas because I liked to talk to strangers and wanted to know more about my country. I did not even take notes of many of the recipes, and when I tried some of the things recently, guided only by my memory of what they should taste like, my family had to eat some strange dishes before I found out how to take the strangeness from some of them.

As indicated on the dedication page, it was Mrs. Hocking—Mrs. William Ernest Hocking—who told me to write this book. So coming now to acknowledgments, I must thank Mrs. Hocking as the first person who kindled this kitchen fire. Whenever Mrs. Hocking tells me to do a thing, I always feel I really must. She believes in me so much that I almost believe in myself. So I began—that was three years ago—and Rulan started to write.

I don't know how many scoldings and answerings-back and quarrels Rulan and I went through, and if kind friends—too many, who helped too much, to thank adequately here—if they had not come to our rescue to get the book done in a last midnight rush, the strained relations between mother and daughter would certainly have been broken. You know how it is with modern daughters and mothers who think we are modern. And it is even more delicate with a mother and a daughter, both having had mixed experiences of eating, cooking, speaking, and writing. Now that we have not neglected to do the making-up with each other after our last recipe, it is safe for me to claim that all the credit for the good points of the book is mine and all the blame for the bad points is Rulan's.

Next, I must blame my husband for all the negative contributions he has made toward the making of the book. In many places, he has changed Rulan's good English into bad, which he thinks Americans like better. His greatest contribution is even more negative. Whenever a dish is not quite right or when it is repeated too often, he simply leaves it alone. That always makes me angry, and in the course of years, I have developed a repertoire of three or four hundred dishes. The only recipe that is really his own is No. 13.1, Stirred Eggs, which I let him write out himself. But he was so long-winded about it that I had to stop him from trying any other dish. Apart from that, his support to my undertaking has been largely oral.

Finally, sincere thanks are due to my fellow provincials Pearl S. Buck and Hu Shih of Anhwei and to Mr. Richard J. Walsh of John Day for introducing this book to the American public.

Buwei Yang Chao

Cambridge, Massachusetts
March, 1945

xxiv

CONVENTIONS AND HINTS

1. Recipe Numbers.—Recipes are numbered by two figures, the first giving the chapter number and the second the number of the particular recipe. Thus, Chapter 8 is Chicken, and Recipe No. 8.17 is the seventeenth chicken dish, namely, Paper-Wrapped Chicken. When the first number is from 1 to 16, it is a dish. 17 is sweet things, 18 is rice, 19 and 20 are mostly flour things.

2. Order of Parts in a Recipe.—

   (a) General description
   (b) List of ingredients
   (c) Readying method
   (d) Cooking method proper
   (e) Method of serving and eating
   (f) Method of using leftovers
   (g) Variations

One or more of these items may of course be absent.

3. Quantities.—Unless otherwise specified, the amount of materials is for serving six, when eating in the American way, with one main dish. When eating in the Chinese way, with several dishes together, the eating materials should be reduced in amount, but the seasoning should be proportionately heavier in order to balance out the large amount of rice eaten as the bulk food at a Chinese meal.

For a smaller number of people eating American-way meals, the amounts given in the recipes can be halved or quartered proportionately.

4. Special Terms of Frequent Occurrence.—

American: abbreviated way of saying "American or European," when referring to cooking and eating.

CONVENTIONS AND HINTS

Cantonese: In most cases, the word is used in the wide sense to include all Kwangtung Province, of which Canton is the capital, especially the Four Districts to the southwest of Canton.

Chinatown: abbreviated way of saying "your nearest place where there are stores primarily for Chinese customers."

Clear-Simmering: slow-cooking without soy sauce.

Cook: Besides the general sense, also used for continued cooking over big fire after wet seasoning has been added after frying.

Ginger: Try to get fresh ginger in Chinatown or at your élite grocer's. Don't substitute with ginger powder, but dried (whole) ginger can do except in recipes (e.g. No. 5.4) where you actually eat the ginger.

Ham: Unless fresh ham is specified, ham is Chinese ham or, as a very plausible substitute, two-year-old Smithfield, Virginia ham.

Hse: my usual way of pronouncing *he* and *she* without distinction when I speak English.

Meat: pork, unless specified otherwise.

Red-Cooking: slow-cooking with soy sauce.

Skillet: flat, thin frying-pan.

Stir(-fry): a big-fire-shallow-fat-continual-stirring-quick-frying of cut-up material with wet seasoning. (See p. 43.)

For other terms, see Index.

5. Chinese Words.—Chinese words in general descriptions are given in the Wade system, to which my husband is opposed. Chinese names for materials to get in Chinatown or dishes to order in American-Chinese restaurants are given in Cantonese. I speak Mandarin with an Anhwei accent and Cantonese with a Mandarin accent. If you want to speak Chinese with an American accent, learn the following approximations:

Letter	*as in*		*Letter*	*as in*
a	almond		*ĕ*	cut (lengthened)
ch	jam		*e*	egg
ch'	chard		*f*	fish

Letter as in		*Letter as in*	
h	*h*am which you try to spit when it is rancid	*p'*	*p*ea
		r	Middle West cu*r*d
hs	between *h*eat and *sh*eet	*s*	*s*oy
i	p*ie*ce	*sh*	*sh*red
ih	Middle West sh*i*r	*t*	*d*ough
j	*r*um	*t'*	*t*ea
k	*g*ame	*ts, tz*	a*dz*e
k'	*k*ohl-rabi	*ts', tz'*	ca*ts*-up
l	*l*ard	*u*	f*oo*d
m	*m*eal	*ŭ*	s*i*zzling
n	*n*oodle	*ü*	French s*u*cre
ng	puddi*ng*	*w*	*w*ine
o	sl*aw*	*y*	*y*um *y*um
p	*b*ean		

In the spelling for words in Cantonese, the letters have about the same values. Cantonese *h* has a smoother quality, as in *fresh ham.* Double *aa* stands for long *a,* as in English *Ah!* The digraph *eu* is the sound of *œu* in *hors d'œuvres.* Cantonese has nine tones, but I can't make them, so I leave them out of the recipes.

6. What to Cook First.—Of various ways of cooking, stir-frying of meat dishes is the hardest. Stir-fried vegetables are a little easier. Red-cooking is the easiest. With red-cooking, so long as you do not burn your stuff with too big a fire, the only danger in cooking too long is that you will have too little to show at the end (though it often tastes better in inverse proportion to the amount.) Whether you want to try the safest dishes or the most characteristically Chinese dishes first, depends upon how adventurous you are. But if you follow the recipes closely, you can begin anywhere among the recipes after having carefully studied the introductory chapters in Part I.

7. What to Eat First.—For beginners in Chinese eating, a good idea is to use Chinese-style food in an American-style meal, instead of going all out for the Chinese way of eating at once. (See pp. 226-228, Chapter 21.)

8. Unexpected Guests.—Because of community eating, that is, eating from common dishes (see pp. 4-5), it is much easier to entertain a few unexpected guests in a Chinese household than is the case in America. You just add an extra bowl and an extra pair of chopsticks for each guest and his dinner is served. If you do it quickly enough, you can say that you expected them in the first place.

9. Chinese Food and Vitamins.—Because of the quickness of the process, stir-frying is particularly good for preserving the vitamins of foods, especially of green vegetables. The vitamins of radishes are however stable even against longer cooking.[1]

10. The Chinese Diet.—Because of emphasis on non-starchy vegetables in Chinese menus and of the small quantities of meat eaten by each person (even among the well-to-do), Chinese food is especially good for the middle-aged. I have no statistics at hand, but I see fewer Chinese (of my class) prone to obesity or rheumatism among the middle-aged. For further details see Chapter 23 on Chinese Diet as Diet.

[1] Since the above was written, special experiments on the recipes of this book conducted at the Massachusetts Institute of Technology have shown that most of the dishes, including the long-cooking ones, keep the vitamins well. It was a surprise to myself that even Red-Cooked Meat lost very little of its vitamin content.

PART ONE

COOKING AND EATING

CHAPTER I

INTRODUCTION

1. Meal Systems.—We eat food during meals or between meals. Most Chinese eat three meals a day, when they can. Rich people have meals between meals. A meal is called *fan*, "a period of rice." Small meals between meals are called *tien-hsin*, something to "dot the heart." Most of my recipes are of dishes for meals, though I should like to describe and eat a few between-meal "dot-hearts" before I finish writing this book.

Meals are eaten quite differently in different parts of China. But a very important idea everywhere is the contrast between *fan* (in a narrow sense) "rice" and *ts'ai*, "dishes." Most people who are poor eat much rice (if that) or other grain food as the main food and only a little *ts'ai* or dishes. The dishes only accompany the rice. So they are the opposite of the American eating system, in which bread accompanies the dish. Whenever they can, Chinese children like to eat little rice and much of the dishes, as American grownups do, but even children in well-to-do families are called good when they are willing to eat much rice. All this to make clear the opposition between rice and dishes in a Chinese meal. If there are noodles or steamed bread, they are considered "rice," that is, grain food.[1]

Different meal systems also go with different kinds of meals. I shall give you sample menus later on (Chapter 21). Here I shall tell you briefly what the meals are like. In the three-meal system places, sometimes all three are alike, consisting of dry boiled rice, accompanied by several dishes. This is what people do in Hunan, or in Anhwei, where I come from. In other places, the first meal is

---

[1] I cannot very well call it cereal, since cereal is breakfast food, and we don't eat breakfast food at breakfast.

a light breakfast. In this kind of breakfast, the rice is not pudding-like, but soup-like. It is called *congee* in English, but most Americans have never heard the word before going to the Orient. The dishes eaten at breakfast are known as "small dishes," being mostly salty and very savory things. This kind of breakfast is common in the lower *Yangtze River* region such as Soochow and Hangchow, the two places next to Heaven one would like to go to, according to a Chinese proverb. *Tien-hsin*, "dot-hearts" are also very good in that part of the country.

In the South and the West, the two-meal system is very common for the common people. They eat in the morning and afternoon, exactly when the three-meal-eating people do not eat. If however you have the means and the time and the space, three light meals can be inserted in between, making really five meals. Thus, in Canton, you can get up with an early light breakfast; then the regular morning meal later; at noon you are ready for tea, with a rich assortment of "dot-hearts" such as Wraplings and Ramblings (Recipes Nos. 20.6 and 20.5); then a second dinner in the afternoon; and, after a busy evening of work or pleasure, a light meal of good-tasting congee or noodles before you go to bed. Some of the most famous restaurants in Canton are more famous for their noonday tea than for their dinners.

Many visitors to China or even long-time residents who never eat a Chinese meal except when invited to a formal dinner with "courses" have no idea what a totally different affair a Chinese family meal is. The typical family meal has several dishes all served at the same time. In families, in shops, and on the farm, people eat together, and share a little of several different dishes, and never have one dish belonging to one person. There are no "courses." Suppose you have on the table a meat, a fish, a vegetable, and a soup with a small-sized family of eight sitting around the table. They do not "serve" themselves to a piece or portion of each and then eat privately. If any child did that, *hse* [1] would be scolded for hogging or hoarding. The dinner is already served when the dishes are on the table. Each person just eats a chopsticks-

[1] See page xvi.

4

ful of this, then a morsel of rice (the rice bowls are always individual), a chopsticksful of that, then a morsel of rice from his own particular bowl, a spoonful of the common soup, and so on, quite casual-like. The result is that you feel you are all the time carrying on a friendly conversation with each other, even though nobody says anything. I wonder if it is because the American way of each eating his own meal is so unsociable that you have to keep on talking to make it more like good manners?

A banquet or *chiu-hsi*, "wine-spread," on the other hand, is a vertical thing. Except at the beginning and at the end, you eat only one course at a time,[1] and you do not eat rice till the end, and maybe you do not eat rice at all, but you drink wine all the time. A typical banquet (see Chapter 21.5 for menu) will start with four or eight small cold dishes, already on the table. The host lifts his wine cup, which is a signal for the guests to thank him. So they all lift their cups and say *"To-hsieh to-hsieh!"* as they drink. The host poises his chopsticks over the dishes and all the guests do the same. Whoever makes his first touching of the food later than the others is more polite. So among very polite company it may take some time before anybody actually gets anything to eat. However, the host can get things going by taking some pieces and offering them to his guests. But men do not usually offer each other food. Ladies do.

The hot dishes come one by one and are the real beginning of the meal. Four medium dishes may come in succession, usually in the form of stir-fried dishes. Then perhaps four larger dishes, some of which may be soup. If one of the dishes is Shark's Fin (Recipe No. 12.13), the guest must say to the host, *Chên t'ai fei-shih lê!* "Really, you should not have put [2] yourself to so much trouble!" Some special dishes like Peking duck with doilies or steamed shad with ham and Kalgan mushrooms come near the end. Last come

[1] To use a musical analogy, a Chinese family meal of four dishes and a soup is a four-part counterpoint with a pedal point, while a Chinese banquet is a long series of solo melodies with a harmonic introduction and a finale in heavy chords.—Y. R. C.

[2] There is no subjunctive perfect in Chinese, but we say it with tones.—Y. R. C.

four heavy dishes together and a few small salted dishes. This is the time to serve rice or congee if you can still eat anything. But most experienced eaters can, because they know the program beforehand and know the motto of *"Tên, jên, hên!"* It means something like: "Await, avoid, attack!" That is, you wait and avoid eating too much of everything, but when something really good comes, attack!

Sometimes you have to wait and avoid, but never attack. That happens if you have to go to another party. For in China a previous engagement is usually no sufficient excuse for not coming. You should at least join the party by having some wine and eating of a dish or two and then leave for another party. Some American-returned students try to stick to one engagement a meal and often offend people by doing so. But they think that they can contribute to improving the custom by sacrificing themselves first. Anyway that is how my husband excuses himself for not going to parties. When people do go to three or four parties in one evening, it is often very hard to get anything to eat, since you have to spend most of the evening in coming and going, in greeting and thanking, and leave taking. To make sure to get something to eat, you would, as an experienced party-goer, often eat a good and hearty meal at home before starting on your rounds, or you can try to catch the last Four Heavies of your last host. The host you visit last feels that you like his party best. But the hosts you visit earlier also feel glad that you went. The understanding is: Better early than not at all.

There are variations on the banquet in different parts of the country. Desserts may be inserted here and there, either in the middle or at the beginning, but never at the end. The habit of eating fruit after the meal is something imported from Europe. In the really Chinese way, fruit is eaten only between meals.

The name *tien-hsin,* "dot-heart," may refer to a small meal or the things you eat at such a meal. A "dot-heart" is never a dish. You may eat noodles, cakes, and other things you cannot call names in English. Most of them are pastry, that is, flour things which are baked, fried, or boiled and may be made sweet or salty. They may form a course in a banquet, but not in a family meal. One thing about a meal of "dot-hearts" is that you can drink tea and you are often said to be drinking tea when you have a meal of "dot-hearts," while you do not drink tea at the table when you eat a regular meal, except in certain southern coastal regions and in American-Chinese restaurants. In some provinces, a light course of "dot-hearts" is served before sitting down at a banquet table.

2. Restaurants at Home and Abroad.—While most of this book has to do with cooking, it will probably interest the eater to know how to eat and what to eat in Chinese restaurants when he goes to China and when he does not go. Since most Chinese eat at home or right where they work, there are few restaurants to eat for business, but mostly restaurants to eat for pleasure. This is true even in the cities. Restaurants serve course dinners as described above or small informal meals. To order an informal meal, you order about as many dishes as there are people in the party, plus one or two soups. You may order more or fewer dishes, depending upon how large the dishes are and how hungry you are and how much you want to spend. If wine is served, you need some cold hors d'œuvres to start with and a few stir-fried dishes before the rice-sending dishes are served. Sometimes certain ready-made menus known as *ho-ts'ai* "harmonized dishes" for various numbers of people and at various prices may be ordered to save the trouble of ordering *à la carte*. This is done only when you are in a hurry. But when you go to a restaurant in China, you are in no hurry.

Big dinners or banquets have to be ordered beforehand except in the largest restaurants. It is of course best to eat in the restaurant unless the host is so well to do as to have a chef who can handle a sixteen-course dinner. A not uncommon practice in cities is to send for a dinner and an assistant chef. Arriving at the house perhaps two hours before the invited time, the slow-cooking dishes have already been done before and need only to be heated. The stir-frying dishes come in the form of readied materials, which need only to "go down the pan" before serving. On such an order, the host's chief worry is to get a good visiting chef and the chef's chief worry is to get a good brisk fire, since the stir-frying dishes are those which show his skill and depend upon a good fire for success.

Styles of food differ a good deal from place to place. You notice it of course when you travel, but you can also taste the foods of all provinces in large centers like Peiping. The only thing about these restaurants is that they lose some of their provincialism if they stay too long, say two hundred years. When the customers all the time ask for not so much hot stuff please, not so much smell please, not so much *hsiang-ts'ai* (a strong Chinese parsley) please, and so forth—after enough years, these restaurants have had to become more and more national and some of them have become more famous in their own name than in the name of their provinces. But if a customer, especially the host, really comes from the province and names the dishes with the right accent, he can get the strongest form of his favorite native dishes. Restaurants in their own locality are of course not called by the name of the place or province. Thus you find in Shanghai signs for *Ching-Su-Ta-ts'ai*, "Peking and Soochow Great Dishes," but no such signs in Peiping or Soochow.

The best-known restaurants which are well represented in the large centers are from Shantung, Honan, Szechwan (where Chungking is), Hunan (where Changsha is), Kiangsu (where Nanking is), Kwangtung (where Canton is), Fukien, etc. Shantung and Honan restaurants excel in general. Szechwan cooking has a fine balance of flavors except that hot pepper is added freely either during cooking or when the dishes are served. Hunan, the rice bowl province, also a hot-stuff-eating province, serves also rich tasting dishes in large vessels with giant-size tablespoons and extra long chopsticks. They tell stories about people in Hunan sitting across the table and feeding each other because the chopsticks are so long they can't bring their ends to their own mouths! Kiangsu cooking contains a lot of sweetening, that is, in salty dishes. Fukien and parts of Chekiang, especially Ningpo, excel in sea food. Kwangtung restaurants are perhaps the most versatile of all and excel in all lines. They also excel in cooking materials for their original flavor with little adornment, such as slow-cooked chicken, paper-sealed mushrooms, etc.

Since most Chinese residents abroad, especially those in America, come from Kwantung, this brings me to the question of eating Chinese food if you do not go to China. With few exceptions, such as a Tientsin restaurant in Washington, a Ningpo and a Tientsin restaurant in New York, a Paoting restaurant in Paris, most restaurants abroad I know of are run by Chinese from Kwangtung, or Cantonese in the wide sense. Now I have often been asked, Do you get real Chinese food in the Chinese restaurants in America? The answer is, you can get it if you ask for it, especially if there is enough demand for it. If you say you want real Chinese dishes and eat the Chinese way, that is, a few dishes to eat in common and with chopsticks, then they know that you know. If you do not know what to order, you can ask for *ho-ts'ai* (*wo-ts'oi* in Cantonese) for so much money and repeat that you want to eat like a Chinese. Many times the trouble is that because the customers do not know what is good in Chinese food they often order things which the Chinese do not eat very much. The restaurant people, on their part, try to serve the public what they think the public wants. So in the course of time a tradition of American-Chinese food and ceremonies of eating has grown up which is different from eating in China, whether in Canton or in any other place. Much of this tradition is interesting and in "good taste," but it is not purely Chinese. This is very like the provincial restaurants getting nationalized in Peiping. Here we see the national restaurants getting internationalized in New York. Or rather in midtown New York, because in the Chinatowns of America, where the customers are mostly Chinese, it is often more like real Chinese food and manner of eating.

3. Table Manners.—The motto that good manners lie in making others feel at ease is as true of Chinese manners as it is true of American manners. But we apply the principle very differently. Sometimes, we seem to be actually quarreling and fighting when we are really each trying to be more polite than everybody else. The important thing is that in that wrangling atmosphere everybody feels happy and at ease, because things are going as they should.

Table manners begin with a fight over yielding precedence in entering the dining room. Among familiar friends, it may come to actual pushing, though never to blows. After a properly long dead-lock, some elder guest will yield and say: *"Kung-ching pu-ju ts'ung-ming,"* "Better obedience than deference." Modern-educated hosts also may break the deadlock by saying allow him to lead the way. After you all enter the dining room, the fight has to be repeated all over again, this time over yielding precedence in seating. The seating system varies too much from place to place to describe fully here. But in general the higher seats are either at the north or at the inner side of the room, while the southern seats or the seats nearest the serving door are the lowest and reserved for the host or hostess. The guest of honor is, therefore, always seated farthest from the host instead of nearest to him. No guest ventures to take the host's seat, as he may finally have to come out on top. Fig. 1 shows three examples of seating.

Except at home, wine must be drunk with somebody. No guest drinks wine unless the host invites him to. If you cannot wait, you should invite the host or some other guest to drink with you. Usually only the host has the right to invite everybody to drink together. Since in finger-guessing games the loser drinks, the dinner-table convention is that everybody is supposed to be reluctant to drink and has to be urged before he accepts to drink.

About the mechanics of eating, I have already told you something in describing the meals. Because of the community form of eating, you often have to reach quite far if there are several dishes on the table. You do not have to excuse yourself for reaching in front of others, although you should not be too obtrusively in another's way. The passing of dishes around the table is strange practice to most Chinese. When you want to be very demure, you simply limit yourself to eating from the dishes nearest to you. This is especially true of womenfolk. On the other hand, hostesses do more offering of food to guests to save their reaching than hosts do.

Recently, a method of using serving chopsticks has been tried, for hygienic reasons, in schools, at parties, and in a few homes. In addition to individual eating chopsticks and spoons, a few pairs of serving chopsticks and spoons are placed in or about the dishes. You use these to serve yourself with whatever you wish to eat and

10

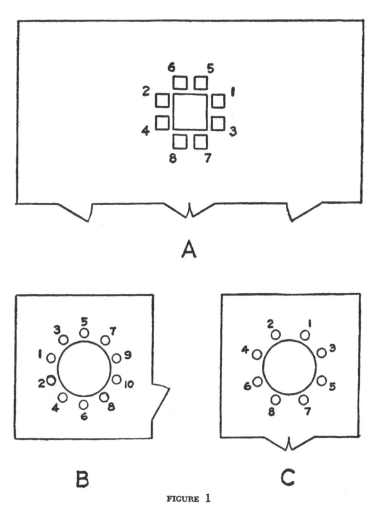

FIGURE 1

EXAMPLES OF PRECEDENCE

A. In a large hall.   B. and C. In small dining rooms.

then eat with your own eating set. Since the Chinese can never conceive of eating from a helping once or twice for all, but are in the habit of taking a morsel at a time and getting more from the common dishes again and again, the use of serving sets makes eating very complicated. At parties where this is done, I constantly forget about it and eat with the serving chopsticks. Then I remember about it, and hurry up to change, and so serve myself with my original eating chopsticks. I am not alone in finding this system difficult, and I have often seen such a dinner end frankly in everybody having two sets of eating chopsticks and spoons. On the other hand, I have also seen it work smoothly in the hands of an alert hostess and one or two well-trained guests seated at strategic points.

Dishes are prepared in relation to the manners of eating them. That is why Americans are at a loss as to what to do when they have stirred whole shrimps, or long, hot soup-noodles. Do as I do. I take hold of a shrimp between my chopsticks. I bite off one half of the shrimp. While keeping the other half between my chopsticks, I shell the first half with my tongue and teeth, spit out the shell noiselessly in my shells-and-bones dish, and eat my shrimp. Now it takes moral courage for me to do this at a largely American party, even when I am hostess, because I was taught before my first visit to America that it was not good American manners to spit anything on the table, or anyway you should spit the shell into your fingers and put it down with them. On the other hand, it takes even more courage for me to follow the American practice and shell the whole greasy shrimp with my fingers or to spit into my hands, since from childhood I was taught not to touch any dinner-food with my fingers or to spit into them. Since the hot towel at a Chinese dinner does not come until the end, what are you going to do with your greasy fingers when you pick up your chopsticks and rice bowl again?

Certain hot foods are best when very hot. The technique for eating them is to draw in air over a narrow opening so as to hasten evaporation and diffuse the flavor. This is most effective when the air roughens the surface of the liquid. That is why hot soup, hot soup-noodles, hot congee, etc., are best when sucked in with as loud a noise as possible. Here, again, I feel an inner conflict when I remember how I was taught that in foreign countries one must drink soup as quietly as possible. On the other hand, I can never bring myself to blowing my nose in public, as people do in America, since this operation tends to be much louder than eating noodles and sounds much less inviting.

Finally, a very important thing about table manners that was drilled into us children is to leave a spot-clean bowl at the end of a meal. It is all right to waste a little vegetable or meat, but not grain. That is the fruit of the sweat of your fellow men. Stories are made up to scare children into eating their rice bowls clean. For example, if you leave any grains in your bowl, you will marry a wife (or a husband if you are a girl) with pockmarks on her face, and the more grains you waste, the more pockmarks *hse* will have. It is very easy to avoid such results. When your rice is getting shallow in your bowl, so that it becomes difficult to scoop out any on your chopsticks, you put your bowl against your lips in a drinking position and shovel the rice with your chopsticks from the side. In this way, it is very easy to eat your rice to the last grain. This is in fact the only way to eat rice if you have put some gravy on it, since the grains will fall apart when wet, and you do not eat rice with a spoon after you are three or four years old. Americans who have lived long in China, especially those who have mixed with the Chinese, like to shovel-eat their rice even when they have returned and eat in American-Chinese restaurants. On the other hand, missionary-educated Chinese students hesitate to go Chinese before Americans because when they learned American manners of eating American food, they acquired the feeling that they are also good manners for eating any food. I share some of this feeling myself, because I was partly missionary-educated myself.

Since we meet and eat with people of so many different experiences and traditions, it is difficult to advise what to do or to tell what is proper. All I can do is to tell you how we do things in China and why. When you know more what the customs are and what kind of company is present, then you can do as you see best by applying the principle that the best manners consist in making everybody feel most at ease.

4. Food and Festivals.—Special foods are associated with special festivals. They are not kinds of dishes, but mostly "dot-hearts," or between-meal refreshments. That is one reason why children are always wishing festivals to come around. In the so-called South (Central East), steamed cakes of glutinous rice flour with meat or sweet stuffing is a New Year's "dot-heart." (Recipe No. 17.7 is an example of it.) On the Fifth of the Fifth Moon on the lunar calendar, the festival food is boiled tetrahedrons of glutinous rice wrapped in leaves of a special kind of rush. The Fifteenth of the Seventh Moon is All Soul's Day, when fried eggplant-tarts are eaten. Around the Mid-Autumn Festival, which is about the time of the harvest moon, mooncake is eaten and sold in Chinatown stores in America. Those with puree-of-jujube stuffing in well-shortened crust are best, though hard to get except in the North.

There are many other ritual meanings of foods besides those eaten at festivals. We don't eat birthday cakes, but eat noodles to wish longevity to the person whose birthday it is. Breads and uncooked noodles are also made into the form of peaches, which are also a symbol of longevity.

If a family moves house, especially into a newly built house, you present them with a very fluffy raised cake called *fa-kao*, "the flourishing cake."

Abstaining from certain foods is sometimes part of religious ritual. Buddhist priests or monks are all vegetarians and do not touch animal food. Some lay believers in Buddhism eat permanent vegetarian food, some go vegetarian on certain days, and some do not express their belief by any kind of abstinence. Mohammedans do not eat pork, so they use chicken fat or duck fat for cooking besides vegetable oil. In many cities, special Mohammedan restaurants are greatly patronized by the general public.

CHAPTER II

EATING MATERIALS

A dish may be Chinese because it is made of Chinese things or because it is cooked in Chinese. I have been in some places in the United States where I can buy nothing but cabbages, lard, pork, pepper, and salt and such like things and have still been able to make Chinese dishes. If you use typically Chinese material, such as soy sauce or bean curd, it will of course make your dishes more interesting and more different.

There are eating materials and there are cooking materials. Garnishes are something in between. The cooking materials are so important that we call them *tso-liao*, "making materials." They will be described in the next chapter. Eating materials are so many that I must leave the details to the recipes. Here I shall only give you some very general descriptions of them.

Eating materials are fresh or preserved. Very often, as with dried scallops, the preserved ones taste "fresher" than the fresh ones. That is because we use the adjective *hsien*, "fresh" for the very savory state of things such as dried shrimps, dried scallops, canned abalone, which have started to spoil just enough to taste good, but not enough to taste bad. Many Chinese foods are in that state.

1. Meat and Poultry.—In Chinese, we speak of *Chi-ya-yü-jou*, "chicken, duck, fish, meat" as the sum total of animal food. But when we say meat, we mean pork unless some other kind of meat is specified, because pork is the most common kind of meat. Different dishes will need different kinds of cuts, as we shall see in the recipes. Beef and mutton are far less common than pork, though they are the chief meats for Mohammedans, to whom pork is unclean.

Chicken means something of a treat, as it does in America. Duck,

15

however, makes a better second and goose a better third than their American cousins.

Of games, wild duck and wild chicken, that is, pheasant, are fairly common. They are very good red-cooked. Bear's paw (usually dried and "developed") and venison are sometimes used at banquets, but much less common. Hare and rabbit are often successful substitutes for pheasant. Though we speak of "mountain rarities" (that is, game) and "sea flavors" as parallel examples of fine food, mountain rarities are really rarer than sea flavors.

There are stories of Chinese eating snakes in the South. They are true. I have eaten them in Canton. They are often shredded and cooked with chicken, and taste something like chicken and something like turtle. There are also stories about mouse-eating, but I have not yet seen anyone eat a mouse or met anyone who has eaten one or who has seen anyone eat one.

Dairy products play a small part in Chinese eating. There is good butter in Inner Mongolia and there is excellent goat's cheese—such as it is—in Yunnan. But in the majority of provinces, people do not drink cow's milk or make or use any dairy product.

The entrails of animals are usually prized more than simple lean meat. Liver was considered a good thing in China long before people talked about vitamins. In Peiping, even cats have long considered liver the standard food to go with their rice. Kidneys, lungs, intestines, tripe, when rightly prepared, are very good indeed. Skin of pork and mutton can be cooked very tender and then it is good. Cowhide is too tough to eat, but tendon attached to stew beef can be stewed into the consistency of jelly. When done right with soy sauce (Recipes Nos. 6.1 & 6.2), then "beef-stew" is not the word at all.

As in America, hen's eggs are the commonest eggs to eat. Next come duck's eggs, then goose's eggs. Pigeon's eggs, with transparent whites when cooked, are a fine delicacy. Eggs are eaten as eggs or form part of cooking material, as we shall see in the recipes.

2. River and Sea Food.—Fish is very good if it is good. Although we speak highly of "sea flavors," actually we like fresh-water food better. We respect the shark, but we love the carp. There is a fish called in Boston "buffalo carp," which abounds in Shanghai under the name of *ch'ing yü* and is greatly relished. But the favorite common fish is the *chi-yü* (*tsik-yü* in Cantonese). It is the fish of which goldfish are cultivated sports. Once in a while it turns up in an American market, but it is so uncommon that it has no definite name. Some fishmen call it "small carp," others call it "sand perch," still others say they do not know what you mean when you ask for small carp or sand perch. I call it give-me-some-of-that fish. It looks like a carp except that the back of its head is not straight but slants off the same way as its facial side. It tastes very fine and mild. Does it help to tell you that it is *Carasius Pekinensis?*

The shad is considered a great delicacy when it swims up the Yangtze River from the sea. We consider it one of the seven regrets of the world that the shad should have so many bones. The Mandarin fish has no small bones and is very good cooked either in Chinese or in American. Fish are so many I must leave them awhile until we cook them by our recipes.

Shellfish are just as good as regular fish. Lobsters, prawns, and shrimps are all called *hsia*, but small river *hsia* or shrimps are the best and very widespread in China. As for crabs, the fresh-water crabs are the best of all. They were introduced into Europe once but have never come to America. They have round shells and grow in lakes and marshes. When shelled they make a very good accompaniment to shark's fin. But the best way to eat crabs is the steamed kind you eat as a separate act, somewhat like your clambake except that they taste a thousand times better. (See Chapter 21.6 f.)

3. Vegetables.—Of fresh vegetables, there is just no end. I must mention lightly those kinds you cannot get in America, since it is no use trying to describe them and make my own mouth water and still cannot make you feel the taste of them. In the recipes, I shall limit myself to the vegetables you can get here. Some are found both here and in China so far as one can remember, like spinach, radishes, cucumbers. Some have been introduced recently from the West to China and made into Chinese dishes, like tomato, asparagus, cabbage, celery. I still regard them as foreign vegetables adapted to Chinese cooking, but to my children they seem to have

17

always grown in China. Indian corn was of course introduced so long ago that even my generation feels that it is a native Chinese grain. Quite a number of Chinese vegetables are planted in America. The Chinese cabbage, or celery cabbage, has been in this country for about twenty-five years, but has not yet been cooked, since you eat it raw. So it remains only to know how to cook it. But few Chinese vegetables come to the general market. Things like bean sprouts, pea sprouts, vegetable marrow or "winter melon," Chinese green cabbage, and a very tender and fat green called *chieh-ts'ai* (*kaai-ts'oi*), are grown on Long Island, in Florida, in the suburbs of San Francisco, Seattle, etc. You go to Chinatown to get them. Tender peas in the pod make a fine crisp green, but they are so expensive here that they can only be used as garnish, as on *Yeungchau Wo-min* (pot-noodles) in American-Chinese restaurants.

An important thing to understand about the place of Chinese vegetables is that potatoes, sweet potatoes, yams, and similar starchy roots are not considered vegetables proper in China, since we get our starch chiefly in rice, wheat and other grains. That is how the word *ts'ai*, "(green) vegetables" gets to mean accompanying dishes while *fan*, "rice" gets to mean the filling part of a meal or simply a meal. Irish potatoes have never been popular in China, and sweet potatoes are chiefly eaten as between-meal refreshments.

4. Preserved Food.—Food is preserved when it is salted, dried, less frequently pickled or candied, and recently also canned. Canned Chinese foods are rather looked down upon, except some specialties such as abalone and phoenix-tail fish. But in this country, the only way of getting certain things, such as winter bamboo shoots or red bean-curd cheese, is to get them canned, and you are lucky nowadays to get them.

There are in China stores specializing in preserved foods. Since the best preserved foods come from the South or from the Shanghai and Ningpo region in the Central East, which also calls itself *the* South, the stores are usually called *nan-huo-p'u*, "southern goods stores," though some of them may actually be made in the North. Almost anything may be preserved. Salted shrimps, shrimps' eggs, salted fish, from tiny one-inch fish to shark's fin, hundred-year-old

18

eggs—which taste best when about 100 days old—Chinese ham (for which two-year-old Smithfield, Virginia ham makes a very like substitute), are the commonest preserved animal foods. Dried lilies or "golden needles," ears of wood, which is a fluffy kind of black fungus, dried mushrooms, bamboo shoots, dried transparent pea-starch noodles, salted vegetables of various kinds, such as *cha-ts'ai* from Szechwan, *hsüeh-li-hung*, "red-in-snow" (for which you may substitute salted mustard green), salted radishes and soy-pickled cucumbers, sauce-pickled vegetables of various kinds—these are the commonest preserved vegetables. For preparing dried foods before cooking, the first step is to *fa* or "develop" them by soaking them in warm water or slightly boiling and then soaking them for several hours to several days; each thing must take its own time. (See Chapter V and the recipes.) Preserved old things you may eat alone or in company with young things. The second way is usually the best. A favorite dish in Shanghai is *ieh to' sieh*, "The Salted Stews the Fresh," consisting of salted and fresh pork clear-simmered together.

5. Fruits and Nuts.—Although fruits and nuts often form the first part of a banquet, they are normally between-meal foods, things that we *ch'ih-chih wa'r*, "eat for fun." In certain dishes, they are used for garnishing or for stuffing, but that is their secondary function. Because of lack of communications, fresh fruit is much limited to its place of growth. In the time of Emperor Hsüan Tsung (eighth century A.D.), litchi "nuts" had to be relayed by fast horses from Szechwan to Chang-an in modern Shensi to please his favorite courtesan. Recently, they have been flown from Canton to Shanghai. But on the whole, even in peacetime, most of the juicy peaches of Hopeh or Shantung are known only in their small locality, at least so far as knowledge of the juice trickling up your wrist is concerned. Dried fruits and nuts go much farther and have found their way into "southern goods stores."

Chinese watermelons have a great many varieties. They are called *hsi-kua*, "west melon" because they were introduced from the extreme west of China. Now they are grown almost everywhere in China. Besides eating melons as a special eating party

(Chapter 21.6 g) you can use the rind of watermelons for a stir-fried dish. Melon-seeds are from special seed-producing melons in which the pulp is not so good or so much. People are sometimes invited to eat the melons so as to get at the seeds. Chinese musk-melons are crisper, tenderer, and more fragrant than cantaloupe.

The lotus is the most versatile plant in China. The stem can be eaten as fruit, sliced and stir-fried, or stuffed with glutinous rice in its flue-shaped holes and steamed as a dessert. Its leaf is a fine wrapper of food. When fresh, it is used to give a delicate scent to congee or steamed meat. Its flower is both majestic and fragrant. Its seeds when young are juicy as fruit, whether eaten raw or boiled with sugar. Young lotus seeds sometimes come to Chinatown in canned form. When ripened into a nut-like state, dried, "developed," and boiled, they make a rich dessert alone or served as part of other sweet or even salt dishes. They not only taste good, but also sound good, since by way of a pun, *lien-tzŭ*, "lotus seed" also means "successive (births of) sons."

The commonest fruits of the northern provinces are peaches, apricots, Chinese pears, apples, crab apples, and persimmons. The Chinese pears are crisp and juicy instead of pulpy. The American pear has been introduced into China recently and known as *Yen-t'ai* (Chefoo) pear, where it has taken root. Chinese apples are not so good as American apples. Persimmons are best in Peiping. They are good and cheap, in normal times, and are a poor man's fruit as well as nourishment. In the southern provinces, there are tangerines, oranges, pomelos (a drier kind of grapefruit), kumquat, loquat, eating sugar canes, bananas, star-fruit, and occasionally papayas. Since the tangerine and not orange is the typical citrus fruit, there is a tendency for translators to render "orange" as *chü-tzŭ*, which is strictly the word for tangerine. A loquat looks like an apricot, but has a different kind of stone or stones. I bought some recently at Haymarket, Boston. The star-fruit is a tree-grown fruit of the Canton region and has star-shaped cross-sections.

For cooking purposes, the water chestnut (often coming canned) and young or ripe water caltrops are very important water fruits or nuts. Water caltrops are sometimes loosely also called water chestnuts. The starch from caltrops is the common binder starch for cooking in China. Here you have to use cornstarch.

There are no dates in China, but jujubes look like dates, and when dried taste less unlike dates than anything else. Though often eaten fresh as fruit, jujubes are much more important when dried and used for making other things, as we shall see in the recipes.

The most important nuts for cooking purposes are chestnuts and walnuts, widely used both in salt dishes and as a part of sweet things. Almonds are less often used in dishes. Peanuts are important for giving cooking oil. As nuts, they are only casual eating nuts and do not often enter dishes.

The sesame seed is an extremely important nut if you call it a nut, or an extremely important grain if you call it a grain. In either case, it is extremely important. Besides forming an important part of many cakes and biscuits and making a jam that looks like peanut-butter but tastes infinitely better, sesame oil is the most important flavoring oil. Salads, stuffings, soups, all need the magic touch of open sesame oil. In this country you have to substitute salad oil for it.

6. Grains.—We have seen that rice and wheat are the two main staples of Chinese food. Corn comes next in importance. Buckwheat, millet, and sorghum are considered coarse grain. Rice usually and millet sometimes are boiled whole. The others are usually ground into flour to make into breads, noodles, etc. Any grain could yield alcohol, but sorghum is very commonly used to distill a colorless liquor. Rice is of course the grain for the famous rice wine that tastes like sherry. More details about rice and wheat when we come to Chapters 18 and 20.

Besides miscellaneous starchy roots and bulbs, there are two important supplementary starch foods. One is the sweet potato. Though it rarely forms a part of dishes, nor is it eaten to replace rice or wheat at meals, it has great staying power when eaten at odd moments. It is a poor man's luxury. The other is beans: red beans, horse beans, and above all soy beans and their products. Bean milk and bean curd are regarded in this country as specialties.

21

But in China, cabbage and bean curd mean a poor family's home cooking. Soy beans not only give starch, but are also the most important source of protein, since most people cannot afford much animal food. Beans and bean products therefore are neither purely *fan*, "grain food" nor purely *ts'ai*, "dishes," but combine something of both and can be regarded as the typical classless kind of eating material in China.

C H A P T E R   I I I

COOKING MATERIALS

Cooking materials are used to bring your eating material to the right eating state, or to add taste to it, or to serve as accompaniment. For the process of cooking proper, we have 1. Heaters, and 2. Binders. For adding taste, or seasoning, we have 3. Salters, 4. Sweeteners, 5. Defishers, 6. Spices, and 7. Flavorers. Finally, we have 8. Garnishes, which form a part of the things to eat but also add to the taste. Several of the cooking materials do more than one thing. For instance, soy sauce is both a salter and a flavorer, and scallion is both a defisher and a garnish. In the following list of things each will be described in one place and referred to elsewhere if necessary.

One very important thing to remember is that the amounts of seasoning I give in the recipes are for eating the dishes in large morsels, such as you do when the "dish" is your main food. In Chinese eating, where the dishes are senders-down for rice, you would want to have the seasoning to a heavier taste, how much heavier depending upon what province you are from.

1. Heaters.—Water and **fat** are the chief heating materials in cooking. They differ in temperature and in giving a different texture to the food. There is not much to say about water except of course that the process of steaming consists in using water in the vaporized state. (On boiling and steaming, see Chapter VI, 1 and 2.)

Lard for Chinese cooking had better be made from leaf lard at the market. It is much better than ready lard in boxes. You cut it into two-inch pieces and heat them in a dry pan. When all melted, press on the pieces gently to squeeze out the liquid. The "leafing" then shrinks into fried pieces and becomes lard leavings. They are good to eat when hot and crisp, and usable to cook with vegetables.

23

When the leavings are brown, the lard is done. Pour into a heat-resisting container and let cool. Scoop as needed. After deep-frying, you have to use your judgment as to what else you can use it for. Few husbands will accept any fat in which fish has been deep-fried, for anything else, unless it is stronger fish. Besides lard, chicken fat is always good where the recipe calls for lard. Duck fat is good, provided you have de-tailed the duck.

The commonest vegetable oils used in China are bean oil and peanut oil; the latter is also obtainable in this country. In Soochow, oil from green cabbage seeds is used. Sesame oil is too precious to cook with and commonly used raw for flavoring, like olive oil. Crisco is not suitable for cooking Chinese dishes, as it tends to jelly when cold and spoil the texture of the food. It may be all right for shortening. Cottonseed oil is very good for Chinese cooking.

Whether lard or vegetable oil or both are to be used will be indicated in the recipes. In general, vegetable-oil-cooked things can be eaten cold or warmed over, while lard-cooked things are good only the first time.

Air is not an important heating material in cooking. In the case of roasting, not a common form of cooking in China anyway, it is really heat radiation that does the cooking.

Sand is a very effective heater for certain things. Roast chestnuts are never good in America. They crack and stay raw because of uneven and interrupted heating. In China chestnuts are roasted in sand. The hot sand, stirred all the time, surrounds the chestnuts on all sides with medium heat. In the course of time, the meat becomes soft and fragrant like well-baked sweet potatoes.

2. Binders.—The most important binder is **starch.** The starch commonly used for cooking in China is from water caltrops (*ling-chiao*), pea flour, or from the drains when flour is washed for getting gluten. Cornstarch is the recommended substitute for cooking in America. Pre-soaking sauces with starch protect the surface of the pieces and keep the juice in on frying. A curious opposite use of starch is that it makes eggs disperse into fine shreds, when so desired, if put into soup before beaten eggs are poured in.

Wheat flour is a heavier binder. Fish is often rubbed with flour so that its skin will hold together better on frying. As in American cooking, deep-frying pieces are often dipped in a thin paste of flour and beaten eggs. Besides fish, hard-boiled eggs (duck's eggs are good) are often sliced and dipped this way and then fried.

In a sense, frying **fats** are binders. In "meeting-cooked" dishes (No. 10 in Chapter VI on Methods), the parts are often pre-fried so as not to fall apart when boiled together.

One form of binder fat is the "net fat" or meshy pork fat from the mesentery of pigs. It is wrapped around shad for steaming to keep all juice in. (See Recipe No. 10.2.)

Some binders are just binders and not part of the food. Examples are Paper-Wrapped Chicken (Recipe No. 8.17.) and rice tetrahedrons wrapped in rush or bamboo leaves.

3. Salters.—Salt is of course the chief salter. Chinese salt is often used in unrefined state and tastes more salty. There is a noticeable difference in strength between cooking and table salt in America. The difference varies with the brand. In extreme cases the difference may be as much as 3 to 4. In giving the amount in the recipes, I am *always referring to cooking salt.*

Soy sauce is a salter in that it contains salt. See § 7. Flavorers, for full description.

One important thing you should understand and remember is that salt is not freely exchangeable with soy sauce. When it is the white kind of cooking, of course salt should be used and the least bit of soy sauce will make it taste wrong, though after the white-cooking is done, it is usually all right to dip-eat the dish in uncooked soy sauce. But even in red-cooking and red-stir-frying, if the recipe says 1 t-sp. salt, and 2 tb-sp. soy sauce, then you must not try to get the same degree of salting with 4 tb-sp. soy sauce and no salt. There is a right proportion of things in each recipe.

4. Sweeteners.—In most parts of China little or no sugar is used in cooking dishes. Only candy and dessert food are sweet. Changchow and Wusih in Kiangsu are known for liberal sweetening of salty dishes. Certain dishes, such as Red-Cooked Meat, always have some sweetening.

In the order of importance, granulated sugar, brown sugar, crystallized sugar are the sweeteners used. Honey is not much used.

5. Defishers.—Half the secret of good cooking lies in defishing the fish, or anything in which you wish to soften down the animal flavor, such as fowl, or duck. The most important part of that is cooking wine. Rice wine of ordinary quality is the cooking wine of China. Ordinary sherry is the nearest substitute for that. Never use distilled liquor for cooking, as it will spoil the taste.

Vinegar is a defisher, besides contributing one of the most interesting tastes itself. The phrase "eat vinegar" in Chinese means "to be jealous." For fish, crabs, etc., vinegar is more frequently used for dip-eating at the table than put in during cooking. One of the best kinds of dipping vinegar is the black vinegar of Chinkiang, once in a while seen in Chinatown.

Ginger is now more available than it used to be. When used in cooking, it is sliced into $\frac{1}{16}$-inch slices. The slices are usually not eaten. When used for dipping together with vinegar, it is in fine shreds or fine dots and as much of it as will stick to the dipping piece will be eaten.

Scallion, or spring onion, is so near the Chinese *ts'ung*—except that it is smaller and not so strong—that it is more *it* than a substitute. Shantung people eat it raw, which is supposed to have made them resistant to germs and grow to heroic statures. In cooking fish, we always mention scallion and ginger in the same breath.

6. Spices.—Under spices I include the rather sharp-tasting cooking materials. When I mention **black pepper** in the recipes, I mean the pepper as in pepper and salt. The usual kind is black, but there is a white kind which tastes almost the same. Black pepper is used in sour-hot soups and is mixed with salt for dipping fried things before eating.

Hot pepper is the vegetable-like fruit, which in the sweet variety (sweet pepper) is simply a vegetable, and in the hot variety forms a very important part of seasoning in the central and southwestern provinces, such as Szechwan and Hunan.

Szechwan pepper, or fagara (*Xanthoxylum piperitum*), is a very ingratiating spice which tastes only faintly hot but brings out the taste of many things very well. Even peanuts boiled with just salt and fagara become a revelation to those who have not had them this way.

Pa-chiao, aniseed, and *ta-liao*, "great spice," are similar to fagara but have a slightly more rounded smell.

Ginger is, of course, also a strong spice. We have already mentioned it as a defisher.

Coriander, Chinese parsley, or *hsiang-ts'ai* (*yinsöi-ts'oi* in Cantonese) is tenderer and has a richer flavor than American parsley. Some people, including Chinese, have to learn to like it. Then they say it's worth learning. It is often put into soups after they come on the table. The slight heat brings out the flavor best. A considerate host asks, "Does everybody like *hsiang-ts'ai?*" before putting it in.

7. **Flavorers.**—The most important flavorer of Chinese food is **soy-bean sauce** or soy sauce for short. With soy sauce, you can cook an untiring series of Chinese dishes with nothing but those foods you can get at any American chain market. In fact even pretty good soy sauce can now be bought at such chain markets. Chinese dishes are called red-cooked or white-cooked according as soy sauce is or is not used. But even in the white-cooked dishes, especially the slow-cooking ones, the morsels, or rather the chopstickles, of food are often dipped in soy sauce before eating. One thing we never do, however, is to pour soy sauce on rice. When Americans do that, it looks funny. It must taste funny too.

Soy sauce is made from fermented boiled soy beans in which salt is added. Several kinds are now seen in this country. The least useful is called in Cantonese *chü-yau*, "pearl sauce," a dark thick sauce without too strong a taste, which lends much color to the dish and is much used in restaurants. Next is *shang-ch'au*, "raw extract," which is light brown, tastes very fine, but is not colorful enough for red-cooking and not available in any great quantity. The sauce most suitable for general purposes is called *ch'au-yau*, "extracted sauce," which fortunately is made by several manufacturers in this country and Canada. All varieties of soy sauce are also called by the general name *shi-yau* in Cantonese.

Similar to but thicker than soy sauce is **soy jam**, available in

27

this country under the trade names of "bean sauce" and "*hoisin* sauce," the latter more savory and sweetish.

There is a whole class of whitish savory powder made mostly from gluten of flour. We shall call it **taste-powder** in the recipes. The oldest form of this is made from dried fermented muscle-of-flour (flour gluten), often made in old Chinese households. Almost thirty years ago, the Japanese manufactured, from hydrolized gluten, a powder called *ajinomoto*, "prime element of taste." Later a Chinese firm manufactured *ve-tsin*, "essence of taste," which is still found on some shelves of Chinatown. "Accent," *mee boan*, etc. are made in this country. All these are essentially monosodium glutamate.

You will note that relatively few recipes of this book call for the use of taste-powder. For good cooking consists in making the best use of eating materials. The cooking materials should enhance the natural taste of the eating material and not take its place. The widespread use of taste-powder in recent years has resulted in a lowering of the standard of right cooking and a leveling of all dishes to one flavor. Persons who have to eat at boarding places complain of declining appetite because all dishes taste alike. If, however, you use taste-powder conservatively and add it only when the other ingredients are very plain, such as spinach and egg soup, then it will be a very welcome and refreshing flavor as one of many different flavors.

Other common flavorers are **oyster sauce, sesame oil,** and **soy bean cheese** (*fu-yü*). Fukien cooking uses **shrimp sauce,** which one has to learn to like. **Chicken** or **meat soup** is often used to impart flavor to other material. In large kitchens, there is a large current pot in which animals for various uses come in and out to get cooked and to contribute their flavor to it. It is called "high soup," or general-purpose soup.

If garnishes like **ham, dried shrimps, bamboo shoots, mushrooms,** and **red-in-snow** are used, little or no flavorer will be needed.

8. Garnishes.—A garnish is something between an eating material and a cooking material. If there is more of it, it is an eating material. If there is less of it, it is a cooking material. For instance, in a boarding place, you often cannot tell whether a dish is meat-shreds garnished with red-in-snow or red-in-snow garnished with meat-shreds. So you call it in Chinese "red-in-snow stirs meat-shreds."

Of eating materials used as garnishes, the commonest are ham slices, dried mushrooms, bamboo shoots, red-in-snow, and hot pepper. The commonest garnishes used only as cooking materials are scallion, garlic, onion, Chinese parsley, ginger, and dried shrimps. As these have been described elsewhere, we shall stop with just mentioning them here.

Following is a list of names to facilitate purchase at Chinese stores:

	Chinese	*Mandarin*	*Cantonese*	*English*
1.	花椒 / 川椒	hua-chiao / ch'uan-chiao	fa-chiu / ch'ün-chiu	fagara, Szechwan pepper
2.	八角	pa-chiao	paat-kok	aniseed, star anise, Chinese anise
3.	芫荽 / 香菜	yen-sui / hsiang-ts'ai	yin-söi / ——	coriander, Chinese parsley
4.	蠔油	hao-yu	hou-yau	oyster sauce
5.	蔴油	ma-yu	ma-yau	sesame oil
6.	醬油 / 豉油 / 抽油	chiang-yu / —— / ——	—— / shi-yau / ch'au-yau	soy sauce, soybean sauce
7.	生抽	sheng-ch'ou	shang-ch'au	(first quality) soy sauce
8.	甜麵醬	t'ienmien-chiang	t'inmin-cheung	flour jam
9.	原豉醬	yuanshih chiang	yünshi-cheung	bean sauce
10.	海鮮醬	haihsien chiang	hoisin-cheung	hoisin sauce

29

CHAPTER IV

COOKING AND EATING UTENSILS

1. Cooking Utensils.—Some of the things to cook and eat with in China are the same as in America. Others are quite different.

A good supply of pots and pans of various sizes should be handy. In general, slow-cooking dishes should have thicker pots and faster cooking things should have thinner ones. In the recipes, the term "skillet" means any shallow, thin pan in which oil can be heated quickly for various forms of frying. Deep-frying, of course, calls for something deep enough in which to float the pieces to be deep-fried.

A Chinese family kitchen may get along fine without an oven, but not without a good steamer. A double boiler in which the steam does not get at the food is not a steamer in the Chinese sense. For dry-steaming, a perforated upper layer is needed. When pastry is steamed, you put a cheesecloth on the perforated upper layer to prevent sticking. Rush leaves and pine needles are often used in China in place of the cheesecloth. In the recipes I use the term "tier" for the perforated partition. If you cannot get a double boiler with a perforated partition, you can make a partition yourself very easily. Get a tin box or a can a size or two smaller and lower than your boiler. With a big nail and a hammer, make a few dozen ¼-inch holes in the bottom. Place the box in the boiler bottom up to serve as a tier. For wet steaming, no special equipment is needed so long as you have a boiler big enough to hold the bowl and still have room for the steam to come over the edges of the bowl.

For the handling of materials being cooked, you can use the ordinary kind of ladles, leaking ladles, and frying shovels with holes in them. We sometimes use chopsticks for putting things into and taking things out of a cooking vessel, but you may use your fingers, forks, or ladles, if you have not learned to use chopsticks.

For the readying of materials, the most important tool is the Chinese *ch'ieh-ts'ai-tao*, "vegetable-cutting knife," which is really a meat-chopping knife. It is about 3 inches wide, 8 inches long, ⅛ inch at the back, and 0 inches at the edge, with a round handle about 3 inches long. With such a "vegetable" knife, you can chop bones, scale carp (but not shad, because shad should not be scaled), mince meat, as well as cut vegetables. For mincing stuffings, two such knives in a pair of skilled hands to the rhythm of some popular folk-song can work very fast. An American meat-grinder is perhaps less tiring than Chinese vegetables knives, but the best stuffing, especially the celery cabbage part in wraplings (Recipe No. 20.6), is hand-chopped, probably because you only cut instead of grinding it. The Chinese "vegetable" knife can sometimes be bought in Chinatown. Sometimes a cook keeps apart a cutting knife from a chopping knife, which has a somewhat different tempered edge. But the difference is not great and the knives all look alike. Don't argue with the cook when he has either of them in his hands, but address him as *Ta-shih-fu*, "the master chef."

Other kitchen accessories such as cutting boards, kneading bowls, rolling pins, are much the same in China as in America. Many things from the kitchen counter at Five-and-Ten's can be quite helpful in a Chinese kitchen, even though we never use them in China. In fact I usually took quite a few of them back after each of my visits to the United States, can-openers, egg-beaters and what not. But I never bought measuring cups, regulation tablespoons, teaspoons, or sweep-dial electric clocks. In spite of my use of thermometers and sweep-dial watches in my medical profession, I am still my Chinese self in the kitchen rather than a dietitian. The Chinese cook or housewife never measures space, time, or matter. *Hse* just pours in a splash of sauce, sprinkles a pinch of salt, does a moment of stirring, and *hse* tastes the frying-hot juice out of the edge of a ladle, perhaps adds a little amendment, and the dish comes out right. It was only when I started on this cookbook that I began to get some measuring things so that I can show you how

31

to do it my way. What my way was I could not tell myself until I measured myself doing it. Now you and I not only have to have the usual measuring things, but also a foot-rule, since I often have to tell how long a slice should be cut or what diameter a cake should be made. Finally, I would advise also the use of an egg-timer for Chinese cooking, since many of the stir-fried dishes take about the time of soft-boiled eggs.

2. Eating and Serving Utensils.—We use trays and tureens and pots, but the serving stage is less important at a Chinese meal eaten in the Chinese way, since you eat out of common bowls filled in the kitchen. In the Chinese way, there are also no serving spoons or ladles or other utensils on the table. In Americanized forms of Chinese meals, a double set of chopsticks and spoons are used, a serving set and an eating set. When there are American guests, forks should also be readied for emergencies, but do not force them on guests who insist on practicing with chopsticks. Small dishes of seasoning for dip-eating are placed at strategic points on the table, so that each kind is within everyone's "boarding-house reach." But except at special eating parties such as Boiled Crabs or Rinsed Lamb, there are fewer dishes of each kind of seasoning than there are guests. When there is wine, there is a wine cup before each guest. Since Chinese rice wine is best warm, some use double-bottom cups with hot water between the two walls. When rice, congee, or soup-noodle is served, there is an individual bowl before each guest. Lately there is a growing practice of having a small dish before each guest for receiving shells and bones. But in the Chinese way of eating, you never use a full-sized eating plate before you, since you are not served portions. A final item commonly found in Chinese restaurants in China is the cup half filled with lukewarm water brought up at the end of a dinner. No, don't drink it, because it is not the finger bowl! You rinse your mouth and spit into cuspidors provided. This is done unobtrusively during the confusion of standing up from the table. Many people—I am one of them—do not like this institution. Another very important equipment is the scalding hot towels served at the end of meals both at home and when dining out. Because of the prevalence of trachoma in China, hygiene-minded persons make a habit of not wiping their eyes when using public hot towels. But the hot towel is such a good thing that those who are used to it always feel their mouth greasy when they have nothing better than a dry piece of cloth to wipe with.

3. Chopsticks are so important as tools of eating that I must give them special mention. Chopsticks used to be called *chu*, related to the word for "help," something to help you eat. But because it has the same pronunciation as the word for "stop," the boatmen

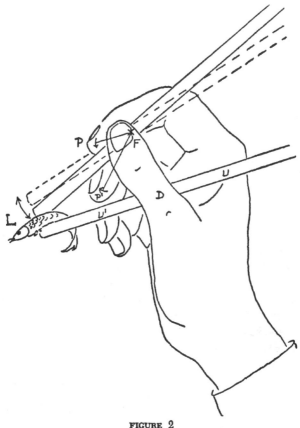

FIGURE 2

HOW TO USE CHOPSTICKS

do not like the sound of it. So they renamed the thing *k'uai-tzŭ*, "something fast," instead of being becalmed. So this is the present name for chopsticks. In Cantonese it is pronounced *faai-tsi*, which is what you would ask for in an American-Chinese restaurant. In using a pair of chopsticks, it is very important to know the difference between the upper and the lower chopsticks. The lower is fixed with the base of the thumb pressing down (D in Figure 2), and the base of the index finger (U) and the thumb side of the end of the ring-finger (U') both pressing upwards. Keep this lower chopstick there and never let it slide or roll. The upper chopstick is held in a floating position. The tip of the thumb holds it down as a fulcrum (F in Fig. 2). The tips of the index and middle fingers pinch and push on both sides of the chopstick farther down toward the food end. When the index finger pushes down harder at P (power), the tip at L (load) comes down and pinches the food against the fixed chopstick. When the middle finger presses up harder at P', the tip is raised (to position shown by dotted lines) and the pincer is opened to make ready to get another morsel. This opening motion, when done firmly, can also separate food, such as meat or chicken, when well done. In moving the upper chopstick up and down, a slight rolling may be caused by its upper part resting on the side of the index finger. But this slight rolling makes no difference in the result. Two important conditions for effective use of chopsticks must be remembered. One is that the two lower ends must be even, that is, one must not protrude over the other. The other condition is that the two chopsticks must be in the same plane. You need not know much geometry to see that unless these conditions are met, you cannot make your two ends meet.

4. Pressure Cookers.—The Chinese do not use pressure cookers. But I have found them so adaptable to Chinese cooking that I want to say something about their uses in this special section. It goes without saying that pressure cookers are suitable only for long-cooking dishes—the good thing about them is that they make long cooking short. For most dishes use 15-lb. pressure and 20 min. *pressurized* time, that is, after the cooker has attained full pressure. The special point to remember, however, is to let the cooker stand, after the fire is turned off, for 20 to 30 min. more. This is necessary in order that the color and taste of the seasoning can get inside the food. Red-Cooked Shoulder (Recipe No. 1.1), however, should stand for 1 hour before opening. If you open the cooker too soon after cooking, the food will taste hasty and un-Chinese.

Pressure cooking is by no means limited to red-cooked dishes. White cooking, such as in Recipe No. 5.6, is also very good with pressure cookers.

Warning: Don't clog the vent and blow off the top! Since the pressure cooker is especially good for foods with thick juice, you should never fill it more than two-thirds full at the most, preferably less. During cooking, some of the stuff tends to splash toward the vent and if too much of it gets collected there, the vent will be stopped up and the pressure will then build up to an explosion. Some cookers have a safety fuse which melts and converts a potential explosion to a geyser. But geysers are better watched outdoors than indoors.

There is however no need to be unduly scared of such eventualities. By taking no more than the usual caution a housewife is expected to take among pots and pans and oil and fire, you will find the pressure cooker a very rewarding cooking utensil.

5. Stoves.—Chinese cooking needs fires which can be brisk, medium, or low, at a moment's notice. For this reason I used to say that gas ranges were the best and electric ranges, with their slow start and lingering heat, were unsuitable for Chinese cooking, while various types of old-fashioned Chinese stoves lay somewhere in between. But with a little experience I have found that the only thing that needs a little attention with an electric range is to remember.to preheat it and be ready for whatever needs a quick fire and to take the pot off to one side whenever a sudden stop is called for. Once you have acquired the right habit, you will find an electric range practically as convenient as a gas range.

6. Freezers.—Freezers are as useful for keeping Chinese foods as American foods. Besides the usual function of freezers to keep raw foods, they can be used to keep pre-cooked foods, parceled to form unit dishes, so that each parcel can be thawed out for the final cooking, as needed. Finished dishes also keep well in deep

34a

freeze. One of my friends was surprised by her hostess with "the very same dish" she had had at my friend's house a few months ago. "When did you learn to make such excellent Red-Cooked Meat, Mrs. Cabot?" "Why, it was the leftover meat you gave me last year, you remember, Mrs. Chin?"

Special uses of the freezer will be mentioned in the recipes, as we come to them, as for example in No. 22.3, Frozen Bean Curd.

CHAPTER V

METHODS OF READYING

Before your things are ready to "go down into the pan," as we say in Chinese, you may have to do a lot of things to them. That is why a three-minute cooking often takes hours to do, though usually only about five minutes.

1. Cleaning.—Food has to be clean of course. There are some apparent exceptions. Szechwan-style Steeped Vegetables (VI.18), for example, should not be washed before steeping. That is because after you take off one or two outside layers, say of a cabbage, the inner part is cleaner than if washed in unsterilized raw water. Most things should of course be washed. Rice is washed in a rice basket, usually with two changes of water, or the equivalent when running water is used. You do not wash noodles, but after boiling, you change the hot water with cold water, or once more with hot water or soup if you want to have them hot. Gizzard, tripe, and intestines are hard to clean. With a gizzard, it is a matter of cutting it open and rinsing off the sandy things. Tripe sometimes comes from the market cleaned. One Chinese method of cleaning the inside of tripe and intestines is to rub them on rough stone surfaces. They are so good as to be worth a lot of trouble-taking.

2. Cutting, Picking, etc.—I did not mention the saw in your kitchen tools, as I take it that you have your butcher do it when it takes that much cutting, such as sectioning a whole Smithfield, Virginia ham or cracking up a pork loin. The heaviest kitchen-scale cutting is with chicken and duck. I refer you to Recipe No. 9.8, Salt-Water Duck, for a description of cutting duck, which also applies to chicken. As to the cutting of meat, there is no problem about large pieces for red-cooking or minced meat for meat balls, but for slicing, which is usually for stir-frying, it is very important to remember to *cut against the grain,* that is, perpendicular to the direction of the fibers. This is especially important for beef, though it applies to all meat and poultry.

A form of vegetable cutting is called *kun-tao-k'uai,* "rolling-knife pieces." Suppose you have a carrot. You cut it across at an angle of 30° from the axis. Roll the rest of your carrot one-third of a turn (120°) and cut it further up so that the new cut will partly cut across the original cut surface and partly cut a new surface. By having the right slant, the right amount of rolling, and right length of advance, you get beautiful combinations of parts of curved cylindrical and plane elliptical surfaces. (See Fig. 3.) Carrots, asparagus, small cucumbers, any cylindrical vegetable can be cut into rolling-knife pieces.

FIGURE 3
ROLLING-KNIFE PIECES

Special manners for cutting specific things will be described in the recipes. I shall mention some very common forms. Any massive thing which you want the juice or oil to enter quickly may be slashed a little on the sides. This applies to whole shoulders, whole large fish, but not usually to poultry. Fresh mushrooms should be sliced into ꟼIꟼ–by–T T T slices, that is, vertically, parallel to the stem. Cylindrical things should be cut by the rolling-knife pieces as described above, but when very thin slices are called for, they are cut at a slant in parallel slices, as with broccoli.

3. Picking.—By picking I mean the separating of parts to throw away from the parts to keep. The general principle seems to be that the Chinese eat everything that can be eaten while the Americans

36

throw away everything that can be thrown away. With large animals the problem is not so difficult. You just buy what you want to eat. The market will throw away beforehand what you do not want, but often also what you do want. This is especially true of fish. The cooking of a Chinese fish dish in America begins with an argument with your fishman. You get a nice fresh carp and tell him to keep his head. But by habit he does it the usual way, and when you open your package after you get home, you find that you have lost your head. Next time you go, you complain about last time, and he is so nice apologizing that you are encouraged to go Chinese one more. So when he cleans the fish, you tell him, twice, to keep its tongue in its cheek, because that is the best part of the fish. Since he has never heard of such a thing, he cannot locate the tongue and throws it away together with the gills. But he is a nice man. Keep your temper and you will soon be able to keep your tongue.

Shrimps are cooked with or without shells according to the dish wanted. It is important to remove the dark gritty line along the back. In the recipes, I sometimes just say "remove sand."

With meat and poultry, the only important difference in Chinese practice is the keeping of the skin for pork, sometimes mutton. We go to great lengths of time in picking hairs and feathers with forceps. With duck, especially in clear-simmering for soup (Recipe No. 15.20), some people object to the too-strong odor from the tail, and unless you know beforehand that everyone likes it, it is better to discard the tail-end, including the oil pouches, before cooking. Some people, however, regard it as good as carp's tongue.

Vegetables are sometimes picked even more radically than in American cooking. That is because stir-frying needs very tender material. When you have string beans, you break off from ¼ to ½ inch from both ends (less off the tip-end), and before breaking one end quite off, try to pull out the strong fibers on the sides of the pod to come out together with the end. For salting or steeping celery cabbage you take off quite a few leaves from the outside, but except for the dirty and withered outermost layer, you can boil for soup leaves which are not tender enough for salting or steeping. Pea sprouts are usually snipped in China, though it may be well to keep them whole here, as they are so hard to get in this country.

4. Mixing and Fixing.—With your eating and cooking materials ready, you sometimes have to do quite a little fixing before they are ready to cook. When I say in the recipes mix such and such things, I always mean mix thoroughly, even though I may forget to say so. For some things, the eating material has to be soaked for a time before going down into the frying pan. Many quick-cooking dishes, such as Fried Spring Chicken (Recipe No. 8.8), use this kind of readying.

Fresh-salting is a very common form of readying. You salt your eating material for a day or so and rinse off some of the salt before cooking. This is done for example with Chinkiang Fresh-Salted Meat (Recipe No. 5.4) and Smoked Carp (Recipe No. 10.12).

I do not need to say much about mechanical mixing such as beating of eggs, kneading of dough, mixing of stuffing. Special mixing such as Fish Balls (Recipe No. 10.10) will be described under the recipes.

5. Pre-cooking.—The most important pre-cooking in Chinese cooking is *fa*, "develop." As I told you, we use a lot of dried and salted things because they keep and because they are more savory than when fresh. Now to get these things ready to cook into dishes, they have to be softened up by heat and moisture. Parboiling, standing, etc., are used for these things and each thing has its own way of "developing" as described in the recipes.

Next in importance is pre-frying. For example, Small Fried Meat Balls (Recipe No. 4.1) dip-eaten in pepper and salt is nice, but very dry and commonplace. Large meat balls are fried only as a pre-cooking readying. They become important when they are finally cooked into Lion's Head (Recipe No. 4.3 *var.*).

Boiling as a form of pre-cooking needs no explanation. Typical of this is the famous Szechwan dish Twice-Cooked Meat (Recipe No. 5.7).

If you plan dishes which call for pre-boiling, and if you have to store the food on refrigeration, it is better to refrigerate after boiling than keep it raw or after complete cooking. This applies, for example, to *Ch'a-shiu* Meat (5.11), Roast Chicken (8.22), Roast Turkey (8.23), and Stirred Crab-Meat (12.14).

C H A P T E R   V I

METHODS OF COOKING

When you have the eating material ready, you can do to it one or more of the following twenty and one things. You can 1. boil it, 2. **steam** [1] it, 3. roast it, 4. **red-cook** it, 5. **clear-simmer** it, 6. pot-stew it, 7. **stir-fry** it, 8. **deep-fry** it, 9. **shallow-fry** it, 10. **meet** it, 11. splash it, 12. plunge it, 13. rinse it, 14. cold-mix it, 15. sizzle it, 16. **salt** it, 17. pickle it, 18. steep it, 19. dry it, 20. smoke it, and, if you have done it right, 21. **eat** it. I shall tell you what you would do in each case.

1. Boiling.—There is very little big-fire boiling, as a complete process, in Chinese cooking. We would not consider eating boiled potatoes. After a thing is boiled, the natural question is, Now what of it? For quick plain boiling is often only a preparatory process for other ways of cooking, as for example in Twice Cooked Meat, Recipe No. 5.7. There are some exceptions, such as plain boiled celery cabbage with salt and a little lard, or boiled yam, to eat with sugar. But celery cabbage and yam are such cook-proof things that they are good in any state. As to more complicated ways of boiling, see the other methods described below.

If you have a scientific-minded husband, such as mine seems to be, who objects strongly to the use of continued big fire after water has started to boil, because water cannot be hotter than 100° C, you can please him, if you want to, by turning the fire to medium. But to make sure that it is at least that hot in all parts, especially in a large tall boiling or steaming pot, the fire must be big enough for you to see the steam come out. This is, however, only for your own reference, as it may start another argument if you say you can see steam, since steam is invisible, you see?

[1] Operations in **bold-face** are the most important ones.

39

2. Steaming.—Steaming is a test of the quality of the eating material. It is therefore a favorite method of cooking very fresh fresh-water fish, though by no means limited to such. Sometimes, the eating material is steamed plain such as ham (or beaten eggs with only salt and water). Sometimes the cooking materials are mixed in first. The steamed bowl is set in the steamer pot, with water enough to last, but not to overboil into the steamed bowl. The length of steaming time varies from ½ hour to 5 hours, depending upon what is steamed. Sometimes no water need be added to the steamed bowl and the natural juice and condensed steam will give just enough juice.

Many forms of "dot-heart" refreshments are steamed dry on steaming tiers or perforated trays. The so-called White-Boiled (Fresh-water) Crabs are really steamed on tiers rather than actually boiled.

3. Roasting.—Roasting is not family cooking in China, since few families have facilities for roasting. Only restaurants go much into roasts and Cantonese restaurants excel especially in these. Chicken, duck, goose—roasted whole—are quite common, roast pig less frequent, roast lamb or roast beef very rare. Instead of ovens, which are used for baking pastries only, roasting is over a charcoal fire, with the roast turning slowly round and round. Sauce is added inside and out from time to time so that the skin remains smooth and shiny, instead of rough and flaky, and the meat remains juicy instead of powdery. The Chinese roast duck, such as Peiping is famous for, is really a sort of soft-broiled duck. Families can go to food shops to buy roast meat or poultry and eat it cold. But for the crisp juicy hot roast duck, one has to go to a restaurant—one of those two-hundred-year-old ones. (See, however, Recipe No. 9.9.)

You will note that there is no mentioning of baking as a form of Chinese cooking. Things like hot biscuits are baked in ovens, but they are not dishes. Baking in the sense of putting made-over material in the oven to cook as a dish is not a usual part of Chinese cooking. Recipes 23.3A, B, and C are exceptions that prove the rule.

4. Red-Cooking.—Red-cooking is stewing with soy sauce, some materials needing pre-frying, some not. It is so-called because the soy-sauce juice gives a reddish color.[1]

Red-cooking is the typical family cooking. It is not what the chef calls a dish-producing way of cooking, since a lot of stuff "boils down" to very little. It has little to show. And then it takes such a long time for most materials. Red-cooked dishes cannot therefore usually be ordered *à la carte* in restaurants unless specially ordered hours beforehand. For the housewife, however, it has the advantage common to slow-cooking dishes that the leftovers keep well and can be eaten cold or warmed over. Cold red-cooked jelly of meat, chicken, etc., is especially good. If you are careful to warm it just to boiling point each time after use, the pot can keep for nearly two weeks. Another household hint is that you can from time to time add in vegetables such as spinach, celery, cabbage, pea-flour noodles, etc., and stretch the dish almost forever.

Usual eating materials good for red-cooking are: pork shoulder, pork sides with skin (fresh bacon), fresh ham, stew beef, especially with tendons, lamb, leg of mutton (skin also good), whole chicken, whole duck, carp, buffalo carp. The cooking time varies from two to six hours, depending upon the thing to be red-cooked and upon how well it has been bought. For details see the various red-cooking recipes.

5. **Clear-Simmering.**—Clear-simmering differs from red-cooking in several ways. It is clear because no soy sauce is used. Secondly, it is less dry and the slow cooking yields clear soup to serve as drink at the table. Except a few "developed" dried vegetables such as dried winter mushrooms, most clear-simmered dishes are meat and fish dishes. As soon as boiling starts, very low fire should be used. Any continued quick boiling will make the soup muddy and uninviting. Commonly clear-simmered materials are: pork shoulder, pork sides (with skin), shoulder, whole chicken, whole duck, whole turtle, whole or half piece of shad. Some people like

[1] If very light-colored sauce is used, it will give a funny taste, just like white port, which always tastes "red" when you drink it with your eyes shut. To avoid this funny feeling, the cook or housewife or the manufacturer often adds coloring to the soy sauce which otherwise would be very light colored.

to skim the scum from pork or duck at first boiling. This lightens the flavor. Some of the fat may also be skimmed if desired. A duck should be de-tailed. Cooking wine is always good for clear-simmered fish or poultry. Slices of ham and winter bamboo will enrich the soup, but they don't make it "too rich."

By clear-simmering, good eating material is brought out and poor eating material is shown up. Good cooks are proud of good clear-simmering, but ordinary cooks hesitate to clear-simmer, since it demands too much quantity, quality, and time. A practical advantage about a clear-simmered dish is that it combines the part of a main dish and that of a drinking soup.

6. Pot-Stewing.—Pot-stewing or *lu* in Chinese is similar to red-cooking, but it is a very-large-scale, long-term operation and uses more spices. Pot-stewing is more a food-shop process than family cooking, though often used by large households. You start with chickens, ducks, and large pieces of meat such as shoulder—skin, bone, and all—and clear-simmer for one hour after boiling. Then add scallion, ginger, aniseed, Szechwan pepper, and a liberal amount of cooking wine and soy sauce. Simmer for a whole day, when all the materials will fall to pieces; then take them out. What remains is the master sauce for future pot-stewing.

To pot-stew anything, cut into medium-size pieces, put in already boiling water and boil for 3 to 5 min., then take out and boil in the master sauce to simmer for one or two hours. Then take out and eat hot or cold.

After three or four uses, the master sauce should be strengthened with soy sauce, salt, wine, and occasionally spices. Before putting away, the sauce should be sterilized by heating each time it has been touched by raw material or unsterilized ladles, etc. Tradition tells of pots with master sauce started two or three hundred years ago. Owners of pot-stew pots fear military upheavals, lest the continuity of the master sauce be broken.

A favorite food with many is Pot-Stewed Eggs—eggs hard-boiled so long that they are soft again. Since eggs only take and do not give much, they are not used in starting a master sauce.

While pot-stewing is a troublesome process, it has the advantage of what we call "Toil once then leisure forever." Especially in China, where you are always expecting unexpected guests.

7. **Stir-Frying.**—Stir-frying is the most characteristic method of cooking in Chinese. This is when you really have to cook *in* Chinese, since the Chinese term *ch'ao*, with its aspiration, low-rising tone and all, cannot be accurately translated into English. Roughly speaking, *ch'ao* may be defined as a big-fire-shallow-fat-continual-stirring-quick-frying of cut-up material with wet seasoning. We shall call it "stir-fry" or "stir" for short. The nearest to this in western cooking is *sauté*.

Materials most suitable for stir-frying are filet or other parts of pork, beef, lamb, where there is no tendon but a lot of uniform meat. With poultry, white meat should be used. In fish, back meat is best. Shrimps and prawns should be shelled. Vegetables should be used young. Tenderness is an important point in stir-frying. Be sure that meat must be cut across or against the grain.

While the stir-frying itself usually takes but two or three minutes, the preparation of the material often takes a lot of trouble.

First you prepare and cut the right ingredients into small pieces, slices, shreds, or cubelets, etc. If different ingredients take different lengths of time to cook, each has to be put in at the right time, so as to come out done together.

The fat must be well heated before anything is put in. Little or no water is used, especially when fresh vegetables are used, which give plenty of their own juice. Everything being timed so as to be done at one common finishing time, the whole thing should be served as soon as done and eaten as soon as served. This is when the hostess often has to stop the men from talking shop. The food is no good when cold and too tough when warmed over. It can be kept warm in a low oven for a short while, but after that it becomes uninteresting.

Because stir-frying has such critical timing and is done so quickly, it can be called "blitz-cooking." Because stirred dishes have to be eaten on time, they also need "blitz-eating." Restaurant chefs like to show off their skill in such dishes, and are often judged by them. Restaurants and cooks with whom you "board" also like stir-frying because it has a lot to show. It is one of the most "dish-producing ways of cooking.

8. Deep-Frying.—Deep-frying in Chinese cooking is more often a preparatory process than a complete dish-making process. "Dot-hearts" are often deep-fried, but they are not dishes.

The commonest way of preparing deep-frying dishes is to cut the material into medium-sized pieces (or make slashes in the case of fish desired to be served whole), soak in prepared seasoning for a while and fry in hot deep fat. Starch or egg-flov dipping sometimes goes with deep-frying. Deep-fried things are often dipped into little sauces of salt and pepper before eating. When deep-fried material is cooked with other things with the addition of wet seasoning, then it is a "meeting," on which see Section 10 below.

9. Shallow-Frying.—Shallow-frying, like deep-frying, is not commonly used as a complete cooking process. Pastry is sometimes shallow-fried, especially after first boiling, such as fried wraplings. In shallow-frying proper, the material is steeped in seasoning and eaten right after frying. When frying is done first and other cooking materials are added later, then it becomes "meeting," "splashing," etc., as described below.

Half-shallow or half-deep frying is often used instead of deep-frying to save oil or to prevent too much drying or just because the pot is not deep enough to keep in oil the whole fish or whatever is to be fried.

10. Meeting.—When pre-cooked materials are put together, usually with some additional seasoning, and cooked together, usually by simple boiling, the process is called meeting. Of two quantities of things, it is the thing of the smaller quantity which is said to meet the other, for example Shrimp Cakes Meet Celery Cabbage, Recipe No. 11.11. You can have a great many things meeting together, as in Arhat's Fast, Recipe No. 14.28, which is a veritable assembly.

11. Splashing.—You will remember that with fried dishes, you sometimes dip the pieces in sauce. Now if before taking the fried stuff out, you splash the seasoning over it in the pan and leave it cooking for 15 seconds, then it is called splashing. Of course you do not splash a deep-frying pan, as that would splash too much.

12. Plunging.—Plunging is a very quick form of soup-cooking on the principle that the more surface is heated the less time it takes. Thus, you cut meat, fish, or poultry to flying-thin slices, dip them in a mixture of soy sauce, wine, and cornstarch, then plunge them into boiling clear soup or water. One or two minutes, and it is done, both tender and savory. The soup also improves after the pieces have been plunged in. Vegetables with thin parts such as spinach need not be sliced, but as they take longer to cook than meat of similar size, they should be boiled a little before the meat slices are plunged in the last minute or so.

Plunging is often done at the table when a fire-pot is served in winter. The famous Chrysanthemum Pot, Recipe No. 16.1 is an example of plunging at the table.

13. Rinsing.—Rinsing is a term applied specifically to a form of plunging lamb slices at the table, for which Peiping is most famous. When you go to a lamb-rinsing restaurant in Peiping, you are served a fire-pot of plain soup with charcoal fire, various sauces with which you mix your own dipping sauce, and dishes of flying-thin lamb slices. When the soup boils, you take a few slices of the lamb with your chopsticks and immerse the lamb in the boiling soup, occasionally making a rinsing motion. Take out as soon as the meat changes color and dip into your dipping sauce. The cooking process ends here.

If you do not wish to take the trouble of holding your rinsed pieces all the time, you can let go of them, except that you may lose track of them and let them get tough, or someone else may fish out your lamb.

For details, see Recipe No. 7.4.

14. Cold-Mixing.—Cold-mixed dishes are the nearest to American salad dishes. But usually we parboil or scald the material, since raw vegetables in China are often not in sufficiently safe condition to eat. Various combinations of sauces of soy sauce, vinegar, pepper, and sugar are used. The best oil is sesame oil. If you cannot get it, substitute American salad oil.

45

15. Sizzling.—Sizzling is the act of throwing fried rice toast into hot clear soup. There are various forms of this. Usually, you make a clear soup with Szechwan *cha-ts'ai*, a tasty, slightly hot salted vegetable. Rice toast is the burned bottom layer of rice which is formed by continued heating after the rice is done. (The burning of neglected rice at the *beginning* of boiling is a different affair and does not give such a good smell.) After the rice toast is dry after some hours, it is deep-fried and then sizzled into the soup at the table. In Chungking this dish has recently been named "Bomb Tokyo."

16. Salting.—Salting in China is about the same process as in America, but it plays a much greater part there. There are three reasons for this. Since there is little refrigeration or canning in most parts, perishable foods have to be salted to keep. Secondly, salted food goes a longer way in "sending down rice" than fresh food and is therefore very economical. Last and most, many things taste better salted than fresh. For example, mustard green is good when fresh, but it becomes wonderful when salted. It is true that food usually loses vitamins when salted. But in the case of poor people, it is a choice of having low-vitamin salted food or having no vegetable or meat.

A common variation is fresh-salting, which consists of salting fresh food for a day or two and cooking right after, for example, Chinkiang Fresh-Salted Meat, Recipe No. 5.4.

Salting is sometimes used as a pre-cooking process, sometimes as a complete dish-forming process. Thus, Salted Celery Cabbage is probably the one best-liked cold dish for many people.

17. Pickling.—The most important forms of pickling are in soy jam (in China often fermented flour jam) or soy sauce. Pickling in vinegar is not so common. Pickling in syrup or honey is for dessert material and not a dish-forming process. Pickled cucumbers in soy sauce are a great delicacy. They are sometimes found canned on the shelves of Chinatown.

18. Steeping.—Steeped vegetable is a Szechwan dish popular in many provinces. The important thing is a steeping urn, earthenware with a circular trough around its neck, so that when the trough is filled with water and an upside-down bowl is placed over the trough, it makes the urn airtight. You start the urn by putting in celery cabbages, large Chinese radishes, sweet pepper, hot pepper, American cabbages, salt, and cold boiled water which would fill half of the urn when empty. Never use greasy utensils with which to take out things. Never wash material to be added in, but peel or cut to get the clean part.

19. Drying.—Next to salting, drying is the commonest way of preserving food in China. It is more difficult than salting, since you must hope the thing will dry before it spoils. Drying is done in Chinese homes like home-canning in America. But since the house is around the yard in China and the yard is around the house in America, it is not so convenient here to hang up your radishes, abalone, scallops, spiced chicken,[1] etc. So I shall not describe the drying of various things in detail. You get your salted and dried things in Chinatown—in "southern-goods stores" in China.

20. Smoking.—We smoke fish, poultry, and tobacco, but not much meat. Brown sugar is the usual smoking material. See Recipe No. 10.12 for an example of smoking.

In the description given above, I have given more details for the less common methods and the methods more difficult to use in American households. On the most important methods, I have said more general things, since the application will come out of the recipes.

One conclusion you may have drawn from reading about these methods is that Chinese cooking needs fire of widely and quickly varying strength. In this respect gas stoves are even better than most Chinese stoves. Electric stoves, however, can also be made serviceable for Chinese cooking, as we have seen (p. 34a).

[1] Called "wind-dried."

PART TWO

RECIPES AND MENUS

CHAPTER 1

RED-COOKED MEAT

This class of dishes is called "Red-Cooked Meat" because the soy sauce used in them gives them a reddish brown color. It looks beautiful if cooked beautifully.

Red-Cooked Meat is not often found in restaurants because it takes them too much meat and time. But in a Chinese family, it is as important as Roast Beef is in an American family.

You can use fresh shoulder of pork, fresh ham, or fresh bacon. Keep the skin on. To many of us, that is the best part of the meat. Fresh shoulder or ham is usually cooked whole. Fresh bacon is usually cut into one- or two-inch cubes, with some skin on each cube to go around for everybody. The reason that we do not use much pork chop in Red-Cooked Meat is that the tissues of pork chop are longer and not loose enough for this kind of cooking.

In the cubed forms of Red-Cooked Meat, other accessories are often added, something like the *à la's* in Western cooking. Thus you can add fresh vegetables, salted or dried sea food, as we shall see in the recipes.

Red-Cooked Meat can be kept on ice. Then it will keep one or two weeks and still keep its flavor. After a few warmings over—but not too many—it even tastes better than on the first day of cooking.

Remember that these recipes serve six people American style and ten people in the Chinese way. You can reduce the quantities proportionately if you are serving fewer people.

HOW TO COOK AND EAT IN CHINESE

1.1. Red-Cooked Whole Pork Shoulder: Plain

1 whole shoulder or fresh ham.	1 cup soy sauce
6-8 lbs. with skin and bone on.	1 tb-sp. sugar
2 cups cold water	2 or 3 slices fresh ginger (if you
¼ cup sherry	can get it)

Leave the whole fresh ham or shoulder with skin and bones on just as it is bought. After washing outside, cut a few long slashes on the sides where there is no skin (so that the sauce will seep in more easily when cooking). Place your shoulder in a heavy pot with the 2 cups water. Turn on big fire and cover pot. When it boils, add the sherry, soy sauce, and maybe ginger. Cover the pot tight again. Change to very low fire and cook for one hour. Then turn skin side down. Still with low fire cook for another hour. After this, add sugar and cook again for another ½ or 1 hour (2½ or 3 hours altogether, depending on the tenderness of the meat bought).

To test your cooking, stick a fork or chopstick through the meat. It is done when the stick goes through very easily. If not, cook over low fire a little longer. Make allowances of course that the prongs of a fork are sharper than most chopsticks.

On second serving, as must be done in a small family, it can be warmed over or eaten cold. Warm over low fire so you won't burn the bottom. When eaten cold, it is stiffer and can be cut into more chewsome slices, with the jelly. (Save the fat on the top for making other dishes.)

1.2. Red-Cooked Meat Proper: Plain

For this type of Red-Cooked Meat, the order of preference of cuts should be: fresh bacon, fresh shoulder, fresh ham, pork chop.

3-4 lbs. pork	1 t-sp. salt
1 cup water	4 slices ginger (if you can get
2 tb-sp. sherry	it)
½ cup soy sauce	½ tb-sp. sugar

52

Wash meat, cut into 1- or 1½-inch cubes. Put meat and 1 cup water in a heavy pot and use big fire. When it boils, add sherry, soy sauce, salt, and ginger. Cover pot tight and cook over very low fire for 1½ hours. (In case of pork chop, use only 1 hour here.) Then add sugar. Again, over low fire, cook for ½ to 1 hour. Test meat same way as for whole shoulder.

1.3. Red-Cooked Meat with Yellow Turnips [1]

3 lbs. pork (see previous recipe for type of cut)
2 lbs. yellow turnips [1]
2 cups water
2 tb-sp. sherry
6 tb-sp. soy sauce
1 t-sp. salt
4 slices ginger (if you can get it)

The Red-Cooked Meat part is the same as above. Wash meat. Cut into 1 inch cubes. Put meat and water in a heavy pot and use big fire. When it boils, add soy sauce, sherry, salt, and ginger. Then cover tightly and turn fire low.

For the turnips part, wash and peel turnips. Cut into any kind of irregular three-dimensional shapes other than cubes, with size about same as the meat.

Add turnips in when meat has its first hour of low fire. (Less time is needed if meat is tender.) Then cook together for another hour.

1.4. Red-Cooked Meat with Carrots

Meat and seasoning same as above.
1 bunch carrots

Peel and wash carrots and cut them in "rolling knife pieces." Roll-knife cuts are made by cutting across the carrot at an angle, rolling the carrot a third of a turn, another cut across part of the first cut, and so on. (See Fig. 3, p. 36.)

Cook meat and carrots as you would meat and turnips.

[1] In China we usually use large radishes.

53

1.5. Red-Cooked Meat with Abalone

Meat and seasoning same as in Recipe No. 1.2.

Except: Use only one cup water, and use juice of abalone for second cup of water.

1 can abalone (get in Chinatown).

Cook meat same as in Recipe No. 1.2.

Cut abalone into slices of about ⅛ to ¼ inch thick.

Put abalone in only 5 min. before serving. Too long cooking would make it tough.

1.6. Red-Cooked Meat and Eggs

Meat and seasoning same as in Recipe No. 1.3

Plus: 1 t-sp. sugar (In case of meat with turnips or carrots, there is already enough sugar in the material).

Eggs: any number up to 12

Cook meat as in Recipe No. 1.3.

Boil eggs for 15 min.; then chill in cold water and shell them.

Put eggs and sugar in meat as you would turnips. Some like to slit the sides of the eggs very slightly to let the juice in.

1.7. Red-Cooked Meat with Chinese Dried Cabbage

Meat and seasoning same as in Recipe No. 1.3

Plus: 2 t-sp. sugar

⅔ lb. dried Chinese cabbage (Get it in Chinatown. Or get canned salted cabbage, in which case omit salt. The flavor of the canned cabbage is different from that of dried cabbage, but some people prefer that. Use 1 can if you can get it.)

Cook meat same as in Recipe No. 1.3 and add cabbage and sugar as you would add turnips.

1.8. Red-Cooked Meat with Dried Lilies

Meat and seasoning same as in Recipe No. 1.3

Plus: 1 t-sp. sugar

¼ lb. dried tiger lilies (called in Chinatown *kam-cham*, "golden needles")

Soak lilies in hot water for 1 hr. Then throw away the water and rinse lilies twice more with cold water.

Cook meat the same way as in Recipe No. 1.3. But put in lilies and sugar ½ hr. later than you would turnips, as lilies always take less time to cook than turnips.

1.9. Red-Cooked Meat with Bamboo Shoots

Meat and seasoning same as in Recipe No. 1.3

Plus: 1 t-sp. sugar

1 can bamboo shoots (Do not keep the juice of canned bamboo shoots.)

Cook meat the same way as in Recipe No. 1.3.

Cut bamboo shoots into irregular three-dimensional shapes of about ½ cubic inch in volume (lumps being more suitable for red-cooking, white slices being better for stir-frying).

Put bamboo shoots in meat only 15 min. before serving.

1.10. Red-Cooked Meat with Squid

Meat and seasoning same as in Recipe No. 1.3

Plus: 1 t-sp. sugar

2 lbs. squid

Wash squids; pull off the skins. Clean everything inside. Keep the "legs." Cut squid into 1 inch pieces.

Cook meat as you do in Recipe No. 1.3 and add squid as you would turnips.

1.11. Red-Cooked Meat with Salted Haddock

Same meat and seasoning as in Recipe No. 1.3

Plus: 1 t-sp. sugar

Except: use only 2 tb-sp. soy sauce (because the haddock is already very salty)

1½ lb. salted haddock or Chinese salted fish

Put fish in a pan of cold water and let it stand for ½ day. Then cut fish into 1-inch sq. pieces.

Cook meat as in Recipe No. 1.3 but put in haddock and sugar ½ hr. earlier than you would turnips.

1.12. Red-Cooked Meat with Peastarch Noodles

Meat and seasoning same as in Recipe No. 1.3

Plus: 1 t-sp. sugar

½ lb. peastarch noodles (get in Chinatown as "long rice")

Boil noodles in hot water for ½ hr. Then turn fire off and stand for another ½ hr.

Cook meat same as in Recipe No. 1.3.

Add in noodles prepared as above, add 2 cups water and complete the cooking as you would with turnips.

1.13. Red-Cooked Meat With Chestnuts

Meat and seasoning same as in Recipe No. 1.3

Plus: 1 lb. dried chestnut meat (the shelled and skinned kind sometimes available in Chinese and Italian foodshops)

Boil chestnuts for 1 hr. or until soft, but not crumbling.

Cook meat same as in Recipe No. 1.3.

Add in chestnuts prepared as above and complete cooking in 15 min. after boiling starts again.

CHAPTER 2

MEAT SLICES

While Red-Cooked Meat dishes consist of big pieces in three dimensions, dishes using Meat Slices (remember *meat* means pork?) consist of meat mostly in two dimensions. For these, we do not use such fat meat as before. The usual cuts used are pork chop, tenderloin, or the lean part of shoulder or fresh ham. The tendons are not suitable for slicing, as you may find out by trying. But I would advise you to take my word for it.

Slice meat into flimsy slices about 1 inch square and $\frac{1}{16}$ inch thick, or thicker if you can't. This needs a lot of patience and skill, but most Chinese wives have them.

Sliced meat is seldom eaten alone, but usually eaten in company with various other materials. The advantages of doing so are rather characteristic of Chinese cooking in general. By adding varying accompanying ingredients, you not only make less meat go further, you also add interest to the taste. I have always wondered why corned beef must always go with cabbage, frankfurters always with sauerkraut, and the same things, when called "hot dogs," must always go with or without mustard. However—er—oh, heavens, my meat slices are burning while I was digressing!

Well, since the meat is sliced thin, it is very easily cooked, or overcooked. The time for cooking is, therefore, more critical, that is, it can go wrong more easily than with the slow-cooking meat dishes. Note carefully that in the recipes, sometimes the accompanying vegetables take longer than the meat and sometimes shorter. Each thing must take its own time.

Most dishes with Meat Slices are *ch'ao* or stir-frying dishes, as described above, though a common soup uses sliced pork, as described under soups. (Recipes Nos. 15.1-5.)

In cooking the following dishes, be sure you have carefully studied the description of *ch'ao* or stir-frying given above (p. 43).

2.1. Bamboo Shoots Stir Meat Slices

1½ lb. meat (or 1 lb. for boneless meat) See introduction of this section on kinds of meat.

1 can bamboo shoots (There seem to be no fresh bamboo shoots in America, at least not the eating kind. There are only canned bamboo shoots, which are already cooked and are good for this purpose. There are two kinds of bamboo shoots—winter and spring shoots. Winter bamboo shoots are more tender and smaller. Get them in Chinatown.)

2½ tb-sp. soy sauce	1 t-sp. salt
1 tb-sp. sherry	1 tb-sp. cornstarch
2 tb-sp. lard or vegetable oil	2 tb-sp. water
1 t-sp. sugar	

Cut meat into thin slices, $\frac{1}{16}$ inch thick and about 1 square inch in area. Mix thoroughly the slices with only 1½ tb-sp. of the soy sauce, the sherry, cornstarch, sugar and water.

Throw away the juice of canned bamboo shoots, cut shoots into slices like the meat.

Heat lard in frying pan till hot. Put flavored meat in the pan and stir constantly to keep meat from burning. After 2 min., put in the bamboo shoot slices. Add the other tb-sp. soy sauce and salt. Cook and stir for 1 min. more.

2.2. Mushrooms Stir Meat Slices

Same meat, sliced same way as in Recipe No. 2.1
1 lb. mushrooms

Prepare meat as before.
Wash and slice mushrooms so that the pieces look like ꟼIIP from one side and like T T T T from another side.
Heat the 2 tb-sp. lard or oil in a skillet till hot. Put in mushrooms,

and keep stirring for 2 min. Then take out mushrooms and put in a dish or bowl. Use another tb-sp. lard or oil and cook the meat as in the preceding recipe. (Mushrooms "eat up" a great deal of oil, therefore we use 2 tb-sp. for mushrooms and only 1 tb-sp. for meat here.)

After meat is cooked for 2 min., add in the mushrooms again and cook together for ½ min. Add salt if desired.

2.3. Cucumbers Stir Meat Slices

Same meat sliced same way as in Recipe No. 2.1
Same seasoning as in Recipe No. 2.1
1-2 large cucumbers (or 3 small ones)

Peel cucumbers. If you have large cucumbers, slit in two lengthwise and scrape out seeds (not necessary for young and tender ones) Slice into $\frac{1}{16}$-inch slices.

Prepare meat as before.

Heat one tb-sp. lard or oil. Put in cucumbers and stir for 2 min.; take them out again.

Cook meat as before with 2 tb-sp. lard or oil. After 2 min. put in cucumbers again and cook together for ½ min. Add salt if desired.

2.4. Sweet Peppers Stir Meat Slices

Same meat sliced same way as in Recipe No. 2.1
Same seasoning as in Recipe No. 2.1
Plus: 1 more tb-sp. lard
5 big sweet peppers

Wash peppers, cut open, and wash out all the seeds. Cut into irregular shapes of about 1 square inch.

Heat 1 tb-sp. lard or oil and cook peppers by constant stirring for 2 min. and take them out.

Cook meat as before with 2 tb-sp. lard or oil. After 2 min. put in the pepper and cook together for ½ min. Add salt if desired.

2.5. Squash Stirs Meat Slices

Same meat sliced same way as in Recipe No. 2.1
Same seasoning as in Recipe No. 2.1
1½ lb. squash (Italian squash)

Cut squash into slices $\frac{1}{16}$ inch thick and a little less than 1 square inch.

Cook squash as you would with peppers but cook for 6 min. instead of 2. Then take it out.

Prepare meat as in Recipe No. 2.1 but add black pepper. Then add in squash. Put in salt if desired.

2.6. String Beans Stir Meat Slices

Same meat sliced same way as in Recipe No. 2.1
Same seasoning as in Recipe No. 2.1
1 lb. string beans

Wash beans. Snip off 2 ends of string beans. Break beans into sections of about 1 inch length.

Heat oil or lard in skillet (but not too hot), put string beans in and keep stirring for about 1 min. Put in ½ cup water (add salt if desired) and put cover on. Wait for 3 min. (when the beans turn into a still fresher green color) then take off cover and stir every 10 seconds for 5 or 6 min. and take out.

Cook meat same as before and add string beans 2 min. after cooking the meat; then cook together for ½ min.

2.7. Tomatoes Stir Meat Slices

Same meat sliced same way as in Recipe No. 2.1
Same seasoning as in Recipe No. 2.1
1½ lb. tomatoes

Cut tomatoes into small slices. Cook meat first and then put in tomatoes (see recipe for meat and bamboo shoots).

2.8. Bean Curd Stirs Meat Slices

Same meat, sliced same way as in Recipe No. 2.1
Same seasoning as in Recipe No. 2.1
1 quart bean curd (get it in Chinatown)

Cut bean curd into slices 1 inch square and ¼-inch thick.
Cook meat first and then add in the bean curd (see recipe for meat and bamboo shoots). Be careful not to mash up the bean curd.

2.9. Cauliflower Stirs Meat Slices

Same meat sliced same way as in Recipe No. 2.1
Same seasoning as in Recipe No. 2.1
1 lb. to 1½ lb. cauliflower

Cut cauliflower into slices of about $\frac{1}{16}$ inch thick and 1 square inch in area.

Heat 1 tb-sp. lard or oil and put cauliflower slices in. Stir for 1 min. and add salt and 1 cup water. Turn to medium fire and cook by constant stirring for 4 min.; then take out.

Cook meat as in Recipe 2.1. After 2 min. add in cauliflower again and cook together for ½ min. more.

2.10. Pea Pods Stir Meat Slices

Same meat sliced same way as in Recipe No. 2.1
Same seasoning as in Recipe No. 2.1, but only ¼ t-sp. salt
½ lb. tender pea pods (now sometimes found in general markets)

Snip off ends of pods, large ones to be cut obliquely in two.
Heat an extra tb-sp. lard, stir-fry pods for 1 min., and take out.
Stir-fry the meat as prepared in Recipe No. 2.1 after 2 min., put in the pods again and cook together for ½ min.

Beef (tenderloin) and chicken slices can be substituted for pork.

CHAPTER 3

MEAT SHREDS

As Meat Slices have one dimension less than the pieces of Red-Cooked Meat, so Meat Shreds have one dimension still less than the Slices. You get Shreds simply by cutting your Slices into sizes of about $1 \times \frac{1}{16} \times \frac{1}{16}$ inch. While Red-Cooked Meat is a slow-cooking dish, Shreds are like Slices in being quick-cooking material. Shreds are never used alone and almost always stir-fried. Meat Shreds are also a favorite form of boarding food, since with the same amount they make a much greater show of meat among the vegetables.

The selection of cut and the basic method of cooking Meat Shreds are the same as for Meat Slices. They should be steeped in seasoning and fried separately before thrown in together with the other things.

3.1. Celery Stirs Meat Shreds

1 bunch celery (about 1-1½ lb.)	1 tb-sp. sherry
1½ lbs. meat (unless it is for boarders in arrears)	1 t-sp. sugar
	3 tb-sp. lard or vegetable oil
2½ tb-sp. soy sauce	1 t-sp. salt

Cut meat into slices and then into shreds. Wash celery and also cut into rather larger shreds than the meat.

Heat 1 tb-sp. lard or oil till hot. Put celery in and stir for 2 min. Then take it out.

Mix thoroughly shreds of meat with 1½ tb-sp. soy sauce, the sherry, and sugar.

Heat another 2 tb-sp. lard or oil till hot and put seasoned meat in and stir for 2 min. Put celery in again with salt and 1 tb-sp. soy sauce. Cook together for ½ min.

3.2. Frozen Peas Stir Meat Shreds

Same meat as in Recipe No. 3.1
Same seasoning as in Recipe No. 3.1
2 packages frozen peas

Thaw out the peas.
Cut meat into shreds.
Mix meat with sherry, sugar and 1½ tb-sp. soy sauce.
Heat 2 tb-sp. lard or oil. Put meat in and stir for 2 min. Without taking meat out, put peas in with salt and another tb-sp. soy sauce. Stir together for 1 min.

3.3. Pea Sprouts Stir Meat Shreds

Same meat as in Recipe No. 3.1
Same seasoning as in Recipe No. 3.1
1 lb. pea sprouts (not bean sprouts)

Cook meat and pea sprouts the same way as with meat and frozen peas but add an extra ½ min. when cooking together.

3.4. Sweet Onions Stir Meat Shreds

Same meat as in Recipe No. 3.1
Same seasoning as in Recipe No. 3.1
1½ lbs. sweet onions

Cut onions into ⅛-inch-thick shreds. Since an onion already grows in slices all around, the best way is to cut horizontally, which is vertical when the onion lies horizontal on the board. If you can't keep it still, use half onions.

Cut meat into shreds and mix thoroughly with sugar, sherry, and 1½ tb-sp. soy sauce.

Heat 1 tb-sp. lard or oil and fry the onions with salt and 1 tb-sp. soy sauce for 3 min., and then take them out. Heat 2 tb-sp. lard or oil. Cook meat by stirring for 2 min. Then put in the onions again and stir together for ½ min.

3.5. Celery Cabbage Stirs Meat Shreds

Same meat as in Recipe No. 3.1
Same seasoning as in Recipe No. 3.1
1 celery cabbage (about 2 lbs.)

Cut the celery cabbage into ⅛-inch-thick shreds. The best way is to cut crosswise at ⅛-inch intervals. Then proceed as in the preceding recipe.

During the process of cooking, a great deal of water will come out of the cabbage. Keep it and serve together with the meat and cabbage. It goes well with rice.

3.6. American Cabbage Stirs Meat Shreds

Same meat as in Recipe No. 3.1
Same seasoning as in Recipe No. 3.1
1 cabbage, about 1 lb.

Cut cabbage into thin shreds as if you were starting to make cole slaw, but stop before you put in any dressing.

Cut meat into shreds and mix thoroughly with sugar, sherry, and 1½ tb-sp. soy sauce.

Heat 1 tb-sp. lard or oil in a skillet till hot and put cabbage in. Stir constantly for 5 min. Then take the cabbage out.

Heat the other 2 tb-sp. lard or oil in the skillet and stir-fry the seasoned meat for 2 min. Then put in the cabbage and add salt and the 1 tb-sp. soy sauce. Cook for ½ min. more.

3.7. Asparagus Stirs Meat Shreds

Same meat as in Recipe No. 3.1
Same seasoning as in Recipe No. 3.1
1 lb. Asparagus

Cut the meat into shreds and add seasonings as in Recipe No. 3.1.
Remove the tough parts (near the roots) of the asparagus. Cut the tender parts obliquely into oblong slices (1 in. long, ¼ in. thick).

Parboil the asparagus slices in water for ½ min. Pour off the water and wash in cold water.

Stir-fry the seasoned meat as in Recipe No. 3.1 for 1 min. Add in the asparagus and stir-fry for 3 min. more.

3.8. Sweet Peppers Stir Meat Shreds

Same meat as in Recipe No. 3.1
Same seasoning as in Recipe No. 3.1
6 big sweet peppers

Cut the meat into shreds as in Recipe No. 3.1.

Split the peppers into halves, remove the seeds, and cut into shreds.

Heat 3 tb-sp. lard in a skillet. Add in the seasoned meat-shreds and stir for 1 min. Add in the pepper. Stir for 3 min. more, then add 1 tb-sp. soy sauce and serve. Better serve the dish right after preparation.

3.9. Green Tea Stirs Meat Shreds

1 lb. pork chops or Boston butts	3 tb-sp. soy sauce
2 tb-sp. green tea leaves	1 t-sp. sugar
1 tb-sp. cornstarch	3 tb-sp. salad oil

Cut meat as described on p. 62. It can be put on refrigeration until ready to use, when it is to be mixed with the cornstarch, soy sauce, and sugar. Steep the tea in 1 cup boiling water for 10 min., then mix the tea with the meat, but leave the leaves aside.

Heat the oil, but not to smoking. Stir in the meat for 3 min. Put in the leaves and stir until well mixed, which should take not more than 5 seconds. Serves six, or four, if very hungry.

CHAPTER 4

MEAT BALLS OR MEAT CAKES

Now we are ready to cut meat down one dimension more and that is the end, because we call it *jou-mo'r* and *mo* is the word for "end." You don't have to cut lumps into slices, slices into shreds, and shreds into ends. What we usually do is to use two of those pound-weight Chinese chopping knives and chop up pieces of pork to a lively rhythm until fine enough. Of course, you can use a rotating meat-grinder or have your butcher grind the pork. For the Chinese dishes described below, better use medium grinding instead of fine.

Ground meat is rarely used in the loose state. It is almost always made into balls or cakes so that you get your three dimensions back again, only in a softer state.

The best cuts for meat balls are those with a little fat in them, such as pork chop. You don't use any skin or tendon. If too lean, the cake will be too dry and stiff.

Meat balls can form a dish alone or in company with other things. We shall start with the basic form.

4.1. Meat Balls or Meat Cakes: Plain

2 lbs. ground pork (see above)	2 tb-sp. soy sauce
1 tb-sp. sherry	2 heaping tb-sp. cornstarch
2 t-sp. sugar	1 t-sp. salt

Mix everything above thoroughly and make into 12 balls, or, if you like, you may press them into flat cakes.

Heat 3 tb-sp. lard (only 2 tb-sp. if cakes are pressed flat) till hot and put balls or cakes in carefully.

Fry (you do not have to turn in the frying pan all the time) about

5 min. on each side over medium fire. They are done when deep brown on all sides.

When meat cakes are eaten without anything, they are eaten with some pepper and salt mixed in small dishes served on the table. When other accompaniments are used, they are then fried for 3 min. instead of 5 min., to leave some time for more cooking with other things.

This kind of meat balls or cakes can be kept for a long time and can be reheated many times.

Variation.—If the meat is ground less fine and the balls or cakes made larger, then this dish is better known as Lion's Head, for which Yangchow and Chinkiang are most famous.

4.2. Meat Balls with Dried Lilies

12 cooked meat balls (see previous Recipe No. 4.1)	2 cups water
	1 t-sp. salt
⅛ lb. dried lilies (called *kamcham* in Chinatown)	1 tb-sp. soy sauce
	1 t-sp. sugar

Wash lilies with hot water and let them stand or lie in hot water for ½ hr. Then pour away water.

Put lilies in a boiling pot. Add 2 cups water, salt, soy sauce and sugar. Then put the meat balls on top of lilies. Cover and cook over big fire till it boils; turn to low fire and cook for 15 min.

4.3. Meat Balls with Celery Cabbage

12 cooked meat balls (see Recipe No. 4.1)	½ cup water
	1 t-sp. salt
2 lbs. celery cabbage	1 tb-sp. soy sauce

Wash and cut cabbage into 1-inch wide strips.

Put cabbage in a pot and add water, salt, soy sauce. Then put the meat balls on top. Cover and cook over big fire till it boils; turn to low fire and cook for 10 min.

Variation.—The Lion's Head is especially good with celery cabbage.

4.4. Steamed Minced Meat .

1 lb. meat (from pork chops, ground fine)	1 tb-sp. sherry
	1 tb-sp. cornstarch
2 tb-sp. soy sauce	½ t-sp. salt

Mix well into a large cake. Steam in a double boiler for 5 min. Add 2 cups of water and put ⅛ lb. of salted cabbage underneath. Steam for 15 min. more.

4.5. A. Cucumbers Stuff Meat

Fat cucumbers (enough to cut into 12 2-inch sections)	1 tb-sp. sherry
	1 tb-sp. cornstarch
½ lb. ground pork (better not so fat as with meat balls)	12 mushroom caps or small pieces of Smithfield, Virginia ham about 1 square
1 egg—beaten	inch
2 t-sp. salt	

Note that no soy sauce is used for cooking cucumbers. It tends to make them sour. But soy sauce is all right in the gravy.

Peel and cut cucumbers into 2-inch-long sections. Use a teaspoon and dig out some of the seeds from *one end. Do not dig through.*

Mix ground meat with the egg, 1 t-sp. salt, sherry and cornstarch, and stuff some in each. Cover each cucumber section with a mushroom cap or a piece of ham.

Stand the cucumbers in a boiling pot, put 1 cup water in, and 1 t-sp. salt.

Use small fire and cook for 40 min. Then put cucumbers carefully in the serving plate. Keep the juice in the pot for making gravy.

Gravy:

2 tb-sp. soy sauce
1 tb-sp. cornstarch
¼ cup water

Mix the 3 things and pour into the pot which has the juice from boiled cucumbers. Stir and boil for about ½ min. until it becomes translucent and sticky, and pour on top of the cucumbers.

4.5. B. Stuffed Cucumber Soup

The dish described above is sometimes made into a soup. For 6 people you need only 6 stuffed cucumbers.

Follow recipe as before without the gravy. After the cucumbers are cooked, add into the pot:

> 6 cups water (depending on number of people).
>   (This serves 6.)
> 1½ t-sp. salt
> ¼ t-sp. taste powder

Cook till it boils.

4.6. Mushrooms Stuff Meat

1 lb. large fresh mushrooms, or better ¼ lb. dried mushrooms from Chinatown, but these must be pre-boiled for 10 min. Keep the water for juice.

1 tb-sp. soy sauce
1 t-sp. salt
1 tb-sp. cornstarch
1 tb-sp. sherry
½ lb. ground pork

Take off stems of mushrooms. (Keep the stems.) Mix thoroughly meat, soy sauce, salt, cornstarch and sherry, and stuff in the cap of mushrooms enough to form a smooth round hump.

Steam the stuffed mushrooms with 2 cups of water for 5-10 min. (depending on the size of the mushrooms). Then take out and put on the serving plate.

Gravy:

Keep 1 cup of the steaming water (if not enough you can add plain water).

> 1 tb-sp. cornstarch   1 t-sp. sugar
> 1 tb-sp. soy sauce   Stems of mushrooms

Cut stems into small round slices, mix everything above, and boil till gravy is sticky and translucent. Pour on the mushrooms in the serving plate.

CHAPTER 5

MEAT SPECIALTIES

Besides balls, shreds, slices, etc., there is one important shape of meat which forms the basis of some very tasty dishes. This is the irregular shape of spare ribs of pork. As this meat needs special cooking, we give it a special heading.

5.1. Dry-Cooked Spare Ribs

2½ lbs. spare ribs. (You can get one whole piece which is about that weight. Ask the butcher to cut the bones into 1-inch lengths.)	2 cups water 4 tb-sp. soy sauce 1 t-sp. salt 1 t-sp. sugar 2 tb-sp. sherry

Wash ribs and cut into separate pieces with a bone and some meat on each.

Put ribs, water, sauce, and salt in a boiling pot. Use big fire till it boils, then turn down fire to simmer for 1 hr. or 40 min. if meat is tenderly bought.

Put ribs together with the juice in a frying pan. Now add the sugar. Use big fire and stir constantly till all the water evaporates and all the sauce seems to have wrapped around the meat.

This can be kept in the oven for a while before eating.

5.2. Sweet Dry-Cooked Ribs

Same ribs as in Recipe No. 5.1 Same seasoning as in Recipe No. 5.1, but add:	2 tb-sp. sugar ¼ can pineapple *or* some fresh fruit

Cook it the same way as in Recipe No. 5.1.

5.3. Sweet-Sour Dry-Cooked Ribs

Same ribs as in Recipe No. 5.1   3 tb-sp. vinegar
Same seasoning as in Recipe No.   2 tb-sp. cornstarch
   5.1, but add: ½ cup water
3 tb-sp. sugar

Mix above and pour over ribs and continue frying and stir for 2 or 3 min. until gravy becomes translucent.

If you like, add in two or three sweet peppers in small slices, ½ can pineapple, or some pickles in the sweet-sour gravy before putting the ribs in.

5.4. Chinkiang Fresh Salted Meat or *Hsiao* [1]

This form of meat is made in big quantities in China. However, if you make it for an American family meal, where you have only one course, a six-pound shoulder or ham may be about right for six.

1 whole shoulder or ham 5-6   4 slices fresh ginger
   lbs., including bone   ½ cup Chinkiang (dark) vinegar
4 tb-sp. salt   (or ¼ cup vinegar and 1 tb-sp.
3 cups water   soy sauce as a substitute)

Leave the shoulder in one piece, but take off the big bone in the middle. Then rub the salt all over and inside the meat. Put it in a pan and cover it. If it is winter, leave it in an unheated room. In warmer weather, put it in an icebox.

After 2 days, wash off slightly the salt on the surface. Then put the whole piece in a heavy pot. Add the 3 cups water and boil over big fire. When it boils, turn to medium fire and boil 1 hr. Then take it out, and put it in a rectangular pan. (You can use a big baking pan.) Put a flat cover on top of the meat and put a heavy object on the cover, the purpose being to press the meat so that it

---

[1] The pronunciation of this word is as palatable as the meat it represents. For in most dialects, this word has an irregular reading pronunciation *yao*, but when applied to this dish it has a phonologically regular pronunciation *hsiao.*—Y. R. C.

becomes tight and has a rectangular shape. Leave it that way for 2 hrs. Then put it in the icebox.

After it becomes thoroughly cold, take out as much as you need and keep the rest in the icebox. Cut the meat into square pieces of about 1¼ inch by ½ inch in area and 1 inch in thickness and spread in a regular design on the serving plate.

Sauce: Cut the ginger slices into thin shreds, mix them with the soy sauce and vinegar (or if you are lucky, some Chinkiang vinegar instead of soy sauce and plain vinegar).

Serve about one tb-sp. to each person. Eat the meat by dipping it in the sauce.

This meat can be kept for 3 or 4 days.

5.5. "Fresh Fried" Sweet-Sour Ribs

3 lbs. ribs (tell butcher to chop into 1-inch lengths)
5 heaping tb-sp. lard or same amount of vegetable oil
4 tb-sp. vinegar
2 heaping tb-sp. cornstarch
5 tb-sp. sugar
4 tb-sp. soy sauce
½ t-sp. salt
1 cup water

Cut ribs so that each piece has a bone and some meat on.

Heat the lard in a skillet and fry the ribs for 10 min. Take out ribs and pour away the oil (you can save it for further cooking), but keep 1 tb-sp. in the pan. Mix the vinegar, cornstarch, sugar and the water in a bowl. Pour it in the skillet. Cook for 1 min. by constant stirring till it becomes translucent. Then put ribs in and cook for 1 min. You can add some green or red sweet peppers, ½ can pineapple or some pickles in the sweet-sour gravy before putting the ribs in.

5.6. White-Cooked Meat

2 petals garlic   4-5 lbs. shoulder meat, fresh
½ cup soy sauce   ham, or pork chops
¼ cup vinegar
½ t-sp. sugar

Use about 1 lb. meat for 3 people.

Boil meat with enough water to cover whole meat. First turn on big fire and turn to small fire when it boils. With small fire, cook for 1 hr. to 3 hrs. (as in the case of a whole shoulder or fresh ham). Test by pricking with a chopstick or fork. It is done when you can prick it all the way through.

Mince the garlic and mix with sugar, soy sauce, and vinegar.

Eat meat either hot or cold by cutting into slices and dipping into the garlic sauce. (If you don't like garlic, you can leave it out, but you don't know what you miss!)

By all means, keep the soup of the boiled meat. You can make many different kinds of good-eating soup from it. It can be kept in the icebox for about a week. See Chapter 15 for soup recipes.

5.7. Twice-Cooked Meat

Twice-Cooked Meat is a Szechwan dish but famous all over China. It is really twice cooked, as you shall see.

2 lbs. pork chops in one piece   1 scallion
3 cups water   4 slices fresh ginger (if you can
1 heaping tb-sp. lard or same   get it)
   amount of oil   1 t-sp. sugar
2 tb-sp. soy jam (get in China-   ½ t-sp. hot pepper sauce (leave
   town or substitute with 2   out if you don't eat hot stuff,
   tb-sp. soy sauce and ½ t-sp.   but start learning now to
   salt)   really appreciate this dish)
4 slices garlic

Boil the whole piece of meat in a pot over big fire until boiling. Then simmer for 1 hr.

Take meat out at the end of the hour and take off the bones. (Put the bones back in the water and boil for another hour, when the soup will be useful for other purposes.) After the meat has cooled, slice it, against the grain, into slices about ¼ inch thick, 2 inches long, and 1 inch wide.

Slightly crush the 4 slices of garlic. Cut scallion into 1-inch sections. Heat the lard or oil in a skillet till hot. Throw in the crushed garlic. After a few seconds, put in the sliced cooled meat and stir for 3 min. Then add in the scallion sections, the soy jam, and the ginger and stir for 2 min. more.

5.8. Red-Cooked Pork Tripe

2 lbs. pork tripe (about 1 lb. or more each)
4 tb-sp. soy sauce
1 tb-sp. sherry
1 t-sp. sugar (optional)
1 onion (halve)
3 slices fresh ginger (if you can get it)

Wash tripe thoroughly, put the whole in a heavy pot, and fill with water. Heat over big fire till it boils. Then throw away all the water. Put in again 3 cups hot water, salt, sherry, sugar, onion, and ginger. Cover tightly and cook over small fire for 2 hrs.

Cut into long strips and serve with the juice.

5.9. Red-Cooked Pig's Feet

6 pig's feet (ask your butcher to cut each into 3 or 4 sections but serve 1 foot to a person)
6 tb-sp. soy sauce
2 pieces ginger (if you can get it)
2 tb-sp. sherry
1 t-sp. salt
2 t-sp. sugar—if preferred. (In China, some places like it and some places don't.)

Wash feet clean. Put in a heavy pot and boil over big fire for 1½ hrs. Then add the soy sauce, ginger, sherry, and salt. With low fire, cook for 2½ hrs. Then add sugar and cook ½ hr. more over low fire.

With young pig's feet, you may need only 2 hrs. for the entire cooking. With old pig's feet you may need 4 or 5 hrs. altogether. However, you can test by pulling at the bones. If the bones can slip out easily then they are done. The skin should also be so soft that it can be easily torn by a fork.

5.10. Sweet-Sour Pig's Feet

Follow all instructions as in Recipe No. 5.9, but at the time when you add sugar, add also:

3 tb-sp. *more* sugar   3 tb-sp. vinegar

5.11A. Ch'a-shiu Meat

If you live far from Chinese stores, you can make your own *ch'a-shiu* meat. If you live near one, the following may taste better:

4 lbs. pork butt, not too lean or too fat

¼ cup soy sauce

¼ cup sherry or equivalent white wine

3 tb-sp. sugar, preferably brown

2 scallions or 1 onion

3 slices ginger, if available

1 pint water

Cut meat with the grain into long slices of about 1 by 2 inches across. Boil meat in seasoning for 15 min., turning over if sauce won't cover all meat. Steep for ½ to 1 hr. Take out meat and broil on wire rack over dripping pan at 400°F for 20 min., turning over after 10 min. Cut against the grain this time, into ⅛ or ¼-inch slices and serve hot or cold.

5.11B. Ch'a-shiu Meat, Variation

Instead of scallions and ginger, use 1 cup *hoisin* sauce (see p. 29). Instead of boiling, rub mixed seasoning well over the large slices of meat, let stand a day or overnight (in refrigerator in summer), and then broil at 450°F for 15 min. on each side. Take out and rub remaining juice and broil each side for 5 min., total time, 15 + 15 + 5 + 5 = 40 min.

5.11C. Ch'a-shiu Ribs

Instead of pork butts, ribs will also make an interesting variation. Since the meat is not so thick, both the steeping time and the broiling time can be reduced. After broiling at 450°F for 15 min., take out and paint over and broil another 15 min. and it is ready to cut and serve.

Ch'a-shiu in any of the above forms is very good for making sandwiches, for cocktails, for picnics, for traveling, and for garnishing soup noodles, rice dishes, etc., as you see in Chinese restaurants. When kept in the freezer, it will stay fresh for 2 or 3 months. Slow thawing before use is advised. For warm eating, bake at 350°F for 20 min.

Beef and lamb can also be made into *ch'a-shiu,* though we usually associate this name with pork and think it tastes better.

5.12. Ancient Old Meat

The dish called "Ancient Old Meat," or *Kwulou Yuk* in Cantonese, is really made of fresh meat, cooked with sugar and vinegar, and is a favorite American Chinese dish for Americans. Get:

1 lb. pork chop or pork tenderloin	½ cup water
4 tb-sp. sugar	1 green (sweet) pepper
3 tb-sp. vinegar	½ small can pineapple
2 tb-sp. cornstarch	1 scallion or small onion
2 tb-sp. soy sauce	4 tb-sp. dry flour
	½ t-sp. salt
vegetable oil for frying	

For garnish and color use strawberries, canned litchi, canned peaches, etc.

Mix above cooking material (except the flour and salt) in a dish, including the water and the pineapple juice from the small can. Cut pepper into irregular 1-in. pieces and the scallion into 1-in. sections, or if onion is used cut it like pepper.

Wash meat and cut into 1-in.-wide by ½-in.-thick strips. When ready to cook, mix the flour and salt and rub on all surfaces.

For pre-frying, fill deep skillet with 1-in.-deep vegetable oil and heat over brisk fire. Put in meat before oil smokes. Fry 3 min. on each side of each strip without stirring until meat is slightly browned. Drain off oil and take out meat in serving platter.

Pour in the mixed sauce in the now practically empty skillet and heat till boiling. When the sauce becomes translucent and jelly-like, put back meat, add in the fruits and scallion and stir once, and the dish is ready to serve four. Increase ingredients proportionally for more or larger eaters.

5.13. Wine Smothers Meat

This dish is similar to 1.1 Red-Cooked Meat, with some interesting variation in the sauces. Obtain:

3-4 lbs. pork shoulder or fresh bacon, better with the skin on	½ cup soy sauce
	1 onion, cut in 4 pieces
1½ cups sherry or 2 full cups white wine	3 slices ginger, if available
	1 tb-sp. honey

Cut meat into 2-in. x 1-in. x 1-in. pieces, preferably with some skin on each piece (so the guests or children won't fight over it). Boil meat in half of the wine over brisk fire. Then put in rest of the ingredients except the honey. After reboiling, turn down fire to simmer for 1 hr. Stir in the honey and simmer for another ½ hr.

5.14. Wine Smothers Meat Slices

This dish is rather special and so I put it here instead of under Meat Slices. Prepare:

2 lbs. boned pork chop	1 t-sp. sugar
½ cup sherry or ¼ cup white wine	½ scallion
3 tb-sp. soy sauce	2 slices ginger, if available
¼ t-sp. salt	

Cut meat into ½-in.-long and $\frac{1}{16}$-in.-thick thin slices. Mix in all the seasoning. Start with low fire and simmer ½ hr. If you are careful to keep the lid fairly tight, the flavor will puff out impressively when served. With rice and a green, this will serve six. The juice on the rice, yes. Soy sauce on the rice, never!

C H A P T E R 6

BEEF

Beef is by far a less common form of meat in China than pork. As we have seen, we mean pork when we say meat. Some people never eat beef, on the ground that cattle work for man on the farm and therefore should not be eaten. There is more eating of beef and mutton by Chinese of Mohammedan faith, by whom pork is considered unclean. One important reason that non-Mohammedans in China do not eat much beef is probably that it is not as versatile a meat as pork from the point of view of Chinese cooking. For, while most of the recipes I have given for pork will make reasonably good dishes with beef, they do not make such easily successful dishes with beef as with pork. Beef meat balls will never be tender enough to be good. In the following recipes, I shall give only such as are specially good for beef; for example, Onions Stir Beef Shreds, Recipe No. 6.6, is better with beef than with pork and is therefore primarily a beef recipe. But you can use your judgment about interchanging the recipes between beef and pork. You know of course that no pork should be eaten that is not well done, while beef can be eaten rare. This compensates in part for the tougher texture of beef than pork. But then beef when too rare will not taste Chinese.

We usually use tenderloin or sirloin for beef slices and shreds. The methods of slicing and shredding are exactly the same as in Pork Meat Slices and Shreds. The general method of cooking is also the same. *No extra time* is needed for cooking beef *slices* and *shreds.* You can add any kind of supplementary material with it as in Pork Meat Slices, but I shall give a list of some combinations which are typical dishes for beef slices and shreds. They have become typical because they are good.

6.1. Red-Cooked Beef (Shin or Shank): Plain

In red-cooked beef, we usually use shin or shank meat in whole pieces or in large cubes. Stew meat is also used but is not as good as shin meat. We do not use other big pieces of muscle meat, because it has longer tissues and they stiffen more on stewing and come out less tender than the shorter fibers of shin meat. On the whole, beef is tougher than pork. When you cook whole pieces of beef or even large cubes, you have to cook from ½ to 1 hr. more than you would with pork.

Look up Recipe No. 1.1 for Red-Cooked Whole Pork Shoulder. Substitute same amount of whole beef shin for whole shoulder.

Cook the beef the same way as in that recipe. Except: Add 1 hr. extra in cooking if necessary. In case the beef is tender you may not need so much time. Anyway, test the beef by pricking with a chopstick or a fork.

This dish is also very good if you put it in the ice box and wait till the juice is all frozen into jelly. Then take out the whole beef with its jelly around it and cut into slices to serve.

6.2. Red-Cooked Beef Proper: Plain

For this recipe, shin (or shank) beef without bones, or stew beef are also preferred.

Follow recipe for Red-Cooked Meat Proper: Plain (remember what "meat" means?) and substitute beef for "meat." Except: the cooking time should be about ½ hr. longer.

6.3. Red-Cooked Beef with Yellow Turnips

Look up Recipe No. 1.3 for Red-Cooked Meat with Yellow Turnips.

Substitute beef for (pork) meat and do everything else according to that recipe. Except: cook the beef about ½ hr. longer.

6.4. Oyster Sauce Beef Slices

Follow Recipe No. 8.7 for seasoning and method of cooking, and substitute beef slices for chicken globules.

Warning: Don't forget to slice beef against the grain. It is even more important for beef than pork.

6.5. Sweet Peppers Stir Beef Shreds

Follow exactly Recipe No. 3.8 but substitute beef for pork.

6.6. Onions Stir Beef Shreds

Follow Recipe No. 3.4 but substitute beef for pork. This is such a good dish that many who do not like beef otherwise like it this way.

6.7. Mushrooms Stir Beef Slices

Follow exactly Recipe No. 2.2, but substitute beef slices for pork slices.

6.8. Frozen Peas Stir Beef Shreds

Follow exactly Recipe No. 3.2, but substitute beef for pork.

6.9. Fried Calves' Brains

3 plates calves brains, about 4½ whole brains	4 tb-sp. flour
	1 scallion or small onion
2 t-sp. salt	3 heaping tb-sp. lard or same
2 cups water	amount of oil
2 beaten eggs	

If you have got some brains, wash them clean, take off the outer skin and small veins, and keep the gray matter. Put in a pot with 2 cups of water and 1 t-sp. salt. Cook over medium fire; move brains a little from time to time to prevent sticking and burning. When boiling begins, turn to low fire and simmer for 20 min. Refrigerate (with the juice) until needed for use.

Just before you are ready to eat, cut the prepared brains into pieces of about 1 square inch by ⅛ inch thick.

Make dip-fry mixture by mixing original juice, which should be less than 1 cup after the boiling, with the beaten eggs, flour, chopped scallion, and 1 t-sp. salt.

Heat the lard or oil in a skillet over big fire till hot. Dip each piece of brain all around in the dipping mixture and fry in the skillet for 5 min. for each piece, turning over from time to time. If there is room on the skillet, you need not wait for the first piece to finish before you start on the second piece.

Variation.—This method applies also to fried pigs' brains.

6.10. Red-Cooked Ox Tongue

1 ox tongue—leave it in one whole piece
Same seasoning as in Recipe No. 6.14

Cook the tongue the same as you would oxtail in Recipe No. 6.14. Only, before adding in the seasoning, take the tongue out for a few minutes and peel off the skin.

Slice before serving. Eat either hot or cold. If you eat it hot, use this juice as gravy.

This dish can also be kept in the icebox for about a week.

6.11. Stirred Beef Heart

2 lbs. beef heart (or veal heart)	4-5 slices fresh ginger (if you
2 tb-sp. soy sauce	can get it)
2 tb-sp. sherry	1 t-sp. salt
2 scallions or a small onion	1 t-sp. sugar
1 tb-sp. cornstarch	2 heaping tb-sp. lard or same
2 tb-sp. water	amount of oil

Cut the heart vertically in two. Then cut across into thin slices about ⅛ inch thick. Take off tough parts (blood vessels) and pieces of fat on it. Then wash it.

Cut the scallions or onion into 1-inch sections. Mix the slices with the scallions or onion, soy sauce, sherry, cornstarch, water, ginger, salt, and sugar.

Heat the lard or oil in a skillet over big fire till hot. Put in the seasoned beef's heart and stir constantly for 3 min.

This dish can be warmed over, though it will not be so good as right after the first cooking.

Variation.—This method applies also to pig's heart.

6.12. Red-Simmered Beef Tripe

2 lbs. fresh beef tripe	½ t-sp. salt
3 cups water	2 tb-sp. sherry
3 tb-sp. soy sauce	1 scallion

Wash the tripe very thoroughly. Put the whole piece of tripe in a pot and add 3 cups water. Start with low fire and simmer for 2 hrs.

Then take it out and cut tripe into strips about ⅛ inch wide by 1½ inches long. Put tripe strips back into the pot.

Cut the scallion in inch-long sections. Then put it in the pot with the soy sauce, salt, and sherry. Simmer for another hour.

If you like it, you can add other materials, for example:

Variation 1.—Red-Simmered Beef Tripe with Carrots.

Cut a bunch of carrots into inch-long rolling-knife pieces (Figure 3, p. 36) and add in the tripe strips together with the other seasonings at the beginning of the last hour.

Variation 2.—Red-Simmered Beef Tripe with Green Pepper.

Cut 4 or 5 green peppers into small pieces, throwing away cores and seeds. Add in the pot 15 min. before the tripe is done.

6.13. Stirred Beef Kidney

3 lbs. beef kidney   2 scallions or a small onion
2 tb-sp. sherry   1 t-sp. salt
2 tb-sp. soy sauce   2 heaping tb-sp. lard
1 tb-sp. cornstarch

The cores of beef kidneys are not good and should be thrown away. Only the outside meaty part is good. Wash the kidneys and slice off as many pieces as you can until you reach the central dark red and white part, which should be thrown away. This leaves about 1 lb. of edible kidney. Put the slices in a big bowl of cold water and let soak for 1 hour, changing water 2 or 3 times. Throw away the water only just before cooking.

This dish should be cooked just before eating.

Cut the scallions or onion into 1-inch sections. Mix it with the sherry, soy sauce, cornstarch, salt, and the kidney slices.

Heat the lard in a skillet over big fire till hot. Put in the seasoned kidneys. Stir constantly for 3 min.

This is not good when cold or warmed over.

Variation.—Same method applies to pig's kidney.

6.14. Red-Cooked Oxtail

3-4 lbs. oxtail—have your butcher   6 tb-sp. soy sauce
   chop it into sections   1 t-sp. salt
5 cups water   3-4 slices fresh ginger
         (if you can get it)

Wash the oxtail and put it in a heavy pot with the 5 cups of water. Heat over big fire until boiling. Then add in the soy sauce, salt, and ginger and simmer for 3 hours.

If you have calf's tail, you need only 1½ hours. Always test by sticking through the meat, with a chopstick or fork. If the meat comes off from the bones easily, it is done.

You can add yellow turnips and other things in as you would

with Red-Cooked Beef. This dish can be reheated and be kept in the icebox for about a week.

6.15. Barbecued Beef

This is a good picnic dish. It is easier than cold chicken salad and tastes better than hot dog sandwich. Barbecued beef is just beef broiled in Chinese seasoning.

2 lbs. tenderloin beef	2 t-sp. sugar
4 tb-sp. soy sauce	1 t-sp. salt
4 slices garlic	

Cut the beef, against the grain, into ¼-inch thick slices. Size the other dimensions as you like.

Peel the garlic skin and crush each slice. Mix it in the soy sauce, sugar, and salt, and soak the beef in the seasonings for about 15 min. (If you are taking soaked beef on a long trip for the picnic, use only 3 tb-sp. soy sauce and only ½ t-sp. salt, as you can trade seasoning for time.)

The best thing to burn for outdoor barbecue is charcoal, though it is all right to burn a little of the beef too. Put a grate on top. Take the beef out of the juice only just before broiling. Put several pieces on the grate and broil on both sides for 4-5 min. Some like it slightly burned.

If you cook this indoors, you can put the beef over a broiling fire in your oven for 3 min., or fry it on both sides in 2 heaping tb-sp. lard or same amount of oil in a skillet over big fire for a total of 3 min.

Variation: Barbecued Lamb.—When this method is applied to lamb, then it is that famous *K'ao-yang-jou* of Peiping. With lamb, the slices are smaller and thinner, the seasoning wetter. There are special broiling grates in Peiping restaurants.

6.16. Rice-Flour Beef

Whoever steams beef? I do. Of course you have to take off the tendons as well as the bones from the chuck roast or rump steak, so that the beef will be tender when steamed.

The rice flour for this dish should be coarse-grained and it will taste better when browned. In China you roast the rice before grinding it. Here you can buy rice flour in Chinese stores, Japanese stores, French stores, certain co-op stores, and occasionally in the regular groceries. You can brown the flour in a pan, but don't if it is fine ground, because it will then burn easily.

1 lb. boned chuck roast or rump steak

8 tb-sp. coarse rice flour, preferably browned

5 tb-sp. soy sauce

2 tb-sp. wine

2 scallions or 1 small onion, cut up

1 t-sp. sugar

Cut meat into $\frac{1}{16}$-in. slices against the grain. Mix it with the seasonings and spread in a pie dish. Steam in already boiling water in a good-sized pot, placing a bowl or wire frame under the dish, so that only steam will come over the meat. Done in 15 minutes. With a green and rice, this will serve four. Increase amounts proportionally if more people eat or if people eat more.

A variation which the Chinese like even better is to use fresh bacon with skin, instead of beef. This will take 3 to 4 hours of steaming.

6.17. Beef Emit-Silk

Beef Emit-Silk looks like hamburger on toast, but isn't. It is so-called because with the Shanghai accent the English word "toast" sounds like *t'u-ssŭ*, which means "emit silk," and the name is suggestive because if you follow directions, it does taste silk-like, especially to go with cocktails.

Use cheap hamburger, which is fatter and will be softer when baked; but if you are very fat-conscious, then you will have to be satisfied with better and therefore leaner meat.

1 lb. hamburger meat	4 slices sandwich bread if used
4 tb-sp. soy sauce	for cocktails, or more slices as
1 t-sp. sugar	main dish
3 scallions	

Mix evenly ingredients and spread over the bread to make open-face sandwiches. Bake in preheated 440°F oven for 10 min., broil until top of meat is brown, which will take 2 to 3 min., depending upon the oven. Serve by cutting diagonally twice into triangular pieces (or larger pieces as main dish).

6.18. Garlic Beef

This is a very popular Chinese dish in Hawaii. It is somewhat strongly flavored, but the seasoning does bring out the flavor of the meat in an interesting way and goes very well with rice. It is simpler to make and tastes richer than beef stroganoff.

1 lb. filet mignon, rump steak, or chuck roast	2 tb-sp. cooking wine
1½ t-sp. sugar	3 or 4 sections of garlic, each section sliced in three
4 tb-sp. soy sauce (or 2 tb-sp. soy sauce plus 1 hpg tb-sp. *hoisin* sauce)	3 tb-sp. vegetable oil

Cut meat against the grain into $\frac{3}{16}$-in. slices and soak in the seasonings for 1 hr. Heat the 3 tb-sp. of oil in skillet over brisk fire. When the oil is hot, but not smoking, put in beef and stir-fry for 2 min. and it is ready to eat or to pour over your rice.

Lamb may be used instead of beef. If pork is used, it should be cooked for 3 min. to make sure it won't be rare.

Above quantity serves six. Leftovers will be good for sandwiches.

CHAPTER 7

MUTTON AND LAMB

Mutton and lamb are both sheep-meat to the mind of the Chinese cook or eater and need not be specified when either will do for the same dish. Mutton, of course, has more taste if you like that taste. Since not everybody likes sheep-meat, it is less widely used than pork. It is used rather more in the northern than in the southern provinces.

7.1. Red-Cooked Lamb

If you can get mutton or lamb with skin on, as you often can in Chinatown, it may turn out to be a pleasant surprise when red-cooked.

> 4 lbs. leg of mutton (or lamb) 6 tb-sp. soy sauce
> with bones (for 6 persons) 1 t-sp. salt
> 3 scallions in 2-inch long sec-
> tions

Chop mutton, with bones, into pieces of about 1½ cubic inches. Wash and put in a heavy pot. Heat over big fire until boiling. Add scallions, soy sauce, and salt. Simmer for 3 hrs.

7.2. Jellied Lamb

Lamb (or mutton) as in Recipe No. 7.1. (Parts with more joints are preferred because they have a great deal of gelatine to jell.)
Same seasoning as in Recipe No. 7.1.
Prepare lamb as in Recipe No. 7.1. After it is done, remove all the bones. Press the meat down so that the juice covers all the

meat. Then put in the icebox. After the juice has jellied, take out and scrape off all the frozen oil on top. Cut the whole—jelly and meat together—into rectangular pieces of 2 inches by 1 inch by ¼ inch.

This dish can be kept in the icebox for 1 or 2 weeks. It is there-fore all right to make enough for future use as well.

The Chinese name *yang-kao* sounds more poetic than the English translation. While "jellied lamb" suggests a cold lunch, *yang-kao* calls for wine and good company. Some people who do not eat sheep-meat in any form may eat it in this form, especially if they are not told until afterward.

7.3. Fried Lamb Slices

The most suitable cuts for this dish are lamb tenderloin and the inside of leg of lamb.

2 lbs. lamb	2 scallions cut into 1-inch-long
2 tb-sp. soy sauce	sections
1 tb-sp. sherry	2 heaping tb-sp. lard
1 t-sp. salt	

Cut the lamb into flying-thin slices and mix with the soy sauce, sherry, salt, and scallions.

Heat the lard in a skillet over big fire until smoking hot, then put in the seasoned lamb slices and stir constantly for 2 min.

This dish must be eaten right after cooking.

7.4. Rinsed Lamb

Rinsed Lamb is such a picturesque as well as a delicious institution that I must describe it in full as it is done in Peiping, after telling you what is the nearest thing to do in America.

First, how can we rinse lamb here and now? Get:

For the pot proper:

Tenderloin lamb, about 1 lb. to a person (you may vary from ½ lb. to 2 lbs. per person). Always try to get the tenderest part of the whole lamb. Slice the lamb extremely thin against the grain.

½ lb. salted *kaai-ts'oi*. Get in Chinatown. This is the nearest substitute for a kind of soured salted-cabbage that we usually use in China. But red-in-snow also can do.

1 tb-sp. salt.

8-10 cups boiling water.

2 lbs. celery cabbage. Cut across into thin shreds.

1 lb. Chinese dried noodles. Get in Chinatown. Put into a big pot of boiling water and heat until they boil again. Turn to low fire and cook almost 1 hr. Add a cup of water, if necessary. If you cannot buy the Chinese dried noodles, use 1 lb. egg noodles instead. Put into a pot of boiling water and cook until they boil again, bring to low fire and cook for 15 min.

½ lb. peastarch noodles. Put into a pot of boiling water and boil over low fire for ½ hr. Turn off the fire but keep the noodles in the water until ready to use. If they "don't have them," ask for "long rice."

For the dip-eating sauce:

1 cup soy sauce

1 cup vinegar

1 cup cooking wine

1 cup hot pepper sauce

1 cup sesame jam (or peanut butter)

1 cup chopped scallions. Use very small scallions. This is a substitute for the stronger smelling *chiu-ts'ai*, or Chinese leeks.

Use large pot and electric stove (hot-plate) and proceed as in the Chrysanthemum Chafing Pot, Recipe No. 16.1.

Mix your dip-eating sauce only shortly before eating.

To make sure that the meat will not be overcooked, keep track of your slices, preferably holding them in the boiling soup and never letting go. The meat is cooked in 10 or 15 seconds. Dip in the dip-eating sauce and eat.

If you ever go to one of the lamb-rinsing places in Peiping (one was started in Nanking too), you will be served a big central-heated chafing pot. (See Chapter 16. Introduction.) While waiting for the pot to boil, sometimes with the aid of a detachable fire-drafter or chimney extension, you mix your dip-eating sauce by taking from the table and putting into your individual bowls spoonfuls of cooking wine, vinegar, sesame jam, shrimp sauce, red bean-curd cheese sauce, soy sauce, and hot pepper sauce. Put in the soured salted-cabbage or red-in-snow served on the table to give the soup an initial taste. Lamb slices are served in small saucers, containing about 2⅔ oz. each, and charged for by counting so many empty saucers at the end of the session. To slice lamb flying-thin is a fine art. The special slicer used to get a salary of two hundred dollars a month, that is, when two hundred dollars were two hundred dollars.

When the soup boils, put into the pot a dish or two of the fatter slices. Let them swim around freely. These are to give the soup "body." Then get a pinch of two or three of the lamb slices between your chopsticks and hold them in the boiling soup, occasionally making a rinsing motion, whence the name Rinsed Lamb. As soon as the meat changes color, which takes between 10 and 15 seconds, it is done. Dip it in your dip-eating sauce, which both cools it and gives it seasoning. It is now ready to eat. Sometimes you can let go of the slices after putting them into the soup. The disadvantage is that they may get lost in the soup and get tough, or someone else may get your lamb.

The *fan* or grain food that usually goes with Rinsed Lamb is hot biscuit with sesame seeds or coarse-cereal noodles. Peastarch noodles are usually put in the soup at the later stages of eating. By the time the dipping sauce gets diluted from dipping the dripping meat, you will have had about enough, and a few spoonfuls of the boiling soup in your bowl will make a fine drinking soup, for we always like to end a meal by drinking good and hot soup.

C H A P T E R   8

CHICKEN

When I say chicken, I mean chicken mostly, though sometimes we use old fowls or very small friers. Then it will be specified. Capons can also be used. For soup chicken, we use big fat hens. When the recipe calls for spring chicken, it is usually young roosters.

One large chicken can often be worked in several different ways. For instance, the white meat can be sliced to make a stir-frying dish. Dark meat and bones can be used for slow-cooking soup. The meat in the soup, if not overcooked, can be used to make White Cut Chicken, or combined with other things to make one form of Red-Cooked Chicken. With young chicken, after the white meat is used in shallow fry, the other parts can be used in deep fry. Thus, we have names like Chicken-in-Three Flavors or three dishes coming from one chicken.

As in America, chickens are considered something a little more special than just meat. Another thing about chicken is that it is very convenient in the country, since one family can use one chicken whenever guests come to justify it, while very often no meat comes until a Fair date comes for slaughtered meat to be brought to the country fair.

8.1. Red-Cooked Chicken

Red-Cooked Chicken has two styles of cooking, depending upon the chicken being a chicken or a fowl. The rule is: While a fowl stews in its own juice, a chicken is fried in somebody else's fat, that it, it has to be fried in lard first. We shall take these up separately.

HOW TO COOK AND EAT IN CHINESE

A. With Fowl

1 fowl, 6-7 lbs., whole piece. Keep the chicken fat. Do not cut.
3 cups water
¼ cup soy sauce
1 tb-sp. sugar
2 tb-sp. sherry
3-4 pieces fresh ginger (if you can get it)
1 small onion or 1 scallion

Wash chicken inside and out. Put chicken in a heavy pot with the chicken fat and the 3 cups of water. Heat over big fire until boiling.

Cut onion into 8 or 10 small sections (if scallion, into 3 or 4 sections) and put them in the pot with the soy sauce, sherry, and ginger as soon as the water boils.

Turn to low fire and cover pot tightly. Cook for 1 hr. Then put sugar in. Continue on low fire for ½ hr. (or 1 hr. if fowl is not tender). Test cooking with chopstick or fork as with meat.

When served in the Chinese way and whole, you break off pieces with your chopsticks to serve your neighbors or to eat yourself. Sometimes it is all right to help out with your fingers if done gracefully, but it is less commonly practiced than in this country. If you want to eat chicken and cannot wait until you have learned to "carve" with chopsticks, you can pre-carve the chicken into egg-size pieces in the kitchen before cooking.

B. With Young Chicken

1 young chicken, 5-6 lbs.
2 tb-sp. lard (because there is little fat in young chicken)
2 cups water
1 tb-sp. sugar
6 tb-sp. soy sauce
2 tb-sp. sherry
3-4 pieces fresh ginger (if you can get it)
1 small onion or 1 scallion

Wash and cut chicken into egg-size pieces (with bones).
Cut onion into 8-10 sections (if scallion, into 3 or 4 sections).
Heat the lard in a heavy pot till hot, put the chicken in, and stir

constantly for 5 min. Then add the water, soy sauce, sherry, ginger and onion.

Turn fire low and cover tight. Boil for ½ hr. Then put in sugar and boil for another 10 to 30 min. (depending on tenderness of chicken).

8.2. Red-Smothered Chicken

One 3-4 lb. chicken (spring   3-4 slices fresh ginger (if you
   chicken)   can get it)
2 cups water   2 tb-sp. soy sauce
1 scallion or 1 small onion   2 t-sp. salt

Wash the chicken and chop into 16 pieces all together.

Put it in a pot with the 2 cups of water. Turn on big fire and cook until it boils. Then add the scallion, ginger, soy sauce, and salt. Turn to medium fire and cook for ½ hr.

Note that the red-smothering is shorter than red-cooking.

8.3. Red-Cooked Chicken with Chestnuts

1 lb. dried chestnuts without outside shells.
Chicken and seasoning same as Red-Cooked Chicken B,
   Recipe No. 8.1 B., but no sugar (because there is enough
   sugar in the chestnuts)
Additional 5 cups of water

Use the 5 cups of water to boil the chestnuts over low fire for 2 hrs. Peel off the inner skin and keep chestnuts in the water.

Cook chicken same as Recipe No. 8.1.A or No. 8.1.B. Then add in the chestnut with its water, cover tight and boil together for 15 min. over low fire.

This can be left over and heated again.

8.4. Red-Cooked Chicken with Bamboo Shoots

1 can bamboo shoots (as mentioned in Red-Cooked Meat and
Bamboo Shoots, winter shoots are preferred)
Chicken and seasoning as Red-Cooked Chicken B, Recipe
No. 8.1.B

Cut bamboo shoots into shapes as close to tetrahedrons as pos
sible. Throw away the juice in the can.

Chop chicken the same as in Red-Cooked Chicken B, Recipe
No. 8.1.B.

Put bamboo shoots in 15 min. before serving.

8.5. Stirred Spring Chicken

2 spring chickens, about 4 lbs.	1 small onion or 1 scallion
3 tb-sp. soy sauce	3 tb-sp. lard or vegetable oil
2 tb-sp. sherry	½ cup of water
2-3 slices fresh ginger (if you can get it)	1 t-sp. salt

Chop chicken into pieces about the size of small plums. Mix
in the soy sauce, sherry, onion, and ginger (leaving the water
alone). Let it stand for 5 min.

Heat the lard in a frying skillet till hot. Put the chicken together
with its juice in the skillet and stir for 2 min. Then add the ½ cup of
water and the salt. Still with big fire cook for 5 more min. under
cover.

8.6. Sweet Peppers Stir Chicken

3 or 4 sweet peppers
Chicken and seasoning same as Stirred Spring Chicken,
Recipe No. 8.5

Wash the peppers and wash away the seeds inside. Cut into
1 square-inch pieces.

Cook chicken as in Recipe No. 8.5. Put peppers in 3 min. before
serving.

8.7. Oyster Sauce Chicken Balls

2 spring chickens, total 4 lbs. with bones (which means only about 1 lb. of big meat)	1 tb-sp. cornstarch
	2 tb-sp. water
	1 small onion or 1 scallion
2 tb-sp. soy sauce	2 tb-sp. lard
1 tb-sp. sherry	2 tb-sp. oyster sauce
½ t-sp. salt	1 t-sp. sugar

Take off all the bones and cut chicken into thick slices. Make a few slashes in the very thick places. Keep chicken meat in refrigeration until just before cooking.

Cut onion into small sections, mix it in the chicken with the soy sauce, sherry, cornstarch, salt, and water, thoroughly.

Heat the lard in a skillet till hot, put the seasoned chicken in and stir constantly for 2 min. (be sure not to scorch the pan) using big fire. Then add the oyster sauce and sugar. Cook and stir for 1 min. more.

Then turn to medium fire and fry for 6 min. more.

After it is done, it can be kept in the oven for a while if necessary, but not too long. or else it will be too dry.

For large chickens, although you cut into the same size and use the same amount as indicated, you have to fry for 10 min. instead of 6 because the meat is not so tender.

8.8. Fried Spring Chicken

2 spring chickens, total 4 lbs. (Fowl is usable but spring chicken is preferred.)	½ t-sp. sugar
	1 cup flour
	1 small onion or 1 scallion
2 tb-sp. sherry	Enough lard or vegetable oil
3 tb-sp. soy sauce	for deep frying (or ½ of a
1 t-sp. salt	pot)

Chop chicken into pieces about the size of eggs.

Cut onion into small sections. Put it in a bowl with the chicken and add the sherry, soy sauce, salt, and sugar. Then let it stand for 1 hr. in the icebox.

Then dip each piece into the cup of flour so that it is all wrapped with flour. Heat enough oil for deep oil frying and put the chicken in. Fry for 2 min.

8.9. *Fu-yung* Chicken Slices

1 large chicken or 2 spring chickens (which will yield about 1½ lbs. white meat)
4 egg whites
½ tb-sp. cornstarch
1 tb-sp. water

1½ tb-sp. sherry
1 t-sp. salt
1 scallion or small sweet onion
3-4 slices fresh ginger (if you can get it)
3 heaping tb-sp. lard

Use only white meat (save the rest for red-cooking or soup). Cut chicken white meat into thin slices (as with meat slices), add in egg whites (unbeaten), cornstarch, water, sherry, and salt. Cut onion into 1-inch sections.

Heat lard in skillet till hot. Put chicken, onion, and ginger in and stir constantly for 2 min.

Be sure to cook this dish just before eating, because it is at its best when hot and it cannot be reheated nor kept in the oven without getting tough. You get the same result also by eating just after cooking.

8.10. Mushrooms Stir Chicken Slices

White meat of one large chicken or two small chickens—about 1 lb.
½ lb. fresh mushrooms
1 tb-sp. cornstarch
2 tb-sp. water
1 tb-sp. sherry

1 t-sp. salt
2 tb-sp. soy sauce
3 tb-sp. lard or oil
1 scallion or 1 small sweet onion
2 or 3 slices fresh ginger (if you can get it)

Cut chicken white meat into thin slices. (Be sure to keep it in the icebox if not used immediately.) Mix with the cornstarch, water, sherry, salt, chopped onion, and ginger.

Wash the mushrooms and cut them vertically into slices. Heat

1 tb-sp. lard in a skillet, put the mushrooms in, add the soy sauce and stir-fry for 2 min. Then take out.

Heat the other 2 tb-sp. lard over big fire and put the chicken in. Stir constantly for 2 min., then add in the mushrooms again. Cook together for ½ min.

8.11. Green Peas Stir Chicken Slices

Same chicken as in Recipe No. 8.10
Same seasoning as in Recipe No. 8.10
Plus: ½ more t-sp. salt (1½ altogether) to replace the 2 tb-sp. soy sauce
1 package frozen green peas
Thaw out the frozen peas
Prepare and cook chicken as in Recipe No. 8.10.

Add in the peas after stirring chicken for 2 min. Then add the extra ½ t-sp. salt. Stir for only 30 *seconds* and take out.

8.12. Bamboo Shoots Stir Chicken Slices

Same chicken as in Recipe No. 8.10
Same seasoning as in Recipe No. 8.10
Plus: ½ t-sp. more salt
1 can bamboo shoots (winter shoots preferred)

Cut bamboo shoots into thin slices. Prepare and cook chicken same way as in Recipe No. 8.10, but put in the bamboo shoot slices after frying the chicken for only 1 min. Add in also the ½ t-sp. salt. Then cook together for 1½ min.

8.13. Colorful Chicken Slices

Same chicken as in Recipe No. 8.10
Same seasoning as in Recipe No. 8.10
Plus enough vegetable oil for deep frying
¼ lb. mushrooms   1 handful frozen green peas
¼ lb. water chestnuts   ¼ lb. dry almonds or dry wal-
¼ can winter bamboo shoots   nuts

Soak the almonds or walnuts in hot water and peel off the inner skin.

Heat the vegetable oil till hot, and deep-fry the nuts for 1 min. (Lard is not good for this purpose.)

Cut mushrooms, water chestnuts, and bamboo shoots into small thin slices.

Fry the mushrooms, water chestnuts, bamboo shoots with 1 tb-sp. lard or oil for 2 min. and then take out.

Prepare and cook chicken as in Recipe No. 8.10; after frying chicken for 2 min., add in the mushrooms, water chestnuts, bamboo shoots, green peas, almonds, and walnuts. Cook together for ½ min.

8.14. Asparagus Stirs Chicken Shreds

Same chicken as in Recipe No. 8.10. (The Chinese use more white meat because those who go in for such dishes at all use more chickens at a time and the other parts can be used for other dishes. However, for convenience in small American families, where fewer chickens are used at a time, we can also use the dark meat of a tender young chicken, together with the white meat, to make up the 1 lb. which Recipe No. 8.10 requires.)

Same seasoning as in Recipe No. 8.10
Except: No soy sauce
Plus: ½ t-sp. salt
1 lb. asparagus

Cut chicken into shreds like meat shreds. Then add in seasoning as in Recipe No. 8.10.

Cut off the root parts of asparagus and cut the tender parts obliquely into thin slices of about 1 inch long and ⅛ inch thick.

Heat 1 tb-sp. lard in a skillet. Put asparagus in and also the ½ t-sp. salt. Fry for 2 min. and take out.

Cook chicken as in Recipe No. 8.10 for 2 min. Add in the asparagus. Cook together for ½ min.

8.15. Bamboo Shoot Shreds Stir Chicken Shreds

This dish is practically the same as Bamboo Shoot Stirs Chicken Slices, except that the chicken and the bamboo shoots are cut into shreds.

Like the slices, the shreds should be eaten right after cooking.

8.16. Paper-Wrapped Chicken

2 young chickens or one large one about 3-4 lbs. with bones

1 tb-sp. sherry

2 tb-sp. soy sauce

¼ t-sp. sugar (if desired)

1 scallion or ⅓ small sweet onion

2 or 3 slices ginger (if you can get it)

Enough veg. oil for deep frying

18 sheets of cellophane paper, 4 by 4 inches

Take off all bones and skins from the chicken (about 1 lb. pure meat left). Cut white and dark meat obliquely to the tissues into slices of about 1 square inch by ⅛ inch thick. (The bones and skins can be used for making soup.)

Put sherry, soy sauce, chopped scallion, and chopped ginger in a bowl with the chicken and let the chicken soak for 10 min.

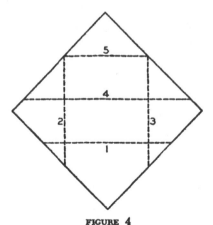

FIGURE 4
How to Paper-Wrap Chicken

Then divide the chicken into 18 portions and wrap each portion in a piece of cellophane in the order of the folds as indicated in Figure 4. Tuck in the corner at No. 5 to prevent the package from falling apart.

Then heat the veg. oil and deep-fry the packages for 2 min. Serve without unwrapping in order to keep the heat and juice in until eating. This dish can be kept in the oven for a few minutes without getting tough but cannot be reheated after getting cold. See also Rec. 23.4B.

8.17. Chicken Cubelets

2 lbs. chicken white meat (or with dark meat if chicken is tender)

1 tb-sp. cornstarch

2 tb-sp. water

2 tb-sp. sherry

1 scallion or 1 small onion

2 or 3 slices fresh ginger (if you can get it)

2 tb-sp. (heaping) soy jam

1 t-sp. sugar

2 heaping tb-sp. lard

Cut chicken into tiny cubes of about ¼ inch cube. Mix it with the cornstarch, water, sherry, and scallion (in 1-inch sections).

Heat the lard in a skillet over big fire, then fry the chicken for 2 min. Mix the soy jam evenly and add into the chicken with the sugar. Fry again for 1 min. Also a quick eating dish.

In China we sometimes like to add in about ¼ t-sp. hot pepper powder. But it is very hot!

8.18. White-Cut Chicken

This is the basic dish of chicken as chicken.

1 chicken about 7-8 lbs. (In this kind of cooking, a hen is preferred.)

2 quarts water

4 tb-sp. soy sauce (for use when serving)

Wash the chicken clean and put in a heavy pot with the 2 quarts of water. Turn on big fire until boiling. Then turn to low fire and cook for 2-2½ hrs. (depending on tenderness of chicken). Keep cover on all the time. After cooking, take chicken out and put in icebox. We usually serve this dish cold by chopping the chicken into small pieces with bones of about 1 cubic inch in volume, e.g., ⅔ inch by 1 inch by 2 inches. (Cf. also p. 105.)

Place in a serving plate and serve with soy sauce. This recipe is for more than 6. The leftovers are good for Variation B below.

Variation A: 15-Min. Chicken.—Instead of starting with old hen in cold water, put a tender, young chicken in boiling water and continue brisk fire for 15 min. Cut and serve as in main recipe.

Variation B: Pepper Chicken.—Heat 20-30 grains of Szechwan pepper or *hua-chiao* in a small pan over medium fire for 1 min. Scoop 3 tb-sp. chicken oil from the top of the soup, add to the pepper seeds, and mix with 4 tb-sp. soy sauce while the mixture is still hot. Stir before pouring over the chicken. In Szechwan, which is famous for this dish, a t-sp. of hot pepper powder is mixed in with the sauce.

8.19. Chicken Meat with Celery—Chinese Chicken Salad

About 1 lb. white cooked chicken meat, such as from leftover white-cut chicken or from the meat of the chicken from clear chicken soup (Recipe No. 15.19)

1 small bunch celery	1 tb-sp. soy sauce
1 tb-sp. salad oil (or sesame oil)	1 t-p. salt
	1 t-sp. sugar

Cut celery obliquely into small strips of about 1 inch long and ⅛-inch thick.

Boil a quart of hot water in a pot. Put the celery strips in and boil for 1 min. Pour off the water and rinse once with cold water.

Take off all the bones from the chicken and tear the meat into small strips. Like many other things, they taste better torn than cut. Tearing gives more surface to taste.

Mix thoroughly the chicken with the seasonings. Serve cold.

Variation.—Try the white meat of Roast Turkey (Recipe No. 8.23).

8.20. Pot-Stewed Chicken

Chickens are pot-stewed as follows:

1 chicken 7-10 lbs. (or two small young chickens)	3-4 slices fresh ginger (if you can get it)
1 cup soy sauce	1 tb-sp. sugar
¼ cup sherry	1 quart water
2-3 scallions or 1 big onion	

Wash chicken clean and put in a heavy pot. Add in the quart of water. Turn on big fire and cook till it boils. Then add the soy sauce, sherry, scallions, ginger, and sugar. Turn to medium fire and cook for 1½-3 hrs., depending on the tenderness of chicken. However, in this method of cooking we do not cook it too soft. In case of two young chickens, cook only 1 hr.

After cooking, take out the chicken, let cool, and cut up to serve. For neat serving, see Salt-Water Duck, Recipe No. 9.8.

The chicken may be kept uncut in the icebox if not used right away.

Pot-Stewed Eggs.—If you have a great deal of sauce left over after eating the chicken you can put in a dozen shelled hard-boiled eggs and boil further for one hour.

8.21. *Fu-yung* Cauliflower

1 cauliflower about 2 lbs.	3 egg whites
2½ cups water	1 tb-sp. cornstarch
1½ t-sp. salt	2 heaping tb-sp. lard
¼ lb. chicken's white meat	

Break the cauliflower into very small branches. Put it into a pot with 2 cups of water and also 1 t-sp. salt. Boil over big fire for 10 min. Then take it out and throw away the water.

Grind finely the chicken's white meat. Add the egg whites, the cornstarch, the salt and 2 tb-sp. of the water. Beat with an egg beater until it puffs up.

CHICKEN

Heat the lard in a skillet over big fire until hot. Put in the beater chicken and egg whites and stir for 2 min. Then add in the cauliflower and stir for 2 min.

Sometimes we like to sprinkle some finely chopped ham and dried shrimps on top when serving.

What We Do with Chicken Livers, Gizzards, etc.

Cook together in red-cooked meat and red-cooked chicken dishes.
Cook with white-cut chicken and slice when serving.
Cut into slices and fry with other materials as with meat slices.
Wrap in flour and deep-fry in oil with fried chicken.

The Chinese often use many gizzards in a dish as the main material. Some like it better than meat and chicken.

8.22. Roast Chicken (Chinese Style)

1 whole tender chicken, 5 lbs.	½ cup sherry
3 cups water	3-4 slices fresh ginger
1 cup soy sauce	1 scallion
1 tb-sp. sugar	1 t-sp. salt

Boil water with seasonings. Then put chicken in. Continue brisk fire for 15 min. Turn off and let steep 20 min. Roast at 500°F. for 15 min. until browned over. Cut chicken in kitchen with bones on (see p. 105), but if you prefer to carve and serve American way —well, do as you like! The juice may be used for gravy and leftover juice may be used in pot-stewing (pp. 42, 98, 103). Hot juice may be poured on second serving, but a second roasting will not be good.

This recipe may be varied by omitting the boiling and roasting for 1 hr., basting with 1 cup water every 15 min. until browned over. Salt and pepper for dip-eating (optional) as in Recipe No. 11.6.

8.23. Roast Turkey[1] (Chinese Style)

1 hen turkey, 15-20 lbs.	3 tb-sp. sugar
12 cups water (not incl. basting)	5 large slices fresh ginger
	3-4 scallions
4 cups soy sauce	2 t-sp. salt
2 cups sherry	

Boil water with seasonings. Put turkey in. Continue brisk fire for 1 hr., turning over, as juice won't cover turkey. Roast at 500°F. for 1 hr., basting with 1 cup water every 20 min., turning over 2 or 3 times until browned over. (Reduce boiling-roasting time for turkeys under 15 lbs.) On use of juice and leftovers, see p. 99.

8.24. Wind-Cured Chicken

To wind-cure chicken, get from the poultry:

1 fresh-killed chicken, about 5 lbs., *with feathers on*	½ t-sp. Szechwan pepper berries (*ch'ün-tsiu*)
	1 hpg. tb-sp. salt

The insides should be cleaned out by cutting an opening under the wing and drying the inside with a piece of cloth. Do not wash chicken with water, cold or warm.

Roast the salt and the Szechwan pepper in a pan until hot. Rub mixture all over the inside of the cleaned chicken.

Now turn the neck of the chicken and tuck the head under one of the wings, tie up with a cord and hang in a cool, shady, airy place, away from rain, sun and cats. The chicken will be wind-cured in two weeks and can be used any time from now on. Before cooking, it will keep for two months in cold weather. In warm weather don't wind-cure chickens.

To cook chicken, remove feathers after scalding with near-boiling

---

[1] I put Turkey under "Chicken" because it is called *huo-chi* (fire-chicken) in Chinese. By my way of roasting, the meat is not powdery, but tender and juicy. (Try also my version of American Roast Turkey: a. Use sherry, scallion, ginger, soy sauce and sugar in the stuffing; b. Less stuffing, so the hot air gets in; c. My roasting time is only ⅔ of American way.)

water. Then heat 4 fresh cups of water and put in chicken for 15 min. of brisk boiling. Serve hot or cold. Instead of cutting the meat, tearing it off seems to make it taste better. The soup can be used separately if desired.

Variations.—Steaming for half an hour is sometimes preferred to boiling. But you get excellent soup from boiling. Another variation consists in putting in 2 or 3 oz. of leaf-lard, cut up and mixed in with the salt and Szechwan pepper and rubbed over the inside of the chicken before sending it to the winds. This keeps in the flavor even better, though it will make the soup a little too rich.

8.25. Salted Turkey

Salted Turkey is not a Chinese dish, because we don't have turkeys, nor an American dish, because Americans don't salt turkeys. It grew out of my idea of trying to wind-cure turkey. It turned out that I did not have to go to the trouble of hanging a big heavy turkey with a rope, but could get perfectly good results with a simpler procedure. All you need to get is:

1 dressed turkey, 15-20 lbs.   6-8 hpg. tb-sp. salt

Cut turkey into 4 large pieces or have it cut at the market. Rub salt all over the pieces. Let stand in a pan or tray in a cool place, but not on refrigeration. After 30 hours, the turkey is ready for use.

Before cooking, wash the turkey lightly with clear water. Boil in enough cold water to immerse the piece or pieces used. For tender turkey boil briskly 40 min. after boiling starts, for older turkey, 1 hr.

Serve sliced hot or cold. Cold salted turkey is much more juicy and savory than leftover roast turkey. It reminds one of wind-cured chicken. As I have told you, it was wind-cured chicken that led me to salt turkey.

Keep the soup.

CHAPTER 9

DUCK

Relative to chicken, duck is more commonly used in China than in America, probably because of the greater variety of ways of preparing it. Ducks are slow-boiled, red-cooked, or roasted, but very rarely stir-fried. There are several ways of salting ducks. One form is to salt them, dry in the sun, and then cook by steaming. Another form is to store in vegetable oil and take out to steam as needed. These forms are very common in Canton. A quick-salted form, known as Salt-Water Duck, is described below. (Recipe No. 9.8.)

9.1. Red-Cooked Duck

1 duck 5-7 lbs.	2 tb-sp. sherry
3 cups water	2 t-sp. sugar
¼ cup soy sauce	1 scallion or 1 small onion

Wash duck and cut off the tail. (Be sure to cut out the oil pouches just above the tail.) You can chop the duck, if you like, into pieces of about 2 cubic inches.

Put it in a heavy pot and add 3 cups water. Cook over big fire till it boils. Then add the soy sauce, sherry, onion, and simmer for 1 hr. Then turn over the duck, if cooked whole, and add 2 t-sp. sugar and let simmer for another hour.

Lengthen or shorten the last hour according to the condition of the duck. Test by pulling the bones. If the meat comes off easily, it is tender enough. We usually like it cooked tenderer than chicken.

9.2. Onion-Cooked Duck

5-7 lb. duck	3 t-sp. sugar
2 bunches scallions or 3-4 onions	3 cups water
(enough to stuff the whole	2 tb-sp. sherry
duck)	3 or 4 slices fresh ginger
8 tb-sp. soy sauce	

Wash duck and cut off the tail, and oil sacs. Leave the scallions whole (but slice the onions). Mix them with 2 tb-sp. soy sauce and 1 t-sp. sugar. Stuff them in the duck. (It is not necessary to sew up the duck.)

Put the stuffed duck in a heavy pot and add 3 cups water, 6 tb-sp. of the soy sauce, the 2 tb-sp. sherry, and the ginger.

Heat till it boils and then simmer for 1 hr. Add the remaining 2 t-sp. sugar and turn over to simmer for another hour or so (depending on tenderness of duck).

9.3. Duck with Five-Spice Cabbage

Same duck and seasoning as in Recipe No. 9.1 Red-Cooked Duck. Except: 2 tb-sp. less soy sauce, because the cabbage is already very salty.

½ can five-spice winter cabbage (called *ng¹-heung tung-ts'oi* in Chinatown).

Cook duck as in recipe for Red-Cooked Duck (Recipe No. 9.1).
After 1 hr. of simmering, add in the ½ can of cabbage, then simmer together for another hour.

[1] This Cantonese word for "five" is to be pronounced through the nose. Just hum it, or rather hung it.—Y. R. C.

9.4. Eight-Jewel Duck

One 5-7 lb. duck
⅓ cup glutinous rice
2 tb-sp. pearl barley (or substitute with common barley)
8 tb-sp. soy sauce
3 t-sp. sugar
3 scallions
15 gingko nuts
15 lotus seeds (or substitute
canned ones)

10 candied jujubes (or substitute dates)
10 fresh chestnuts
2 tb-sp. raisins
2 tb-sp. sherry
3 or 4 slices fresh ginger
5 cups water

Wash the duck clean and cut off the tail and oil sacs.

Shell the gingko nuts, soak in hot water for about ½ min. and peel off the soft skin.

Boil the rice and barley together in 2 cups water for ½ hr. over low fire.

Then mix thoroughly the boiled rice and barley with 2 tb-sp. of the soy sauce, 1 t-sp. of the sugar, 1 chopped scallion, the gingko, lotus seeds, jujubes, dates, chestnuts, and the raisins. Stuff it in the duck and place in a heavy pot.

Put 3 cups water in the pot with duck and also add the remaining 6 tb-sp. soy sauce, 2 tb-sp. sherry, 2 scallions (not necessarily chopped) and ginger.

Heat over big fire till the water boils, then turn fire low and simmer for 1 hr. Then add 2 t-sp. sugar, and turn over to simmer another hour.

The last hour may be stretched or shrunken, depending upon the tenderness of the duck. In any case, for the same kind of duck, a stuffed duck takes ½ hr. longer than an ordinary Red-Cooked Duck.

This duck can be kept in the icebox for almost one week.

9.5. Pot-Stewed Duck

This recipe is very much like Recipe No. 9.1 for Red-Cooked Duck, except add:

2 extra tb-sp. sherry   2 extra tb-sp. soy sauce

Do not use big fire. Use medium fire and cook for 1 hr. Take the duck out and put it in a refrigerator. (The gravy should be saved for preparing other dishes like Pot-Stewed Meat, Pot-Stewed Eggs, and Pot-Stewed Chicken.)

Cut the cold duck with the bones into slices of about ⅛ inch in thickness and 1 inch in length.

(This dish may also be served hot. Remove the bones if you do not mind the trouble.)

9.6. Pot-Stuck Duck

2 lbs. breast and legs of duck   2 eggs
  (A 6-7 lb. duck will give this   4 tb-sp. cornstarch
  much meat.)   ½ t-sp. salt
2 tb-sp. soy sauce   4 tb-sp. water
1 tb-sp. sherry   3 tb-sp. lard or the same amount
1 scallion   of vegetable oil
4 slices fresh ginger

Put the duck's breast and legs with the soy sauce, sherry, chopped scallion, and chopped ginger in a big bowl and let stand for ½ hr.

Mix the eggs, cornstarch, salt, and water together into a paste and apply a coating of the paste on the duck.

Heat the lard in a skillet over big fire until hot. Fry the duck (2 min. for each of the two sides). Turn to medium fire and fry for 10 min. on each side (altogether 24 min.) until the skin becomes crisp.

Cut the duck into ½-inch slices. Serve each person with 5 or 6 slices.

(Mix 3 tb-sp. salt and ½ t-sp. black pepper in a small dish for dipping before eating.)

9.7. Fresh Ginger Stirs Duck Shreds

Since fresh ginger can be obtained only during certain seasons, this dish can be prepared only when fresh ginger is on the Chinese market. However, other accompaniments like mushrooms, peas, asparagus, winter bamboo shoots, etc., may be used if you cannot get the ginger.

1 duck, about 2 lbs. of meat	1 tb-sp. cornstarch
2 oz. fresh ginger	1 t-sp. salt
2 tb-sp. soy sauce	1 scallion (in 1-inch sections)
2 tb-sp. sherry	2 tb-sp. lard

Wash the fresh ginger and cut it into shreds.

Cut the meat from the breast and the legs into shreds.

Mix the soy sauce, sherry, cornstarch, salt, scallion sections with the duck shreds.

Heat the lard in a skillet till hot. Put the seasoned duck shreds in and stir for 1 min. Add in the fresh ginger shreds and stir for another 3 min.

(This dish should be served right after cooking, otherwise it would get very "fishy" which, for ducks, is even more "fishy" than fish. The bones, neck, etc., from the duck can be red-cooked or made into soups. Since duck meat is very fat, red-cooking is preferred.)

9.8. Salt-Water Duck

"Salt-Water Duck" is not a kind of sea gull, but a land-based duck. It is simply the Nanking name for fresh salted duck, which is one of the good things of Nanking. It is a cold dish and different from heavily long-salted duck.

One 5-7 lb. duck

3-4 tb-sp. salt

1 t-sp. Szechwan pepper (Get in Chinatown under the name of *ch'ün-tsiu* or *fa-tsiu*, or substitute with cinnamon.)

8 cups water.

Mix pepper with salt. Rub it on the duck all over, neck and all, both inside and outside. If it is winter, you can simply put the duck in a pan and keep it in an unheated room. If it is summer, put it in the icebox. Let it stand for 1-2 days. Then rinse off slightly with cold water the salt on the surface of the duck.

Put the duck in a pot with the water and heat with big fire; when it boils, turn to medium fire and boil for 1 hr. If the duck is bought tender, boil only 40 min., as this kind of duck is good when it is not too soft. After cooking, cool or chill before serving.

Method of Serving: Chop each leg, including upper leg, into 6 pieces. Pull off each wing and chop into 3 sections. Separate chest from back. Chop back into small pieces. Then comes the best part of the duck, the white meat, which is now reddish. First cut lengthwise in two. Then chop sidewise into ½-inch-wide pieces.

Now, lay the back bones, wings and neck on the plate as foundation, then the leg pieces all around, finally the 2 rows of white meat on top. Now is the time for rice wine (but substitute sherry).

The bones, however, are far from being the worst part of the duck because the most savorous part is in the bones. Very often, we enjoy sucking the bones more than eating the meat.[1]

Warning: This dish will keep for only 3 days—if it goes that far.

9.9. Roast Duck (Peking Style)

Whether the famous old city is called Peking or by its ancient name Peiping, Peking duck will always be Peking duck. The best part of Peking duck, like the best part of many other Chinese foods, is its crisp skin. You always offer the guest or guests of honor the well-browned skin. To eat the meat and discard the skin would be as ungracious, or just plain silly, as to eat the pulp and throw away the skin of kumquats.

Eating Peking duck in a 200-year-old restaurant is quite an event. The waiter shows the dressed duck to the host, who nods approval to the duck as one would nod to the wine. Then the party will drink with Chinese *hors d'oeuvres* while the duck is roasting. When

[1] That's fine, darling, I'll have the meat, please.—Y. R. C.

done, the duck is again shown to the host before being carved on a side table into very thin slices, each slice with some skin and a little of the meat. Another style of serving is to start with skins only and the meat later, but the drumsticks and wings and the neck and the tail assembly (for whoever likes it) are usually served as wholes. The skin and/or meat is dipped in sauce and scallion and wrapped in doilies (Recipe No. 20.9) or lotus buns (see below) to eat like sandwiches. The restaurant usually serves a steamed custard (like Recipe No. 13.6, but without meat) with the duck's fat and a large soup with celery cabbage boiled from the duck's carcass. But since bones take hours of boiling to make soup, it is usually from a previous customer's bones that you get the soup, while your bones will go to a subsequent customer's soup. But how did the first customers get their soup? Well, 200 years ago, life was more leisurely and they could probably wait.

In American Chinese restaurants Peking duck usually needs 24 hours' notice for preparation. It is usually served with steamed buns (Recipe No. 20.1) and *hoisin* sauce (Item 10, p. 29) is used for dipping. If the waiter omits shreds of scallion from the sauce for fear some customers do not like scallion—well, I do, don't you?

If you live far from Chinese restaurants, roasting your own Peking duck can be very rewarding. Get:

1 Long Island duck, about 6 lbs.	½ cup water
2 tb-sp. sugar	3 scallions
1 tb-sp. soy sauce	1 small dish *hoisin* sauce

If the duck is bought frozen, it should be slow-thawed for a day or two. Wash duck clean and dry in oven in very low fire for 10 min. The way to make the skin crisp is to separate it from the meat before roasting. In China, this is done by sewing the emptied tailend airtight and pumping air between the skin and the meat, until the duck looks puffed up. Actually it is not necessary to have it puffed up all the time so long as the skin has been separated. A simple way to do this is to insert a stiff plastic straw and blow in some air in several places. If the air stays, well and good, if not, no matter.

Peking duck is called in Cantonese *k'ualou-aap,* "hang-oven duck,"

because it is suspended in the oven. You should roast it on a large
wire frame over a dripping pan, so that no oil or juice will collect
on the skin to make it soggy. Before putting the duck on the frame,
make basting juice with the sugar, soy sauce and the ½ cup of water
and rub it all over the skin. Roast at 400°F with back down, ab-
domen up, with an additional cup of water and 2 scallions inside
(Cantonese style with spice, coriander, and salt inside, but not in
Peking). After ¼ hr. the water inside will have been absorbed or
evaporated. Turn duck around and baste with juice. Repeat process
every ¼ hr. During the last ¼ hr. turn heat up to 450°F for browning.
Total time should be 1 hr. for 6 lbs. and longer if larger.

Lotus Buns

Lotus buns are a kind of pastry, but we cannot wait until Chapter
20, since we need them to go with Peking duck. Use:

| 4 cups flour | 1½ cups lukewarm water |
| 1 packet fresh yeast | small quantity of vegetable oil |

Dissolve yeast in water and stir evenly with a spoon. Mix in the
flour and knead evenly and divide dough into 12 pieces. With a
rolling pin, roll them into about 4-inch discs (Fig. Aa). Rub each
piece around lightly with the vegetable oil, so that it will not stick
when folded and will easily open when steamed. Fold discs over
into semicircles, as in Fig. Ab, and score the tops with the teeth of
a comb and the result will look like half a lotus leaf, as in Fig. Ac.
Let raise for 20 min., then steam on steaming tier for 10 min. With
good timing, the lotus buns should come steaming hot when the
duck is served, ready to go into the fold of the bun, together with
the *hoisin* sauce, and with scallion, of course.

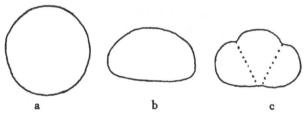

FIG. A. LOTUS BUNS

a   b   c

HOW TO COOK AND EAT IN CHINESE

9.10. Roast Duck (Szechwan Style)

1 Long Island (or L.I. type) duck 3 or more lbs.

Wash (after thawing if frozen).

Mix:

3 cups water	1 tb-sp. sugar
4 tb-sp. soy sauce	1 onion, cut in four
¼ cup sherry or ½ cup wine (either white or red)	1 t-sp. salt (if you like it more salty)

(If more ducks are used, do not add seasonings proportionately, but add only 1/3 of above for each additional duck.)

Boil duck in big covered pot over brisk fire for 30 min., starting from boiling water, turning over at half time. Leave duck in sauce for 1 hr. before taking out. (Same length of time for boiling one or more ducks.) Sauce can be saved for future ducks or other food.

If not roasted right away, duck can be put on refrigeration for a week or two before roasting. If put in freezer, it can wait for one or two months before coming out to be thawed for roasting.

For basting sauce use:

3 tb-sp. soy sauce
1 tb-sp. honey or 1 tb-sp. sugar
1 t-sp. cinnamon powder

Preheat oven to 450° and roast duck on rack for 5 min. or until warm. Mix basting sauce and baste over skin. Roast with breast up for 15 min. Baste again on all sides and roast back side up for 15 min. Baste again and roast with breast up again for 10 min. and the duck is done. Same length of time for more ducks as for one duck.

To serve one duck to four Americans, cut and serve in large pieces and let them cut themselves as they eat. To serve the Chinese way,

105c

cut into pieces (with the bones) small enough to be taken with
chopsticks.

CHAPTER 10

FISH

Fish is a greater delicacy than meat and poultry. The cooking of fish is also a more delicate matter. Fish tastes as fish should only when cooked just right, otherwise it tastes fishy. A restaurant is often known by the chef's skill in fish. A new cook is also often tested by his fish.

Sea fish is much used along the coastal provinces and travels inland quite far when salted. But fresh-water fish plays a much greater part in Chinese cooking than in America. The Chinese ways of cooking probably make it so. Restaurants and even households often buy live fish and keep them swimming in vats until needed for use. Because of the limited variety of fish in American markets, I shall give only a few recipes of fish which can easily be got in this country.

Of sea fish, bluefish, whitefish, flounder, cod, salmon, bass, skate-fish, fresh sardine, scup, and butterfish can make good Chinese dishes. Shad and mullet are partly sea and partly river fish. Shad is a great delicacy in China. Of fresh-water fish, carp and buffalo carp are the most important in Chinese fish dishes. (See also Chapter II.)

There are almost as many ways of cooking fish as there are ways of cooking. Fish is even eaten raw, for which salmon and cod are good. The most important part of cooking fish the Chinese way is to use wine and other defishers. Many American fish dishes taste fishy because they have no wine, ginger, or scallion in them. For further details, try to cook some of the following dishes.

10.1. Red-Cooked Fish (Carp)

Red-cooking is one of the most popular forms of fish dishes in China. Carp, buffalo carp, scup, butterfish, perch, shad, mullet, skate fish, fish cheeks, etc., are commonly used. Since the size of fish varies, the time and the method required are also different.

l carp or buffalo carp about 3-4 lbs.	5-6 slices fresh ginger
	2 scallions (in 1-inch sections)
5 tb-sp. soy sauce	1¼ cups water
3 tb-sp. sherry	Pinch of flour
1 tb-sp. sugar	Lard enough to make 1 inch
2 t-sp. salt	deep in the skillet

Clean the fish but leave its tongue in its cheek. Make some slashes crosswise in the back of the fish. This is to make the oil and heat go deeper in. Rub the surface of the fish with some dry flour. This is to avoid sticking of the fish skin to the hot bottom of the frying pan; also this reduces danger of burning the skin.

Deep-fry the fish in about 1 inch of heated lard or oil. Use a big fire to fry for about 1 min. on each of the 2 sides. Turn to medium fire and fry for 3 min. on each side. Total 8 min. Pour off the lard or oil until about 1 tb-sp. of it remains. Add the sauce, sherry, sugar, salt, ginger, scallions, and water. Cover and cook over big fire for 10 min.

This dish can be put in an oven for several min. before serving. However, the red-cooking part had better be put off until just before serving. It is also good to serve the dish cold with the jelly.

Variation 1: Red-Cooked Perch or Butterfish

2 lbs. perch or butterfish	2 t-sp. sugar
5 tb-sp. soy sauce	3 slices fresh ginger
4 tb-sp. vegetable oil	1 scallion (in 1-inch sections)
1 t-sp. salt	1 cup water

Clean the fish. Put 2 tb-sp. soy sauce in a saucer and wet the fish in it on both sides.

Heat the vegetable oil in a skillet till hot. Put the fish in and then turn it over as often as necessary to keep it from sticking to the bottom and losing its skin. Add in the scallion, ginger, soy sauce, sugar, and water. Cover and cook for 10 min. May be served either warm or cold.

Variation 2: Red-Cooked Mullet, Bass or Scup

Same seasoning as in Recipe No. 101.

For small-sized fish, treat them as the butterfish is treated in Variation 1 above. For big-sized fish, follow the recipe for carp.

For this dish the time required for frying is less than in the case of carp. A frying of 2 min. on each of the 2 sides will do.

Occasionally bean curd may be added to this dish. In that case, cut 1 pint of bean curd into slices about ¼ inch thick by 1 inch square. After the fried fish has been cooked for 8 min., add the bean curd in and cook for 2 min. more. With bean curd, this dish should be served right after cooking in order to taste its best.

Variation 3: Red-Cooked Fish Cheeks and Tongues

3 lbs. fish cheeks and tongues	4 or 5 slices fresh ginger
2 heaping tb-sp. lard	1 scallion
4 slices garlic	1 t-sp. sugar
3 tb-sp. soy sauce	½ cup water
1 tb-sp. sherry	

Heat the lard in a skillet. Add in the garlic first, then the cheeks. Fry for 2 min. Add in all the other seasoning. Boil vigorously for 2 min. and then simmer for 5 more min.

This dish (when covered) may be stored in an oven for 10 min. before serving.

10.2. Clear-Simmered (or Steamed) Fish (Shad)

There are two ways of cooking fish plain in China, steaming and simmering. With the first, the fish is placed in a bowl with seasoning and very little water, and the whole thing is placed in

108

a steaming pot to steam. Since only a good-sized fish is worth cooking in this way and would need a better-sized bowl to contain it and a still better-sized pot to contain the bowl, it is usually not practical to do such steaming in American home kitchens. An alternate method apparently just as good is to clear-simmer it. You put the fish together with the small amount of liquid seasoning directly into the pot and bring to boiling over a big (but not too big) fire and turn fire down to simmer as soon as boiling starts. Never let boiling continue hard. Shad, bass, pike, and mullet are suitable for clear-simmering.

We shall now take shad as the typical clear-simmered fish. To cook shad right, you must begin at the market. For the first thing is to tell your fishman to *keep the scales on*. If the scales are removed, the skin will become dryish and the taste will be wrong, and you might as well cook it the American way. If the fish is too long for the pot, you may have to cut it in two, but the whole fish looks much nicer.

1 shad, 3-5 lbs. with scales on	5 slices fresh ginger
Net-fat (from pork mesentery) enough to wrap around the fish thinly	1 scallion
	2 cups water
2 tb-sp. soy sauce	5 thin slices of Smithfield, Virginia ham
2 tb-sp. sherry	2 t-sp. salt

Wrap a thin layer of net-fat around the shad. Add in all the seasonings. Bring to boiling over moderately big fire. Then simmer for 40 min.

Dip-eating sauce is made by mixing soy sauce, vinegar, and ginger finely chopped.

As said above, it may be a shade better to bowl-steam the shad if you have large enough utensils, but there is so much difference in the quality of the fish you start with that the slight difference between steaming and simmering, if any, is not worth the extra trouble.

Hint: Enjoy the fat abdominal part first, while you are still hungry, and eat the leaner back and tail parts as you become fuller.

Variation: Clear-Simmered Bass, Pike, Mullet, Whitefish, or Bluefish

Follow Recipe No. 10.2, but remove the scales of the fish. Also omit the net-fat. Use the same amount of seasonings for the same weight of fish.

10.3. Five-Willow Fish

Bass, pike, and mullet are best suited for this dish.

3-4 lbs. bass, pike, or mullet	2 tb-sp. sherry
⅓ can or jar of Chinese pickles (sold in Chinatown, containing pickled ginger, cucumber, turnips, etc.), cut into shreds	2 tb-sp. cornstarch
	3 (or 2) cups water
	2 t-sp. salt
	1 scallion cut into 1-inch sections
5 tb-sp. sugar	1 tb-sp. lard
5 tb-sp. vinegar	

Put fish on steaming tier (or in the pot) and heat the 3 (or 2) cups of water to boiling. Then steam (or simmer) for 20 more min. Transfer fish to a serving plate.

Heat the lard in a skillet. Mix the other seasonings together and add into the skillet. Heat for 1 or 2 min. until the juice becomes translucent. Pour over the fish, and the dish is ready to serve.

This dish may be put in the oven for 5-10 min. before serving. Better serve right after cooking, and eat right after serving.

10.4. Sweet-Sour Fish

Carp, buffalo carp, and mullet are best suited for making Sweet-Sour Fish

1 fish about 3-4 lbs.	1 t-sp. salt
8 tb-sp. sugar	4 tb-sp. soy sauce
8 tb-sp. vinegar	4-5 slices fresh ginger
3 tb-sp. sherry	1 scallion (in 1-inch sections about 1½ inch apart)
4 tb-sp. cornstarch	
2 cups water	

Clean the fish and make some slashes in its back. Rub some dry flour on the outside of the fish. Deep-fry in about 1 inch of lard or oil. Use a big fire at first and fry for 2 min. on each side. Turn to medium fire and fry for 4 min. on each side. Then turn to big fire again and fry for 1 more min. on each side. Total 14 min. By now the outside of the fish will be very crisp while the inside is just right in softness for eating. Take the pieces out and put it on a plate.

Pour off most of the oil until about 1 tb-sp. of it remains. Put in the scallion and ginger first. Turn on fire. Then add in the mixed seasoning. When the mixture becomes translucent, pour it on the fried fish and serve.

If you like, you can add some sweet pepper shreds or sweet pickle shreds into the seasonings.

This dish may be put in the oven for 5-10 min. before eating. However, too long standing may reduce the crispness of the skin and spoil the dish.

10.5. Tile-Piece Fish

When a fish is cut up in large pieces and prepared in the above manner, it is called Tile-Piece Fish, for which Honan is famous.

Same ingredients as in Sweet-Sour Fish.

Remove head, which may be separately red-cooked. Split fish from the back into halves. Cut crosswise into about 10 sections. Coat each section with dry flour. Proceed as in the above recipe for Sweet-Sour Fish.

The cooking materials should not be reduced since the head is mostly bones and absorbs less juice.

10.6. Pineapple Fish

2 lbs. fillet of flounder	2 eggs
2 tb-sp. soy sauce	2 tb-sp. lard
½ t-sp. salt	1 tb-sp. sugar
1 tb-sp. sherry	½ cup water
1 scallion	10 oz. canned pineapple
2 tb-sp. cornstarch	

Cut each fillet into 2 or 3 pieces. Shred the scallion. Mix the soy sauce, salt, sherry, and scallion shreds and soak the fish pieces in the mixture for 10 min.

Heat the lard in a skillet till hot. Mix the cornstarch and the eggs. Dip the fish pieces in this mixture just before frying. Fry for 2 min. for each of the 2 sides. Transfer the fried pieces to a plate.

Mix the water, sugar, and pineapple with the starch paste left and boil till the mixture becomes translucent. Pour it over the fried fish.

This dish may be left in an oven for several min. before serving, but long standing and too high temperature would make it tough.

10.7. Splashed Fried Fish

2 lbs. butterfish, scup, or fresh sardine	1 t-sp. sugar
3 tb-sp. vegetable oil	1 scallion (chopped very fine)
2 tb-sp. soy sauce	3 or 4 slices ginger (chopped very fine)
1 tb-sp. sherry	6 tb-sp. water
1 t-sp. salt	

Wash the fish, drain the water, and let the skin dry a little (otherwise the skin will stick to the hot bottom of the pan).

Heat the oil until very hot. Put in the fish and fry for 5 min. on each side. (For sardine 3 min. are used.) Take out the fish and leave the oil in. Stir in the mixture of soy sauce, sherry, salt, sugar, scallion, ginger, and water. Heat to boiling, splash hot sauce over the fish (but not yourself) and serve.

This dish may also be served cold or warm. It is the vegetable oil that makes it still good when cold.

10.8. *Fu-yung* Fish Slices

In China quite a number of fresh-water fishes can be used for this dish. In America, where salt-water fish is the more common thing, the choice of fish is difficult, as the meat of most salt-water fish will disintegrate after frying. Fillet of sole, however, may be used.

3 lbs. fillet of sole	4 egg whites
3 tb-sp. lard	1 tb-sp. sherry
1½ t-sp. salt	1 scallion (in 1-inch sections)
4 tb-sp. water	2-3 slices fresh ginger
1½ tb-sp. cornstarch	

Cut each fillet into 3 or 4 pieces. Mix with ½ t-sp. salt, 2 tb-sp. cornstarch and 4 egg whites.

Heat the lard in a skillet till hot. Fry the fish for about 2 min. on each side.

Mix the starch paste left with the sherry, 1 t-sp. salt, 1 tb-sp. cornstarch, scallion, ginger, and water. Add to the fried fish, turn it gently several times, and cook for 2 more min. until the liquid becomes translucent. (Total time about 5 min.)

10.9. Raw Fish

Salmon, tuna or stripped bass may be eaten raw. However, for this recipe, the fish has to be very fresh and has to be very clean.

2 lbs. salmon, tuna or stripped bass	½ t-sp. black pepper
2 tb-sp. sherry	1 scallion (chopped very fine)
2 tb-sp. soy sauce	1 tb-sp. sesame oil (or salad oil if you cannot get sesame oil)
½ t-sp. salt	

Remove the bones and skins. Cut the fish into very thin slices. Mix with the seasonings. Let stand 10 min. before serving. If the news says there is an epidemic around, cook the fish.

10.10. Soup Fish Balls

1 carp (about 5 lbs.)	2 t-sp. melted lard
6 egg whites	1 t-sp. taste powder
2 t-sp. cornstarch	1 scallion
2 t-sp. salt	5-6 slices fresh ginger
2 tb-sp. sherry	8 cups water

Remove the head of the fish and split the fish from the back into 2 halves. Your fishman will be glad to do it without your cutting your fingers. Remove the big bones. With a vertically held blunt knife, scrape the inside of the fish from tail toward head. (Don't scrape in the reverse direction, as then the fine bones will turn loose.) In this way, the fish meat can be made into a fine paste, suitable for the preparation of fish balls. (The skins left after the scraping may be used for preparing salted fish, Recipe No. 10.11, etc.)

Crush the scallion and ginger in 1 cup of water. Grind (but better chop) the scraped fish meat with the scallion-ginger pulp. Mix with the other seasoning. Beat with an egg beater for 10 min. during which time 2 cups of water are added gradually.

Heat 5 cups of water in a pot to about 85-90 degrees Centigrade (just before boiling). Take a fistful of the beaten and seasoned fish meat. Squeeze fish through the hole formed by the index finger and the root of the thumb and scoop with a big spoon. In this way a fish ball will be formed which can be put into the very hot water. (About 50 balls can be made out of the materials used in this recipe.) Boil for 3 min., when the balls will be slightly enlarged in size.

The fish balls may be cooked by "meeting" with chicken soup or meat soup, if either one is handy. Otherwise you may add to the soup with which you cooked the fish balls:

6 beaten egg yolks (the whites have been used in this recipe)
2 t-sp. salt
1 t-sp. taste powder

The fish balls can be stored in a refrigerator for days. They can be red-cooked with mushrooms, bamboo shoots, etc. They can also be added to Sour-Hot Soup (Recipe No. 15.13).

10.11. Fresh Salted Fish

For this recipe, carp, scup, butterfish, etc., can be used. Rub both the outside and inside of the fish with salt. About ½ t-sp. salt is required for each butterfish; about 3 tb-sp. salt is needed for a carp or scup weighing 3-4 lbs. Let the treated fish stand for 24 hrs. Wash in cold water. Drain until the skin is more or less dry. Fry in 3 tb-sp. of vegetable-oil for 5 min. on each side.

Carp is preferably cut into sections (10-12 depending upon size) before salting. Scup may be cut into 3 or 4 sections.

10.12. Smoked Fish

Same fish as in Recipe No. 10.11. Whitefish or bluefish, which can often be obtained in American markets, may be used.

Prepare the fish just as in Recipe No. 10.11. Put the fried fish on a perforated plate or tin steaming tier (see Chapter IV.1). Add 3 tb-sp. brown sugar in a heavy iron pot (one that will stand dry heating without being ruined) and put in the fish on the tier. Cover tightly and apply a big fire. After about 3 min. the fish will be smoked to a light brown color and is ready to serve.

(Better open the windows of the kitchen when you are doing this experiment. Remember that the smoke will sneak into anything it can reach, including your best clothes. So wear a laboratory coat if you have one. Another good idea is to smoke your fish shortly before a scheduled shampoo.)

CHAPTER 11

SHRIMPS

Whenever an American and a Chinese talk about shrimps and things, sooner or later they will start talking at cross purposes. In Chinese there is only one word *hsia* for what are quite different things to English-speaking persons. But because "shrimp" is the commonest thing of this type, that gets to be the conventional translation of *hsia*. Therefore you get such varieties as lobster, *lung-hsia,* "dragon shrimp"; large Chefoo prawns and Ningpo prawns, *tui-hsia,* "paired shrimps," because they are sold in pairs; ordinary American shrimp called *hsia* (*ha* in Cantonese) in American-Chinese restaurants; and finally the river shrimps, the usual kind of *hsia* eaten in China but not often seen here. Add to this the fact that the American salt-water shrimps used to be called prawns here twenty or thirty years ago.

Call them what you will, the American prawns are not so tender or savory as the Chinese fresh-water shrimps. The difference is, however, not so killing as that between fresh-water and salt-water crabs. So I think it will still be interesting enough to cook American prawns by the recipes for Chinese shrimps. Recipe No. 11.6 is a dish for Ningpo or Chefoo prawns, and is not so bad with American prawns. For the other dishes, we can help out by a little imagination, especially if we call a prawn a shrimp.

Proper cooking begins with marketing, and this is especially true of shrimps. In China you judge by testing whether they jump. The "Drunken Shrimps" of Hangchow, freshly pickled in liquor, sauce, and ginger, must jump in your mouth as you eat them. Here you have to judge by color. The fresher ones are more bluish, while they get whitish and pinkish as they become less fresh. They have to be kept in the icebox until used. When the recipe says "remove sand," it means to slit open the back of the shrimp (or take off the whole shell if the recipe calls for shelling), and take off the dark thread or line along the back, which would give an unpleasant gritty chew if left there.

11.1 Stirred Shelled Shrimps

There are two ways of stirring shelled shrimps, white-stirring and red-stirring. In white-stirring, you use no soy sauce. In red-stirring soy sauce is used liberally. It is as simple as that. Shelled shrimps may be stirred plain or with the addition of bamboo shoots, water chestnuts, etc.

(A) White-Stirred:

2 lbs. fresh shrimps	3 or 4 slices fresh ginger (if
1 tb-sp. cornstarch	you can get it)
1¼ t-sp. salt	3 tb-sp. lard
2 tb-sp. sherry	1 scallion or small onion

Shell the shrimps. Remove sand. Rinse in water and drain.

Mix the shrimp meat with the starch, salt, sherry, scallion, and ginger.

Heat the lard in a skillet till very hot. Add the seasoned shrimp meat and stir vigorously. Fry for 3 or 5 min. depending upon whether the shrimps are small or large.

(B) Red-Stirred:

Same shrimps
Same seasoning, except: Omit the salt

Use 2 tb-sp. soy sauce instead. Proceed just as in the above recipe.

11.2. Mushrooms Stir Shelled Shrimps

Add ⅓ lb. mushrooms, same shrimps as in Recipe No. 11.1 B.,
same seasoning as in Recipe No. 11.1 B.

Cut the mushrooms vertically into slices.

Proceed as in Recipe No. 11.1 B. After frying the seasoned shrimps
for 1 min., add in the mushrooms and extra tb-sp. soy sauce. Stir
together for 4 min.

In China, dried Kalgan mushrooms are used.

11.3. Peas Stir Shelled Shrimps

Same shrimps as in Recipe No. 11.1 A
Same seasoning as in Recipe No. 11.1 A
Plus 1 package frozen peas
½ t-sp. salt

Follow the same procedure as in Recipe No. 11.1 A. After stir-frying the seasoned shrimp meat for 2 min., add in the peas and salt.
Cook together over continued big fire for 2 or 3 min. more.

11.4. Bean Curd Stirs Shelled Shrimps

Same shrimps as in Recipe No. 11.1 B
Same seasoning as in Recipe No. 11.1 B
Plus 1 pint bean curd
1 t-sp. salt

Cut the bean curd into slices ¼ inch thick. After stir-frying the
seasoned shrimp meat for 2 min., add in the bean curd and salt
and cook over continued big fire for 3 min. more.

11.5. Shrimp *Fu-yung*

Same shrimps and seasoning as in Recipe No. 11.1 B
Plus ¼ lb. ground pork
2 eggs
1 tb-sp. soy sauce

Treat the shrimps as in Recipe No. 11.1 B., mix together with the ground pork, eggs, and soy sauce.

Fry together for 3 min.

11.6. (Fried) Phoenix-Tail Shrimps

This dish is about like American fried shrimps. Since it is popular in Chinese meals in China, it is included here.

1 lb. fresh shrimps	4 tb-sp. water
1 egg	1 tb-sp. salt
4 tb-sp. flour	lard for 1-inch deep frying

Shell the shrimps, but keep tails on, they are the "phoenix tails" which turn a beautiful red when fried. With a small knife open up the back of each shrimp just enough to take out the dark, gritty thread along the back, but not so as to let the shrimp fall apart in two.

Mix and beat the egg, flour, water, and salt for 2 min.

Heat the lard in a skillet till hot. Take each shrimp by its tail, dip in the mixture, and fry in the oil. Be sure to fry both sides of the shrimps. Each shrimp should stay in the heated oil for about 3 min.

This dish may be put in an oven for several min. before serving.

A mixture of 1 tb-sp. salt and ¼ t-sp. black pepper may be served with the shrimps but in a separate dish. Dip the shrimp in the mixture and then decide whether you like it that way or not.

11.7. Fried Shrimp Cakes

2 lbs. fresh shrimps	1 t-sp. salt
1 lb. ground pork	2 t-sp. sugar
2 eggs	8 tb-sp. water
2 tb-sp. cornstarch	2 tb-sp. oil
2 tb-sp. sherry	2 scallions, sectioned
2 tb-sp. soy sauce	

Shell and clean the shrimps. Divide roughly in three portions all the ingredients, except the pork, scallions, and oil and grind well in the blender in three installments. Then mix by hand the whole thing with the pork and the scallions in a bowl. Form cakes about 1½ in. across and ⅜ in. thick in the middle.

Heat the oil in a skillet till hot. Turn to medium fire and put in the formed cakes. Fry for 3 min. on each side (but 2 min. for Recipes Nos. 11.8-12 & 14). Do not use big fire, as this tends to burn the outside of the cakes while leaving the inside too rare.

This dish is preferably served right after cooking, but it can be put in an oven for 5 min. before serving. As for reheating—well, if you must. Nevertheless shrimp cakes are good as sandwich filling. They can also be meeting-cooked, as in the following recipes, in which they give a quite different feel.

11.8. Mushrooms Meet Shrimp Cakes

Same shrimps as in Recipe No. 11.7	½ lb. mushrooms
	2 tb-sp. soy sauce
Same seasoning as in Recipe No. 11.7	1 cup water

Cut the mushrooms vertically into slices, about ¼ inch thick.

Make the shrimp cakes or balls as in Recipe No. 11.7, and simmer them with the 1 cup of water for 15 min.

Add in the mushroom slices with the soy sauce. Cook for 3 more min.

This dish can be stored in a refrigerator and served after reheating. However, the mushroom slices are preferably added just before final reheating.

11.9. Shrimp Cakes Meet Spinach

Same shrimps as in Recipe No. 11.7	1 lb. spinach
	1 cup water
Same seasoning as in Recipe No. 11.7	1 t-sp. salt

Prepare shrimp balls or cakes as in Recipe No. 11.7. Wash spinach and use it whole.

Add the cup of water to the fried shrimp balls or cakes and simmer for 15 min. Then add in the spinach with the 1 t-sp. salt. Cook for 3 min. more.

This dish can be prepared long before serving, but the spinach is preferably added in just before the final reheating.

11.10. Shrimp Cakes Meet Tiger Lilies

Same shrimps as in Recipe No. 11.7

Same seasoning as in Recipe No. 11.7

⅓ lb. dried tiger lilies (called *kam-cham* in Chinatown)

2 tb-sp. soy sauce

2 cups water

Prepare the shrimp balls as in Recipe No. 11.7.

Soak the dried lilies in very hot water for ⅓ hr. Pour the water off. Wash 2 or 3 times and drain. Lay the lilies on the bottom of a skillet and put the shrimp balls or cakes over them. Add the water and the soy sauce. Simmer for 20 min.

This dish may be prepared long before serving. Reheat just before eating.

11.11. Shrimp Cakes Meet Celery Cabbage

Same seasoned shrimps as in Recipe No. 11.7

2 lbs. celery cabbage

1 t-sp. salt

1 cup water

Make shrimp balls or cakes as in Recipe No. 11.7. Since they are to be cooked after frying, the time required for frying should be shorter. Usually 1 min. on each side is enough.

Wash the celery cabbage and cut into 1-inch sections. Lay them flat on the bottom of a frying pan and then put the shrimp balls or cakes over the cabbage. Add in the cup of water with the salt. Bring to boiling. Then simmer for 15 min.

This dish may be prepared long before serving. Reheat just before eating.

11.12. Shrimp Cakes Meet Cucumbers

Same shrimps as in Recipe No. 11.7	Plus 2 big cucumbers or same amount of small ones
Same seasoning as in Recipe No. 11.7	2 cups water
	2 tb-sp. soy sauce

Prepare the shrimp cakes or balls as in Recipe No. 11.7.

Peel the cucumbers. Cut into 1-inch sections. Lay them on the bottom of the frying pan. Then put the shrimp cakes over them.

Add in the water and soy sauce. Bring to boiling. Then simmer for 10 min.

This is also a dish that can be reheated just before serving.

11.13. Splashed Shrimps

2 lbs. shrimps	1 t-sp. salt
2 tb-sp. lard or the same amount of vegetable oil	2 tb-sp. sherry
	1 scallion or 1 onion
1 tb-sp. sugar	2 or 3 slices fresh ginger
2 tb-sp. soy sauce	(if you can get it)

Wash the shrimps (with the shells on) and drain off the water.

Heat the lard or oil in a skillet till hot. Put in the shrimps and chop the scallion and ginger.

Fry 8 min. (If the shrimps are small, 5 or 6 min. may be enough.) Stir in the sugar first and then the soy sauce, the salt, the sherry and the chopped scallion and ginger. Cook together for ½ min. after everything is in.

If vegetable oil is used, this dish may be stored in the refrigerator and served cold, or with sandwiches for a picnic. It will last 2 or 3 days at American room temperatures. It can be wrapped in wax paper and carried as a very pleasant and tasty companion during traveling. But take some paper napkins along.

11.14. Raw-Stirred Shrimps

Same shrimps as in Recipe No. 11.13
Same seasoning as in Recipe No. 11.13

The time used for the pre-frying should be about half that for Recipe No. 11.13, but the final half min. stays the same. Another difference is that splashed shrimps are not good without any sugar, but Raw-Stirred Shrimps may be cooked without sugar if you prefer it.

Very fresh shrimps have to be used for this dish. It can be left over in a refrigerator, or put in an oven for 10-20 min. before serving.

CHAPTER 12

SEA FOOD

When I say that fresh-water food is more important in China than it is in America, it is not to be inferred that sea food is unimportant there. The common phrase for fine food is "mountain rarities and sea flavors." You think of shark's fin, of course.

Now the trouble with sea food is that it is never completely fresh, since it has been salted from birth. Instead of trying to compare freshness with fresh-water food, why not make a virtue of its being salt-water food and have it salted and dried until it gets that class of exotic flavors we call *hsien?* Thus, the most typical sea foods we eat in China are canned abalone, dried razor clams, dried mussels, dried scallops, dried squids, which are in each case more savory than the corresponding fresh ones. Dried scallops are widely used as a soup maker.

Since in this country dried sea food in the Chinese form is not generally obtainable and since fresh sea food is plentiful, I shall give you, in this chapter, recipes for making Chinese dishes with fresh sea food. You do make such dishes in China, too, and they are good, when you make them good.

In the first edition of this book I said, "You come to China and I'll show you how to cook crab dishes with real crabs," and with that I consistently avoided touching crabs for the rest of the book. But with further experimentation, I have been able to adapt sea crabs to Chinese cooking, too. California crabs prepared the Chinese way almost give an illusion of fresh-water crabs. It goes without saying that for the Special Eating Parties (p. 225, f.), live crabs must be used. But even for crab-meat dishes, as in Recipe No. 12.14, it is fully worth the trouble to buy live crabs and boil and shell them yourself. Large crabs should be boiled half an hour, small ones 15 minutes.

Lobsters, or "dragon shrimps," as they are called in Chinese, are not commonly eaten in China. They are found only in certain coastal provinces. Since, however, many Chinese restaurants in America excel in lobsters, I shall give a few recipes for lobsters.

At a Chinese meal, where there are usually several dishes, each person will eat one or two pieces of a lobster. More will, of course, be needed on the American main-dish plan. The following recipes are usual for 6 main-dish portions.

5 lbs. live lobsters (large or small)	¼ lb. ground pork chop
	2 tb-sp. sherry
2 beaten eggs	2 tb-sp. cornstarch
1 scallion finely chopped	½ cup water
2 tb-sp. soy sauce	2 heaping tb-sp. lard
1 t-sp. salt	5 slices fresh ginger

Steam the lobsters in a big steamer for 5-8 min., depending upon the size of the lobsters, larger ones taking longer. With shells on, cut each body lengthwise in two, then across into 1½-inch-long sections. Chop each head into 4 parts and each claw into 3 sections.

Mix thoroughly the eggs, scallion, ginger, soy sauce, salt, meat, sherry, cornstarch, and water.

Heat the lard in a skillet till hot. Then put in the pieces of lobsters and pour the mixed sauce on them right after and stir for 5 min.

Variation: As done in Chinese restaurants in America.—Get from Chinatown 2 tb-sp. salted small black beans. Wash off visible salt, boil 10 min., crush, and add to the stirring sauce.

12.2. Meat Sauce Stirs Lobsters

The difference between a stir-fried dish and a meeting-cooked dish is that in stir-frying you do not pre-cook your material. When lobsters are stirred, they are tenderer than those you meet after steaming. The limitations are that you have to have tender lobsters and you must use them the day you buy them. Another difference is that you will probably want to have your marketman cut each lobster in two halves and take out the dark gritty stuff in the head.

Use the same amount of lobsters and cooking materials as in Recipe No. 12.1 and cut the raw lobsters into the same kind of pieces as with steamed ones.

Mix thoroughly the ingredients of the meat sauce as in the preceding recipe.

Heat the lard in a skillet over big fire till hot. Put in the lobsters and stir-fry for 5-7 min., the tougher lobsters taking longer time. (For lobsters of different sizes, even though cut up to pieces of the same size, those of larger lobsters should be cooked longer.) Then pour in the meat sauce mixture and stir over big fire for 3 min.

Variation: Same as in preceding recipe.

12.3. Steamed Lobsters

3 one-pound lobsters. Tell your marketman to cut each lobster lengthwise into two and take out the dark sand-like stuff in the head.

2 tb-sp. soy sauce

1 tb-sp. sherry

1 scallion finely chopped

3 or 4 slices fresh ginger finely chopped

2 tb-sp. water

Place all the half lobsters with shells on the tier of a steamer with the shells underneath.

Mix the soy sauce, sherry, scallion, ginger, and water together. Put a little of it on each lobster.

Cover the steamer and steam over big fire for 10 min., counting from the time the water begins to boil.

12.4. Lobster Steams Eggs

Any amount of lobsters up to 6 half-lobsters (⅙ to ⅓ for each person). Tell your marketman to cut each lobster lengthwise and take out the dark sand-like stuff in the head.

8 beaten eggs   3 cups cold water   2 t-sp. salt

Take off the shells but leave meat of the half-lobsters whole that is, in whole halves.

After the first beating, add 3 cups of cold water and the 2 t-sp. of salt to the eggs and beat thoroughly again. Put the eggs in a large bowl or any presentable serving container that will stand steam-heat. Place bowl with the eggs in a big pot with enough water to last through the steaming, but not to splash into the bowl when boiling. The amount depends upon the size and shape of the pot and the bowl, but 3 cups is usually right. Cover the pot, but not the bowl.

Heat over big fire. After boiling starts, keep steaming for 10 min. Stop the fire so as not to burn your hand. Open the cover. By this time, the eggs should have coagulated already. Lay the big pieces of the lobsters on top of the eggs. Then cover again and steam for 10 more min.

12.5. Stirred Squids

The Chinese squid or *yu-yü* is rather shorter than the American squid, that is, even before they are dried, as they usually are in China. The Chinese kind is *Ommastrephes Pacificus*, while the American kind is *Ommastrephes Illecebrosus*. But at the market they call a squid a squid. Chinese dried squids may be developed and stirred or boiled to make a very tasty soup. Fresh squid, because it has a light taste, should best be stir-fried.

3 lbs. squids. (Small squids better. Big squids go better with Red-Cooked Meat.)

2 heaping tb-sp. lard or same amount of oil

1 scallion cut into 1-inch sections

2-3 slices fresh ginger

2 tb-sp. soy sauce

1 tb-sp. sherry

1 tb-sp. cornstarch

2 tb-sp. water

Pull out the center bones of the squids and take off the skin. Clean out everything inside. Cut off and keep the tentacles too. Slit open and then cut into 1½-inch squares. If you have big squids, cut a few slashes lengthwise and crosswise on each square piece.

Heat the lard or oil over big fire till hot. Then put in the squids. Put in the scallion and ginger and stir for 1 min. Then add the soy sauce and sherry. Stir again for 2 more min. Put the squids in the serving dish but leave the juice behind in the skillet. Mix the cornstarch with the water, and pour it into the skillet and cook until it becomes translucent. Then pour it on the squids.

Do not cook until assured that eating will be done promptly after cooking.

12.6. Celery Mixes with Abalone Shreds

Many like abalone cold better than hot, as the flavor seems to have a better chance to show. In this as in other abalone dishes, don't forget to save the juice in the can. It makes wonderful soup.

2 cans abalone (*pou-yü* in Cantonese)	1 tb-sp. sugar
1 bunch celery, about 1 lb.	1 tb-sp. sesame oil or salad oil
3 cups water	1 tb-sp. salt
2 tb-sp. soy sauce	

Cut the abalone into 2-inch-long shreds, about ⅛-inch thick.

Cut each stem of the celery into rolling-knife pieces (Fig. 3, p. 36) of about 1 inch long. Parboil the celery, that is, throw into boiling water and continue to boil for 1 min. after boiling starts again. Take out and chill with cold water. Shake off as much water as possible.

Mix celery in with the abalone shreds, the soy sauce, sugar, salt, and sesame oil or salad oil, in other words, mix up everything. If desired, you can chill it in the icebox before serving.

12.7. Stirred Fresh Scallops

2 lbs. fresh scallops	3-4 slices fresh ginger
1 heaping tb-sp. lard	1 tb-sp. cornstarch
2 t-sp. salt	4 tb-sp. water
1 scallion cut in 1-inch sections	

Wash the scallops and take off the small tough muscle on the side of each scallop. Cut each into 4 round slices.

Mix the cornstarch with the water. Heat the lard in a skillet over big fire and put the scallops in. Stir for 1 min. Add in the scallion, the salt, and the ginger slices. Stir again for 2 min. Then mix the cornstarch with water, add in the starch mixture, and stir for ½ min. more, when the juice will become translucent and the scallops are done.

12.8. Sweet Peppers Stir Scallops

1½ lbs. scallops
Same seasoning as in previous recipe
Except: no cornstarch and water
Plus: 3-4 sweet peppers

Prepare the scallops as in the previous recipe.

Cut sweet peppers into irregular pieces of about 1 inch square.

Cook the scallops as before, but when you add in the seasoning add in also the sweet peppers. Then stir and cook for 2 min. more. The last ½ min. is omitted, since no starch is used.

12.9. Mushrooms Stir Scallops

1½ lbs. fresh scallops	1 t-sp. sugar
½ lb. fresh mushrooms	1 scallion cut in 1-inch sec-
1 t-sp. salt	tions
2 tb-sp. soy sauce	3-4 slices fresh ginger
	1 heaping tb-sp. lard

Clean and cut scallops as in Recipe No. 12.7.

Cut mushrooms into ⅛-inch-thick slices.

Heat the lard in a skillet over big fire. Then put in the scallops and stir-fry for 1 min. Add in mushroom slices, scallion, ginger, soy sauce, salt, and sugar. Stir-fry for 2 min. more.

12.10. Plain-Steamed Clams or Razor Clams

3 doz. clams or razor clams

Wash the clams. Heat water to boiling in a steamer (with perforated inner bottom). Put the clams in and steam for 5-10 min. until the bivalves open.

In a small bowl, mix:

2 tb-sp. soy sauce	3-4 slices fresh ginger, chopped
1 tb-sp. sherry	fine
1 scallion, chopped very fine	1 tb-sp. sesame oil or salad oil

Dip the clam meat into this sauce and then eat it.
Sand may be rinsed in the same way as in America.

12.11. Cold-Mixed Clams (or Razor Clams)

3 doz. clams or razor clams	2-3 slices fresh ginger,
2 tb-sp. soy sauce	chopped fine
1 tb-sp. sherry	1 scallion, chopped fine
1 tb-sp. sesame oil or salad oil	

Treat the clams as in Recipe No. 12.10.

Mix the clam meat with the sauce, sherry, sesame oil, ginger, and scallion. Put into refrigerator and serve cold.

12.12. Meet the Clams (or Razor Clams)

1½ doz. clams or razor clams	½ pkg. frozen peas
¼ lb. pork chops (in slices)	2 tb-sp. lard
¼ lb. mushrooms (in vertical	2 tb-sp. soy sauce
slices, ⅛ inch thick)	1 tb-sp. cornstarch

Boil the clams in 2 cups of water for 3 min. By then the bivalves should have opened. Pick out the meat and wash away any grit or sand.

Heat 2 tb-sp. lard in a skillet till hot. Put in the pork slices, mushrooms, and peas, and stir-fry for two min. Add in the clam meat and then a well-mixed mixture of the soy sauce, cornstarch, and 1 cup of soup from the clam-boiler. Heat for half a minute more.

This dish tastes best immediately after preparation. Better have everything ready and do the final cooking just before serving.

12.13. Shark's Fin

Shark's Fin is one of those few sea foods which we regard as better than fresh-water food. It is not limited to fins but includes the tails too. It is from the soup-shark, which has been found to have very potent vitamins in its liver and has attracted many fishermen to the West Coast. Shark's fin comes dried. You "develop" it by boiling and soaking. It is best when cooked with red-cooked things such as meat, chicken, or duck. Shark's fin with fresh-water crab-meat is usually eaten up soon after it comes on the table.

Shark's fin goes to Chinatown in two forms, one with and the other without the original rough skin of the shark.

For fin without the original rough skin, prepare like this: Soak ½ lb. of the skinless fin in warm water for ½ hr., add 1 t-sp. bicarbonate of soda, and simmer in a pot for 2 more hrs., until the fin has become soft and frail. Then remove the fin from the thick soup in which it has been simmering.

For fin with original rough skin still on, the preparation is more troublesome. Use 2 lbs. of these fins with the skin. Boil for one hour in water deep enough to cover the fins. Take out and wash away sand, removing any fish meat and soft bones that may still be clinging to the fins. Return the fins to the pot, add 1 t-sp. bicarbonate of soda to the water, and boil for 3 hrs., by which time the fins will be soft. Remove fins from soup and soak in clear warm water until used or stored in refrigerator. (Since fins melt with over-developing, younger fins should be boiled in soda for fewer hours.)

A. Red-Cooked Shark's Fin

Put into the pot 2 cups of gravy from red-cooked meat or red cooked chicken. (Some people like to make use of the thick soup that results from the preliminary cooking of the shark's fin; some do not like it. If you use it, the recipe calls for ½ cup of the thick soup and 1½ cups of the gravy.) Pour on the already softened shark's fin, cook for 10 min., and add 2 tb-sp. soy sauce and ½ t-sp. taste powder. Eat it, and you will find that there is something in it that is neither in the fin alone nor in the chicken or meat alone. More interest can also come by adding 1 lb. of celery cabbage (in 2-inch strips) when you bring the shark's fin and the gravy together.

The use of fresh-water crab-meat, as I said, will make the dish good beyond words. Also acceptable: meat from fresh sea crabs.

B.　Clear-Soup Shark's Fin

Use clear chicken soup or clear meat soup. Add 1 t-sp. salt and ½ t-sp. taste powder. Pour in the already softened shark's fin and cook 10 min. before serving. One pound of celery cabbage, cut in 2-inch strips, may also be added along with the shark's fin.

12.14.　Stirred Crab-Meat

1½ lb. crab-meat (cf. p. 124)	1 cup water
3 heaping tb-sp. lard	½ t-sp. salt
2 heaping tb-sp. cornstarch	10 slices fresh ginger
4 tb-sp. sherry	2 scallions, in ½-inch sections

Heat lard hot. Put crab-meat and seasonings in and stir for 2 min. Mix starch in water, pour on crab and stir another min. Serves 6.

Six beaten eggs in place of one third of the crab-meat (½ lb.) will make a more substantial dish, also very good.

We usually add vinegar to our spoonfuls just before eating.

CHAPTER 13

EGGS

Hen's eggs occupy about the same place in Chinese cooking as in American. They make either the main thing in a dish or go with other main dishes. Because eggs are nourishing and easily digested almost in any form, they have always been regarded as good for the young and the frail.

We have boiled eggs, fried eggs, etc., but they do not usually mean breakfast nor are they usually made the same way as American dishes of the same names. Boiled eggs are usually hard-boiled and usually dip-eaten with soy sauce at breakfast. As part of other dishes, they are hard-boiled so long that they become soft inside again. Fried eggs are usually sprinkled with soy sauce. Dropped eggs are dropped in soup instead of on toast, and eaten wet. We have no shirred eggs but have stirred eggs, which is something between scrambled eggs and egg-omelet. (See below.)

Eggs are preserved by salting or lime-treating, for which duck's eggs are more commonly used. Lime-preserved eggs are the so-called 100-year-old eggs, which are best when about 100 days old.

I shall now give a few very common egg recipes, each containing some variations.

13.1. Stirred Eggs

Stirred eggs may be said to be the most everyday dish made by applying the most everyday method to the most everyday material. Learning to stir-fry eggs is the ABC of cooking. As this is the only dish my husband cooks well, and he says that he either cooks a thing well or not at all, I shall let him tell how it is done:

"Obtain:

6 average-sized fresh eggs (for this is the maximum number of eggs I have cooked at one time)

3 grammes of cooking salt (or, as an alternative, 4 grammes of table salt)

50 c.c. fresh lard, which will approximately equal the content of 4 level tablespoonfuls

1 plant of Chinese ts'ung (substitute with scallion if ts'ung is unobtainable) about 30 cm. long by 7 mm. in average diameter. (This ingredient is optional.)

"Either shell or unshell the eggs by knocking one against another in any order.[1] Be sure to have a bowl below to catch the contents. With a pair of chopsticks, strike the same with a quick, vigorous motion known as 'beating the eggs.' This motion should, however, be made repeatedly and not just once. Automatic machines, aptly named as 'egg-beaters,' have been invented for this purpose.

"Make cross sections of the ts'ung at intervals of about 7.5 mm., making 40 sections altogether. Throw in the ts'ung and the measured amount of salt during the final phase of the 'beating.'

"Heat the lard in a large flat-bottomed pan over a brisk fire until it (the lard) begins to give off a faint trace of smoke. Pour the contents of the bowl into the oil at once.

"The next phase of the operation is the most critical for the successful stir-frying of eggs. When the bottom part of the mixture becomes a puffed-up soft mass on contact with the heat, the upper part will remain quite liquid. Preferably using a thin flat piece of metal attached to a handle, the operator should push the mixture to one side so as to allow the uncooked liquid portion to flow onto the hot fat on the now exposed portion of the bottom. (Sometimes this may be facilitated by slightly tipping the pan.) Quickly repeat this

[1] Since, when two eggs collide, only one of them will break, it will be necessary to use a seventh egg with which to break the sixth. If, as it may very well happen, the seventh egg breaks first instead of the sixth, an expedient will be simply to use the seventh one and put away the sixth. An alternate procedure is to delay your numbering system and define that egg as the sixth egg which breaks after the fifth egg.

until abut 90 per cent of the liquid has come in contact with the hot fat and becomes puffed. Then, still using the flat piece of metal, make the entire content of the pan revolve through 180 degrees about a horizontal axis. This delicate operation is known as 'turning it over,' which in the hands of a beginner may easily become a flop. It can be done neatly and without waste only after repeated practice with different sets of eggs.

"If the turning over has been successfully carried out, wait for 5 seconds, which is about the time it takes to count from 1 to 12, then transfer the contents to the bowl or a platter, when the dish is said to be done.

"To test whether the cooking has been done properly, observe the person served. If he utters a voiced bilabial nasal consonant with a slow falling intonation, it is good. If he utters the syllable *yum* in reduplicated form, it is very good."—Y. R. C.

Stirred eggs are really much simpler to make than to tell. It is a very handy dish to fill the table when unexpected guests come. Remember that only lard or any animal fat is good for this dish. It is therefore only good for once, in fact only when it is hot.

13.2. Egg *Fu-yung* (with Meat Shreds)

This is the recipe as it is used in China. For the form used in American-Chinese restaurants, see Recipe No. 13.8.

8 eggs	2 scallions or an onion
1 t-sp. salt	3 heaping tb-sp. lard
¼ lb. meat shreds	2 tb-sp. soy sauce
¼ bunch celery	2 t-sp. sugar
¼ lb. pea sprouts (get in China-town)	

Beat the 8 eggs with the salt.

Cut scallions or onion and celery across obliquely into shreds about 1 inch long.

Wash the pea sprouts clean.

Heat 1 tb-sp. lard in the skillet over big fire, put the meat shreds

135

in, and stir for 1 min. Then add in the celery and scallions and stir 1 min. more. Then add in 2 tb-sp. soy sauce and 2 t-sp. sugar. Again stir and cook 1 min., and then take out. Big fire all the time.

With the same skillet, heat 2 more tb-sp. lard till hot. Turn to medium fire and pour in all the eggs. Do not stir or break the mass. Leave it whole. Lift the bottom occasionally to make sure that it does not stick or burn. After 1 min., when the eggs are still partly liquid, put the meat, celery, scallions, and pea sprouts in again. (Do not pour in the juice. Keep it for further cooking.) Fold one edge of the egg over the other so as to make a half pie, with the meat shreds and things as stuffing. Cook each face of the half pie 1½ min.

If you like to have some gravy, heat the juice of the meat and celery, etc. Mix 1 tb-sp. cornstarch with 2 tb-sp. water, pour into the heated juice, and continue to heat till translucent. Pour this gravy on the eggs in the serving plate.

Though this dish can be kept in the oven for a few minutes, it is best eaten immediately after cooking. Sometimes in the midst of a meal we ask our guests to excuse us so that we can go to the kitchen to prepare this dish. If some guest wishes to give a helping hand, she is welcome to do so.

Variations.—In place of meat shreds, various other things may be used.

(a) Egg *Fu-yung* with Shrimps.—Use ½ lb. fresh shrimps in place of the meat. Clean shrimps by removing shells and the dark, gritty thread at the back. Stir-fry the shrimps with the seasonings as with the meat shreds. The rest is the same as with the preceding recipe.

(b) Egg *Fu-yung* with Fish.—Use ½ lb. fillet of flounder. Cut into small pieces and proceed as above.

(c) Egg *Fu-yung* with Chicken Shreds. Use ½ lb. of white chicken meat and cut into shreds. Stir-fry as with meat shreds.

(d) Clam Meat, (e) Oysters, and (f) Crab Meat may also be used, though ¼ lb. will be enough, as these are not such suitable big-morsel food as meat and fish.

13.3. Grown Eggs

Grown Eggs are also called Iron-Pot Eggs, as they are often made in a heavy iron pot. This dish has the appearance of an American egg custard, but don't believe in appearances. Various accompaniments may be put into Grown Eggs. I shall now describe the basic dish, which in the simple form also tastes quite wonderful.

10 beaten eggs	1 tb-sp. melted lard
1 t-sp. salt	½ lb. ground pork meat
2 tb-sp. soy sauce	1 cup water

Put all these things together and mix evenly. Put mixture into a pyrex dish with volume of about 3 times the volume of the mixture. Cover the bowl and put the bowl directly over the fire. Start with a very low flame and cook for ½ hr. The eggs are done when they have grown enough to push up the lid. Keep over low fire until ready to serve. The grown-up, puffed state will last only a couple of minutes on the table, and that only when the stove is not too far from the table. Nothing annoys the hostess more than talking away and not noticing the beautiful Grown Eggs [1] until the dish has shrunken cold.

13.4. Thin-Flowing Eggs

This is not an easy dish, but worth the trouble if it comes out right.

8 beaten eggs	4 cups water
2 oz. dried shrimps	3 heaping tb-sp lard
⅔ cup flour	

Either { ½ lb. cod or fillet of flounder
        1½ t-sp. salt

or { ¼ lb. Virginia ham
     1 t-sp. salt

[1] Not noticing? Oh, yes, aren't they beautiful? How old are they?—er—as I was saying, Dr. Li, you have not yet proved conclusively that the high-frequency tones are ...—Y. R. C.

137

Put the dried shrimps in a small pot with 1 cup of water. Heat till it boils. Stop the fire and let stand for 20 min. Then take the shrimps out and chop into very small pieces. Put both the shrimps' boiling juice and the chopped shrimps in the beaten eggs.

Cut the fish into tiny bits and put in the eggs with 1½ t-sp. salt. (Or cut the ham into tiny bits and put in the egg with 1 t-sp, salt.)

Mix the flour with 3 cups water and also add into the eggs.

Now beat the eggs with shrimps, fish or ham, and flour together very evenly,

Heat the lard in a skillet over big fire. When it is hot, pour in all the mixed eggs. Stir quickly and constantly until it looks more scrambled than scrambled eggs, when it is done. This takes 5-7 min. on big fire.

This dish can be kept in the oven for only a few minutes before serving.

Sometimes we do not mix in the ham and shrimps in the eggs before cooking, but cook the eggs and flour separately first, and then sprinkle the ham or shrimps on top when serving. This looks brighter, but does not taste so good, since the flavor of the shrimps or the ham will not be in the eggs, you see?

13.5. Pork Omelet

This dish is very well liked in China and is a very common dish in the home.

1 lb. pork chops	1 t-sp. salt
2 tb-sp. soy sauce	3 tb-sp. lard
8 eggs	

Cut the pork into very thin slices. Mix well with the 2 tb-sp. of soy sauce. Beat the eggs and the salt together. Heat the lard in a skillet till very hot. Add in the seasoned pork slices, fry for 2 min., add the eggs and fry for 2 more min.

This dish should be served immediately after being prepared. When cold it loses much of its savor. Any leftover, however, may be made into a soup by boiling it with the proper amount of water.

13.6. Steamed Custard

This dish looks like the American custard but has its own good points.

       ½ lb. ground meat
or ½ lb. ground cod meat
or ½ lb. ground shrimp meat
or ¼ pint ground or chopped clam meat
or ¼ pint chopped oyster meat
or 1 doz. razor clam meat (ground)
or ½ lb. lobster meat (cut into ½-inch cubes)

Beat together 10 eggs
              3 cups water
              2 t-sp. salt
              2 tb-sp. sherry

add your meat and beat again, then pour the mixture into a pyrex dish. Place the pyrex dish on a stand over water in a pot 2 inches wider than the pyrex dish, cover the pot, and steam over big fire for 20 min. Take out the pyrex dish just before serving.

13.7. Tea Eggs

Tea eggs are one of those ways of hard-boiling eggs so long that they are soft again. They are not so much a dish as a breakfast "dot-heart" or between-meal "dot-heart," though sometimes also eaten at big meals. They are especially good for traveling and for picnics. Serve cold or hot.

2 dozen eggs
2 t-sp. black tea (used leaves usable, though fresh leaves are better)
1½ to 2 tb-sp. salt
1 tangerine rind

Boil the eggs for 1 hr. Cool in cold water and crackle the shells, but do not detach. Boil again in enough water (about 6 cups) to cover all the eggs. Add in the tea, salt, and the tangerine rind. Simmer for 2 more hrs. and stop the fire, but keep the eggs in the juice. Serve cold or hot. The juice is only for external use by the eggs.

The eggs are usually best on the first or second day, if they are not too good to last that long. So long as these eggs are immersed, there is no need to keep them in the icebox except in extremely hot weather. If the eggs get too salty from soaking, their taste can be lightened by soaking in fresh water.

13.8. Egg *Fu-yung* (American-Chinese)

To make Egg *Fu-yung* as served in Chinese restaurants in America, start with the same ingredients as in Recipe No. 13.2, except that lard should be increased to 1-inch deep-frying amount. Now, instead of stirring the eggs separately from the other things, mix them together and scoop large table-spoonfuls or ladlefuls to deep-fry in the heated lard, medium fire. After ½ to 2 min., when one side is browned, turn over the pieces to brown the other side. Take out with a leaking ladle, pressing with another ladle to strain excessive oil back into pan. As many pieces can fry together as the pan will hold. The lard should be replenished when it gets too shallow.

If sauce is desired, follow Recipe No. 13.2 (sauce on p. 136).

The same variations (a, b, c, d, p. 136) can be used with deep-frying. Leftover roast meat, turkey, etc. can be shredded and used in both forms of Egg *Fu-yung*.

CHAPTER 14

VEGETABLES

In vegetables, as in some other things, the Chinese are both poorer and richer than Americans. Poorer, because a smaller part of the population can afford any great variety of vegetables, or anything else, and because lack of communication makes many good Chinese things limited to a small region, and lack of refrigeration and canning limit the use of certain things to certain brief seasons of the year. Richer, because there are on the whole a greater variety of things, and because we eat more of the things which Americans have but do not eat. We try everything, watermelon rind, radish top, pea vines, and what not. On my first trip to America twenty-odd years ago, I was so homesick for the tender vines of sweet peas that I bought a bunch of them for a dollar at a flower shop and took it home to cook, but it turned out to be different from the Chinese pea vines! Typical of seasonal food, we have in spring spring bamboo shoots, pea-pods, horse beans (eaten with skin). In summer too many things can be named. A vegetable melon, *tsit-kua* "(inter-) festival melon," is a reminder of later summer or early autumn and has been introduced from Canton to other parts of China and is occasionally seen in Chinatown. In many parts, winter is a good vegetable season. The *p'iao-êrh-ts'ai* of Nanking (a flat-top chard-like green vegetable), the *pai-ts'ai* or green cabbage of Changchow and Soochow, and the purple vegetable top that looks like broccoli—these are the reminders of winter. And of course the winter bamboo shoots of Hangchow and Ningpo!

Whenever needed for use or for trade, the vegetable gardener lifts up the straw cover, perhaps together with a little snow on top, and digs up the plants or the bamboo shoots as needed. On democratic principles, I do hope for the time when anybody can have anything anywhere at any time of the year, but the now privileged people will then probably look back with some wistfulness at the good old times when spring was spring and winter was winter. Meantime let's look over some vegetables you can cook in America.

14.1. Stirred String Beans

1 lb. string beans	2 tb-sp. vegetable oil or
1 t-sp. salt	chicken oil or 2 heaping
¾ cup water	tb-sp. lard

Wash beans. Snip off both ends of string beans, then break the string beans into sections of about 1 inch long.

Heat oil or lard in skillet (but not too hot). Put string beans in and keep stirring for about 1 min. Then put in the water and salt, and cover the skillet. Wait for 3 min. (when the beans will turn into a still fresher green color), then take off the cover and stir every ten seconds for 5 or 6 min. By this time, the water will be gone and all the flavor is still in the beans.

14.2A. Stirred Cabbage

This method is usually for new American cabbage.

2 lbs. new American cabbage	1¾ t-sp. salt
2 heaping tb-sp. lard or the	¾ cup water
same amount of vegetable oil	

Wash the cabbage and cut it into strips of about ¼ of an inch wide.

Heat oil or lard in skillet till hot, put the cabbage in and stir for 1 min. Then add salt and water. Keep on stirring for 3 min. more.

14.2B. Boiled Cabbage

This method is usually for older cabbages.

3 lbs. old American cabbage (This type of cooking needs more
  cabbage.)
2 heaping tb-sp. lard or the same amount of vegetable oil
2 t-sp. salt
1 cup water

Wash the cabbage and cut into pieces of about 1 inch square.
Heat in a skillet or a boiling pot (not a heavy pot) the lard or
oil till hot; then put in the cabbage.[1] Stir for 1 min. Then put salt
and water in. Turn fire low and cover the skillet or pot for about
15 or 20 min.

14.2C. Sweet-Sour Cabbage

This method is for either new or old cabbage. The special name
for this dish is "Sweet and Sour Cabbage."

2 lbs. American cabbage	1½ cup water
2 heaping tb-sp. lard or the	3 tb-sp. sugar
same amount of vegetable oil	3 tb-sp. vinegar
1½ t-sp. salt	1 tb-sp. cornstarch

Do everything same as in Recipe No. 14.2A for American cabbage, except that you cut the cabbage leaves into 1 square inch
pieces instead of into strips.

Mix the vinegar, sugar and cornstarch together with an additional cup of water. When the cabbage is done according to Recipe
No. 14.2A, put the mixture in and stir. It is done when the juice
becomes translucent.

[1] My variation (B') is as follows: Put everything in at the same time, and
turn on the fire neither very big nor very small. The advantage of this is that
you can leave it alone and go away until it is done or until you smell it burning. If you remember it in time, as I sometimes do, it is almost as good as
Variation B. Yes, this is the only other dish I cook besides Stirred
Eggs.—Y. R. C.

14.3. Stirred Spinach

2 lbs. spinach
3 tb-sp. vegetable oil or chicken oil or 2 heaping tb-sp. lard
1 full t-sp. salt

Wash the spinach and shake off as much water as possible, because a great deal of water will come out of the spinach itself during cooking. Do not cut spinach.

Heat oil or lard in a skillet until hot. Put the spinach in and put salt in immediately. Keep stirring for 3 min. and it is done. In this way, the spinach still has its green color and also keeps its flavor, instead of tasting like "spinach," as understood by American children. It can be kept in an oven for a few minutes before serving.[1]

14.4. Cold Spinach with Dried Shrimps

2 lbs. spinach	2 tb-sp. soy sauce
2 oz. dried shrimps	1 cup cold water
1 t-sp. salt	5 cups boiling water
2 tb-sp. salad oil	

Wash the spinach; don't cut. Put it in a pot with 5 cups of boiling water. Heat until it boils again. Then throw away the water. Chill with running cold water and shake away as much water as possible. Then chop up all the spinach.

Put the dried shrimps in a small pot with 1 cup of cold water. Heat over big fire until boiling. Then turn off fire and let stand for 20 min. Take the shrimps out, but *keep* the water. Chop up the shrimps and put them in the spinach with the shrimp water. Then add in the salt, soy sauce, and salad oil. Mix and serve.

[1] This was one of the few things I learned to cook from Mother, when I was only ten. When I went to a grade school in Washington and made this dish in my cooking class, my schoolmates liked to eat it better than either their teachers' or their mothers' spinach.—Rulan.

That's nothing, Rulan. I can tell a better one. When I first visited America, I learned to eat a kind of vegetable called "spinach" for three years. One day I saw some Chinese *po-ts'ai* in a market. Being always interested in words and names, I asked the market man what the English name of that Chinese vegetable was. "Chinese vegetable?" he said, "why, that's spinach!"—Daddy.

14.5A. Stirred Celery Cabbage

Celery cabbage is also called Chinese cabbage and is often found in American markets.

> 3 lbs. celery cabbage
> 2 heaping tb-sp. lard or the same amount of oil
> 1¼ t-sp. salt

No water is needed because a great deal of water will come out of the cabbage itself.

Wash the cabbage and cut into 1-inch sections.

Heat the lard or oil and put in ⅔ of the cabbage near the root. Stir-fry for 2 min. and add in the salt. Then add in the other ⅓, which is mostly leaves. Cook for 2 min. more.

14.5B. Sweet-Sour Celery Cabbage

> Same celery cabbage as in Recipe No. 14.5A
> Same seasoning as in Recipe No. 14.5A
> Plus:
> 3 tb-sp. sugar
> 3 tb-sp. vinegar
> 2 tb-sp. cornstarch
> ½ cup water

Follow Recipe No. 14.5A. After adding in the salt, mix the sugar, vinegar, cornstarch, and water together and add the mixture into the cabbage. Stir and cook for 3 min. more.

14.6. Stirred *Kaai-Ts'oi*

Kaai-ts'oi in Cantonese, or *chieh-ts'ai* in Mandarin, is another of those vegetables grown by Chinese in America for Chinese and sold only in Chinatown. It is all green and has a little bitter taste. There are two varieties, the winter *kaai-ts'oi* and the spring *kaai-ts'oi*.

The winter *kaai-ts'oi* has a shape similar to that of an American cabbage.

> 2 lbs. *kaai-ts'oi*
> 2 heaping tb-sp. lard or the same amount of oil
> 1 t-sp. salt
> 1 t-sp. sugar
> (⅛ cup water in case of winter *kaai-ts'oi*)

Wash the *kaai-ts'oi* clean and cut into 1-inch squares.

Heat the lard or oil in a skillet and put the *kaai-ts'oi* in. Stir-fry for 1 min., and add in the salt, and sugar (with water, in case of winter *kaai-ts'oi*). Cook again for 4 min.

14.7. Stirred Chinese Green Cabbage

Do not confuse this with the celery cabbage, which you often see in American grocery stores. This Chinese green cabbage has a main stem in the center. It is white at the stems but dark green at the leaves, and so like Swiss chard in appearance. They are grown by the Chinese on Long Island, N.Y., and on the West Coast, and sold in Chinatown and in some general markets under the Cantonese name of *Bock Choy*.

> 2 lbs. Chinese green cabbage
> 2 heaping tb-sp. lard or the same amount of oil
> 1 t-sp. salt
> ⅛ cup water

Wash the cabbage clean and cut into 1-inch sections. Separate the white stems and green leaves.

Heat lard or oil in a skillet, and then put in the white stems. Stir for 1 min., and then add the salt and water. Cover the skillet and let it cook for 3 min. more. Then add in the leaves and cook together for 2 min. Serve with the juice.

14.8. Stirred Mustard Green

There are two kinds of mustard green. One is tender; the other is tougher and has a central stem with flowers, but they are both good.

The method of cooking is the same as in Recipe No. 14.6.

But the best way to use mustard green in Chinese cooking is to salt it.

14.9. Stirred Celery

1 bunch celery   1 t-sp. salt
1 tb-sp. vegetable oil   1 t-sp. sugar (if desired)

Wash the celery and cut each piece obliquely into small slices. (Celery in China is tubular and much thinner and needs only to be cut into small sections.)

Heat the oil in a skillet till hot, then add in the celery. Stir for 1 min., then add in salt (and add sugar if you do). Cook again for 2 min.

14.10. Cold Celery

1 bunch celery,   ½ t-sp. salt
1 quart boiling water   1 t-sp. sesame oil, or salad oil
1 tb-sp. soy sauce   1 t-sp. sugar (optional)

Cut celery across into 1-inch sections. Then slit each section in three.

Scald celery in the quart of boiling water for 2 min. Then take out. In this way the celery is more tender and most of the vitamins are still kept. Put the celery in cold water (ice cold if preferred) for about 1 min.

Then throw away all the water, put celery in a bowl and mix with the soy sauce, salt, and salad oil.

This is like an American salad dish, but the scalding makes it different.

14.11. Celery Stirs Mushrooms

1 bunch celery	2 tb-sp. soy sauce
½ lb. fresh mushrooms	1 t-sp. salt
2 tb-sp. vegetable oil	1 t-sp. sugar

Wash the celery and cut into inch-long oblique cuts.

Wash mushrooms and cut into ¼-inch-thick slices.

Heat the vegetable oil in a skillet over big fire until hot. Then put the mushroom slices in first and stir for 1 min. Then add in the soy sauce, salt, and sugar, and then add in the celery right after and cook together by constantly stirring for 3 min.

14.12. Stirred Fresh Mushrooms

2 lbs. fresh mushrooms	1 t-sp. sugar
4 tb-sp. vegetable oil	1 tb-sp. cornstarch
2 tb-sp. soy sauce	2 tb-sp. water
½ t-sp. salt	

Wash the mushrooms and cut vertically into thin slices ⅛ inch thick.

Heat the vegetable oil in a skillet till hot, then put in the mushrooms and stir for 2 min. Put in the soy sauce and stir again for 2 min. Then mix the salt, sugar, cornstarch, and water together and add in. Cook together for ½ more min. until the juice becomes translucent.

14.13. Stirred Swiss Chard

This vegetable looks something like Chinese green cabbage, only the stems are longer, rougher, tougher, and less juicy.

> 2 lbs. Swiss chard
> 3 heaping tb-sp. lard or vegetable oil
> 1 t-sp. salt
> ½ cup water

Wash chard clean and cut into 1-inch sections.

Heat the lard or oil in a skillet and put in the $\frac{2}{3}$ near the root first, and stir for 1 min. Then add salt and water and cover the skillet. Turn to medium fire and let it cook for 5 min., then take off the cover and put in the top end $\frac{1}{3}$ of the chard, turn on big fire again and cook for 2 more min.

14.14. Boiled Cucumbers with Dried Shrimps

Cucumbers with dried shrimps is a vegetable dish, though not a vegetarian dish, since dried shrimps are animal food and yet only used as flavoring.

> 3 large cucumbers, or the same amount in small ones
> 2-2½ oz. dried shrimps
> 2 cups water
> 1 t-sp. salt

Peel cucumbers, cut each into 1½-inch sections, and then slit each section vertically in two. It will save time if you slit each cucumber before cutting across, but be sure not to cut your fingers when the cucumber tries to roll away.

Put the dried shrimps with the cucumbers and the water in a pot. Heat over big fire till boiling. Then simmer for ½ hr.

If you like a thick gravy in the dish, mix:

> 1 tb-sp. cornstarch   2 tb-sp. cold water

and pour mixture into the pot with the cooked cucumbers and stir over big fire until juice becomes translucent.

14.15. Cold Cucumbers

2 big cucumbers or their equivalent	2 tb-sp. vinegar
	2 tb-sp. sugar
1 t-sp. salt	1 tb-sp. sesame oil or salad
2 tb-sp. soy sauce	oil

Peel the cucumbers and cut into small round slices about ⅛ inch thick. If the cucumbers are big, slit vertically into two and then cut into semicircular slices.

Mix with the salt, soy sauce, vinegar and sugar.

Sometimes we like to have cucumbers and cold radishes together.[1]

14.16. Cold Sweet-Sour Radishes

40 small radishes	1½ tb-sp. sugar
1 t-sp. salt	2 t-sp. sesame oil. (If you can-
½ tb-sp. soy sauce	not get it in Chinatown, use
1½ tb-sp. vinegar	salad oil.)

Wash the radishes and cut off both ends. Use the back or side of a heavy knife (or anything heavy and flat), and smash each radish gently. Do not break it into small pieces, but leave it so that you can still pick each up as a whole radish.

Mix in 1 t-sp. salt and let it stand for 5 min. Then mix in the soy sauce, vinegar, sugar, and sesame oil.

(If the green tops are young and fresh, wash them clean and cut into ¼-inch sections. Mix with another t-sp. salt and scrub hard. Then squeeze out the water. Add the leaves into the radishes and also add in 2 more t-sp. sesame oil.)

14.17. Hot Sweet-Sour Carrots

1 big bunch or 2 small bunches of carrots	1½ cups water
	2 tb-sp. vinegar
1 heaping tb-sp. lard or the same amount of oil	2 tb-sp. sugar
	1 tb-sp. cornstarch
1 t-sp. salt	

Wash the carrots but do not peel them. Cut into slices obliquely. Heat the tb-sp. of lard or oil in a skillet and stir-fry the carrots

---

[1] In that case, I wish you would remember to soak the radishes a few hours beforehand, Buwei.—Y. R. C.

for 1 min. Then add the salt and ¼ cup water and let it boil for 5 min. If the carrots are big and old, cook a little longer.

Mix the vinegar, sugar, cornstarch, and 1 cup water. Add in the carrots and cook until the gravy is all translucent.

14.18. Stirred Broccoli

2 lbs. broccoli	1½ t-sp. salt
2 heaping tb-sp. lard or the same amount of vegetable oil	1 t-sp. sugar (optional)
	1 cup water

Break off the small branches of the broccoli from the big stem one by one. Peel off the tough skin on the stem and cut into slices obliquely. Wash the stem slices together with the small branches.

Heat the lard or oil in a skillet. Put the broccoli in and stir for 1 min. Then add the salt, sugar, and water. Cover the skillet and let it cook for 3 min. Then take off the cover, stir every ¼ min. for 5 min. (About 8 or 9 min. altogether.)

14.19. Stirred Dandelion

2 lbs. dandelion	1 t-sp. salt
3 heaping tb-sp. lard or the same amount of vegetable oil	1 tb-sp. sugar

Wash the dandelion very thoroughly. Be sure to get rid of all the sand. Do not cut.

Heat the lard or oil in a skillet till hot; then put in the dandelion. Stir for 1 min. and then add in the salt and sugar. (No water is needed, as water will come out of the dandelion itself.) Cook for 3 min., stirring constantly.

14.20. Cold Asparagus

2 lbs. asparagus	1 t-sp. sugar
4 cups boiling water	1 tb-sp. salad oil
2 tb-sp. soy sauce	

Break off the tough part of the asparagus near the root.

Cut into long, rolling-knife pieces. (See Fig. 3, p. 36.)

Put all the asparagus in the 4 cups of hot water in a pot and then heat till it boils again. Let it boil for 2 min. Then throw away the water and chill with cold running water. (You can keep the asparagus in the icebox if it is not for serving right away.)

Mix the asparagus with the soy sauce, sugar, and salad oil.

14.21. Red-Cooked Eggplant

1 big eggplant (about 2 lbs.)	2 tb-sp. soy sauce
3 heaping tb-sp. lard or the same amount of oil	¼ t-sp. salt
	4 or 5 slices of garlic
1 cup water	

Cut the eggplant lengthwise into 4 sections; then slice each section crosswise into a little over ½-inch slices.

Heat the lard or oil in a skillet. Put the eggplant slices in and fry on both sides for 2 min. altogether. Peel off the thin skin from the garlic and crush each slice into an absorbent, or rather juice-yielding state. Add it into the eggplant with the cup of water, soy sauce, and salt. Turn to low fire and cover the skillet to cook for 15 min.

(If you have small dried shrimplets, you can boil 2 oz. of them in the cup of water with low fire for 10 min. When the eggplant is ready for adding the seasoning and the cup of water, add in the seasoning and the shrimplets with their boiling water instead. Then proceed as above.)

14.22. Stirred Summer Squash or Italian Squash

This is sold in American markets but not very frequently. There are two kinds, one with dark green color and one with light green color (Coccazelli and Zuchini).

2 lbs. summer squash or Italian squash	2 tb-sp. soy sauce
	1 t-sp. salt
2 heaping tb-sp. lard or same amount of vegetable oil	¼ t-sp. black pepper
	½ cup water

Wash the squash. Cut across into very thin slices, about ⅛ inch thick.

Heat the lard or oil in a skillet. Put the squash in and stir for 2 min. Then add salt, pepper, and water. Stir again for 5 min.

This is very good with meat slices. See Recipe No. 2.5 for Squash Stirs Meat Slices.

14.23. Stirred Bean Sprouts

Bean sprouts are from soy beans. Sometimes we can grow the sprouts ourselves at home with simple materials. However, the room temperature must be accurately adjusted and the process is too complicated to be worth while for a small family.

2 lbs. bean sprouts (called *tou-nga* in Chinatown)	2 tb-sp. soy sauce
	½ t-sp. salt
2 tb-sp. vegetable oil	

Wash the bean sprouts. (In China we sometimes break off all the roots from each of the bean sprouts.)

Heat the oil in a skillet and put in the bean sprouts. Stir for 1 min., then add the soy sauce and salt. Cover the skillet and turn on low fire. Let it cook for 5 min. Then take off the cover and stir for 1 min. more.

Sometimes you can use lard instead of vegetable oil if you do not plan to have leftovers for eating cold.

14.24. Bean Sprouts Stir Red-in-Snow

Same bean sprouts as above
Same seasoning as above
Except: Omit the salt
Plus: 1 t-sp. sugar
1 cup red-in-snow (or salted mustard green) (get in Chinatown)

Prepare and begin to cook bean sprouts as above. When you are ready to add in the soy sauce, add in also the salted mustard green. Add sugar and then continue as above.

14.25. Stirred Pea Sprouts

The pea sprouts are quite different from the bean sprouts. Pea sprouts are grown from tiny green peas. They are more tender and constitute the common ingredients in American-Chinese dishes.

2 lbs. pea sprouts (called *nga-ts'oi* in Chinatown)
2 heaping tb-sp. lard or same amount of vegetable oil
2 t-sp. salt

Put all the sprouts in a big pan of water. The shells of the peas will float on the top of water. In this way you can get rid of all the shells after changing water a couple of times.

Heat the lard or oil in a skillet and put the pea sprouts in. Stir for 1 min. and then add in 2 t-sp. salt. Then cook for 3 more min., still with big fire, and stir constantly.

This is not very good when left over.

14.26. Red-in-Snow Stirs Peas

Peas in China are used in the fresh state in vegetable dishes. When preserved, they are dry and not suitable for making vegetable dishes. They are rarely canned and never frozen. Here are two recipes for peas in different states.

(A) With Fresh Peas

3-4 lbs. fresh peas in pods	1 cup red-in-snow, or salted
2 tb-sp. vegetable oil	mustard green
1 cup cold water	2 tb-sp. soy sauce

Shell the peas.

Heat the vegetable oil in a skillet until hot and put the peas in. Add in the cup of water and cover the skillet. Continue on big fire for 5 min. Then add in the red-in-snow and the soy sauce. Stir for 2 or 3 min., when the juice will have all been wrapped around the peas and red-in-snow.

(B) With Frozen Peas

2 packages frozen peas	1 tb-sp. soy sauce
2 tb-sp. vegetable oil	1 t-sp. sugar
1 cup red-in-snow	

Thaw out the frozen peas.

Heat the vegetable oil in a skillet. Put in the red-in-snow first and stir for 2 min. with the fire still big. Add the soy sauce and sugar, and the thawed frozen peas right after. Stir together for 2 min.

14.27. Red-in-Snow Stirs Fava Beans

Horse beans look like lima beans but are not. They are also called Fava beans and frequently sold by Italians. In China they are known as "silkworm beans." They are used fresh or dried. For this dish, use fresh beans.

> 3-4 lbs. horse beans
> Other ingredients same as (A) above

Shell and skin the beans and leave just the inner kernels. (But the skin is very good when the beans are very tender.)

Proceed as with (A) above.

14.28. Arhat's Fast or Vegetarian's Ten Varieties

The Arhats are Buddhist Saints. Hence this dish is "food for the saints." Arhat's Fast consists of a number of specified vegetable ingredients, some of which are dried materials. There are, however, some local variations depending upon availability. In this dish, many of the ingredients have to be prepared separately before they are put together. Here are the separate and ensemble steps in the cooking.

(a) Hair vegetable. This is a black hair-like seaweed. Get about 40 cents' worth in Chinatown. Soak in hot water for ½ hr., rinse several times to get rid of all the sand. Pull it apart into small groups (this step is optional).

(b) Dried Tiger Lilies. Get ⅛ lb. in Chinatown. Soak in hot water for ½ hr. and rinse clean.

(c) Peastarch noodles. These are a kind of transparent noodles, made of the starch of a kind of tiny green peas, the same kind from which pea sprouts are raised. They are very common in China and can be got in Chinatown. Put ¼ lb. in a pot full of boiling water and cook over low fire for ½ hr. Then turn off fire and let it stand and cool off.

(d) *Gingko* or *paak-kwo* in Cantonese. Get ⅓ lb. in Chinatown. When bought, they have white, hard shells outside. Crack shells with nutcracker. Soak nuts in a big bowl of hot water and peel off inner skin.

(e) Mushrooms. Get ¼ lb. Properly you should use dried mushrooms, which are more savory than fresh ones. Since they are not generally available in this country, fresh ones have to be substituted. Cut vertically into thin slices. It is possible to dry fresh mushrooms and later soak them, but that takes days.

(f) Gluten of Flour, or skin of bean curd. Get ⅓ lb., both from Chinatown. If you get gluten of flour, cut it into pieces of 1 cubic inch. If you get bean curd skin, put it in a pot of boiling water and keep boiling for ½ hr. Then cut into 1½-inch wide strips.

(g) Chinese cabbage; 3 lbs. Either Chinese green cabbage or celery cabbage (which you cut into pieces about 2 inches long).

(h) 1 package of frozen peas. Thaw them out.

(i) ½ can winter bamboo shoots. Cut into slices of about 1 square inch.

(j) Fried puffy bean curd; 6 pieces (or 12 pieces if small). Get in Chinatown. The best is to get them ready fried, but if you cannot, get 1 pint fresh bean curd and cut each into 4 pieces and fry it in deep vegetable oil until it is brown.

Cooking material:

4 tb-sp. vegetable oil	2 t-sp. taste powder
2 t-sp. salt	2 cups water
½ cup soy sauce	

Direction for ensembles:

Heat the vegetable oil in a pot (not necessarily heavy, but big), put the cabbage in first (item g) and stir for 1 min. Then add in everything from (a) to (j), then also add in the soy sauce, salt, taste powder, and water. Boil together for 20 min.

This can be a main dish on meatless days. It looks rather complicated, but as you practically get everything in Chinatown, you need make only one trip to shop for these things, When you give the salesman the list, he will immediately know what you are making and may give you some suggestions and tell you why his combination is certainly better than mine.

If you cannot get some of the items from this list, you can add in something of your own, such as chestnuts, string beans, carrots, etc. Sometimes we do not use so many things. As few as four or five kinds are sometimes used and the dish is still called Vegetarian's Ten Varieties. But better have things nearly right to taste nearly right.

A beauty of this dish is that it can be kept as long as one week without losing flavor.

14.29. Red-Cooked Bean Curd

8 3 x 3 x 1-in. pieces bean curd	1½ cups water
4 tb-sp. soy sauce	2 tb-sp. vegetable oil
1 tb-sp. sugar	1 scallion (optional), sectioned

Cut bean curd to size, if bought or made in larger sizes. Heat oil in skillet over medium fire and put in bean curd flat before oil gets too hot. Use a spatula to turn over bean curd so that both sides are slightly browned. Mix above ingredients and pour in until gravy becomes translucent, separating the bean curd occasionally from the bottom to prevent burning. Throw in scallion last, if desired.

This is a basic vegetarian dish. For various combinations with meat things see recipes below.

14.30. Bean Curd with Ground Meat

Make Red-Cooked Bean Curd as in Recipe 14.29. In addition, use:

1 lb. pork or beef, medium grind	½ tb-sp. vegetable oil
1 tb-sp. cornstarch	½ cup water

Mix meat with the cornstarch and water. After the red-cooked bean curd is taken out of the skillet, add the ½ tb-sp. oil and stir in the meat until cooked. Then put in the bean curd, turning a little, but don't stir, and it is done. Add scallion last, if desired.

14.31A. Fried Bean Curd

The most convenient size of pieces for this is 1-in. cube or 1 x ½ x 2 in. Use enough vegetable oil for deep frying. The main thing about frying bean curd is to have the outside browned and slightly crisp and the inside still soft. This requires hot oil over moderate fire and fairly quick frying. Since bean curd is always wet, it is well to protect your face by having a lid to cover the pot as soon as the pieces are in and take off the lid only when the frying sound quiets down a bit.

14.31B. Oyster Sauce Fried Bean Curd

The recipe for this dish consists of buying a bottle of oyster sauce from Chinatown for the dipping sauce for Fried Bean Curd. This is not to be confused with Recipe No. 14.33 for Oyster Sauce (unfried) Bean Curd.

14.31C. Sweet-Sour Fried Bean Curd

This is not so common in China, but many Americans like it. Use:

2 tb-sp. soy sauce   ½ t-sp. taste powder
3 hpg tb-sp. sugar   ½ cup water
2 tb-sp. vinegar   1 tb-sp. cornstarch

Mix and boil to translucency to make a dipping sauce for Rec. 14.31A.

14.32. Cold Mixed Bean Curd

6 pieces bean curd about 3 x 3   1½ tb-sp. vegetable oil, prefer-
   x 1 in. size or equivalent   ably sesame oil
4 tb-sp. soy sauce   1½ t-sp. sugar
     ½ t-sp. salt if desired

Mix everything together and you have a salad. Some like the curd not so broken up. In China it is often eaten with the tender buds of *hsiang-ch'un* or fragrant cedar (*Cedrela chinensis*), but don't pick by mistake from the similar-looking tree stinking cedar (*Ailanthus glanulosa*).

14.33. Oyster Sauce Bean Curd

Same bean curd as in Recipe No. 14.29
Same seasoning as in Recipe No. 14.29
Except: Omit the salt
Plus: 2 tb-sp. oyster sauce

Follow directions in Recipe No. 14.29 and add the oyster sauce during the last ½ min.

14.34. Mushrooms Stir Bean Curd

½ lb. fresh mushrooms	2 tb-sp. soy sauce
1 quart fresh bean curd	½ t-sp. salt
2 heaping tb-sp. lard or same amount of vegetable oil	1 tb-sp. cornstarch
	3 tb-sp. cold water

Wash mushrooms and cut vertically into ¼-inch-thick slices. Also cut bean curd into ¼-inch-thick slices.

Heat the lard or oil in a skillet over big fire until hot. Put the mushrooms in first and stir for 2 min. Then add in the bean curd, the soy sauce, and salt. Stir gently (so as not to break the bean curd), but constantly, for 3 min. Then mix the cornstarch with the water first and pour mixture in. Stir for another ½ min. until the juice becomes translucent.

14.35. Scallions Stir Bean Curd

2 pints bean curd

1 bunch scallions

2 heaping tb-sp. lard or same amount of vegetable oil

2 tb-sp. soy sauce

1½ t-sp. salt

Cut each piece of bean curd into 5-6 pieces.

Wash scallions and cut off the roots and cut into inch-long sections.

Heat the lard or oil in a skillet over big fire until hot. Then put the scallions in and stir for 1 min. Then put in the bean curd and stir gently for 2 min. Then add the soy sauce and salt. Continue big fire and stirring for 1 min. more.

This dish is not good when recooked. When done, the sooner eaten the better.

14.36. Pot-Stuck Bean Curd

2 pints bean curd	4 tb-sp. cold water
4 eggs	½ t-sp. taste powder
2 t-sp. salt	4 tb-sp. lard
2 tb-sp. cornstarch	

Beat the eggs thoroughly along with the salt, cornstarch, water, and taste powder.

Cut bean curds into slices of about 2 square inches in area and ¼ inch thick.

Heat half of the lard in a big skillet over medium fire.

Dip each piece of bean curd in the mixed eggs first and then shallow-fry it in the skillet for 2 min. Add in more lard as used up until all is finished. As many pieces may of course be laid on the skillet as there is room for them to be spread out.

This is also best when served tongue-burning hot. It can be kept good in the oven for not more than 5 min.

14.37. Red-in-Snow (Salted Mustard Green)

Salted Mustard Green is so important you must learn to make it. Buy the kind without flowers. Wash, dry in air until no water shows. Cut into 2-inch sections. Rub with salt, kneading slightly, 1 tb-sp. to 1 lb. of green. Can in glass jars, driving out excess liquid and all bubbles. Stand in cool place for 2 weeks or until it turns yellow, when it will be ready to eat or go into many of the recipes calling for Red-in-Snow. Squeeze off brine lightly before use.

CHAPTER 15

SOUPS

By this time, you will expect me to say that in China a soup is not a soup, but something quite different. Well, soups will be soups, but they are used very differently. At big dinners, they come several times and always once at the end. At ordinary meals, there is usually a common bowl of soup on the table of which you partake with your spoon any time of the meal, especially toward the end. Since water is never and tea rarely served on the table, soup is the only drink. If at any time you find soup served in individual bowls at the beginning of the meal and then removed before other dishes or rice is started on, you know you are in Americanized company, such as some of my parties are.

Soups may be divided into light soups and heavy soups. A light soup is just a drink. Its ingredients are more for flavoring than for eating. When you count the number of dishes to figure out the amount of food, light soups are sometimes not counted, because there is so little in them. At formal dinners, light soups come in between courses and are especially welcome after a dish, say, of deep-fried shrimps. Heavy soups, on the other hand, are usually more than one dish. A whole chicken, a whole shad, a turtle, or a central square from a whole ham called *hsiao-chien*, "a small affair," is usually enough as a main dish. Add two or four small stir-fried side dishes and you have a first quality dinner (Chapter 21.4). When a friend says to you, "Drop in, I have some soup tonight," you can be sure that he has something very substantial in his soup. A heavy soup or two often comes at the end of a formal dinner. It is, however, not so well appreciated as at an informal meal, since many guests forget to observe the motto of "await, avoid, attack" for banquets. When you have a pot (Chapter 16), it takes the place of a heavy soup.

A soup gets its name from what is in it, but not necessarily its taste. In a restaurant or with a cook you "board" with, the taste of the soup often has nothing to do with what you see in the soup. Thus, a "ham and chicken soup" may have the taste of simmered pork shoulder. For what we call the "original soup" of the chicken is often used in improving the taste of other dishes. In a restaurant, where they often boil or reheat pork, beef, chicken, duck, and various bones, there is a common soup stock, usually very dilute, that can be served with anything else and is called "high soup." In recent years, the use of taste powder is very widespread.

In home cooking, of course, a soup does get its taste from what is in it. In some of the recipes for light soups I indicate the use of some taste powder, but I am very conservative in its use. (See Chapter III.7).

I. SIMPLE SOUPS

15.0. Soup for the Gods

When you are absolutely out of soups, you can always make *shên-hsien-t'ang*, Soup for the Gods. Since it is too simple to count as a dish, I am numbering it as 15.0.

8 cups boiling water
2 tb-sp. soy sauce
Some dozen ½-inch sections of garlic shoots or 1 scallion cut in ⅛-inch sections
1 t-sp. sesame oil or salad oil or lard
1 t-sp. salt

Put seasonings in a bowl and pour the boiling water into it.

Soup for the Gods is a good drink to go with rich foods, such as Egg Stirs Rice (Recipe No. 18.5).

15.1. Cucumber and Meat-Slice Soup

1 small or ½ large cucumber	2 tb-sp. soy sauce
½ lb. pork meat (boneless, usu-	½ tb-sp. sherry
ally from pork chops)	7 cups water
½ tb-sp. cornstarch	½ t-sp. salt

Peel cucumbers and cut into very thin slices.

Cut meat into very thin slices and mix meat with the cornstarch, 1 tb-sp. of the soy sauce, and the sherry.

First get the 7 cups of water boiling, then put in the ½ t-sp. salt and the 1 tb-sp. soy sauce. When it boils again, put in cucumber slices and boil for 1 min. Then add in the meat and boil for 2 min. more.

15.2. Scallops and Meat-Slice Soup

Same meat as in Recipe No. 15.1
Same seasoning as in Recipe No. 15.1
Except: only 1 tb-sp. soy sauce
1 (instead of ½) t-sp. salt
½ lb. scallops

Prepare meat as in Recipe No. 15.1.

Clean off the small tough part on the side of each scallop. Cut each scallop into 4 round slices.

Put scallops in a pot with 7 cups water. Heat over big fire till it boils. Then turn fire low and cook for 3 more min. Then add in 1 t-sp. salt and the seasoned meat and cook together for 2 min.

15.3. Mushrooms and Meat-Slice Soup

Same meat as in Recipe No. 15.1
Same seasoning as in Recipe No. 15.1
½ lb. mushrooms

Prepare meat as in Recipe No. 15.1.

Cut mushrooms vertically into thin slices.

First get the 7 cups of water boiling, then put in the mushrooms and boil again for 1 min. Then add the ¼ t-sp. salt, the remaining 1 tb-sp. soy sauce, and the seasoned meat. Boil together for 3 min.

15.4. Bean Curd and Meat-Slice Soup

Same meat as in Recipe No. 15.1
Same seasoning as in Recipe No. 15.1
Plus: ⅓ t-sp. taste powder
1 pint bean curd

Prepare meat as in Recipe No. 15.1.

Cut bean curd into small ½-inch cubes.

First get the 7 cups water boiling. Then put in the bean curd and boil for 2 min. Then add the ¼ t-sp. salt, 1 tb-sp. soy sauce, the ⅓ t-sp. taste powder. Add the seasoned meat. Boil for 3 min.

15.5. Egg and Meat-Slice Soup

Same meat as in Recipe No. 15.1
Same seasoning as in Recipe No. 15.1
2 eggs
2 tb-sp. cornstarch

Prepare meat as in Recipe 15.1.

Then put seasoned meat in 6 cups of boiling water and boil for 2 min. Mix the cornstarch with ¼ cup of water and add to the boiling mixture. Beat the 2 eggs and pour into the soup very slowly while stirring the water all the time. Then add in the salt and soy sauce and boil for 1 more min.

15.6. Ham and Winter Melon Soup

¼ lb. two-year-old Smithfield, Virginia ham—in whole piece with bones
1 lb. winter melon (get it in Chinatown)
8 cups water

Wash and take off the skin of the ham but keep the bones.

Peel off the skin of the melon and cut into slices of about ¼ inch thick and 1½ square-inch area. (This is convenient for small individual serving. When served in the Chinese way, much larger slices are used.)

Put ham and melon in 8 cups cold water and turn on big fire till it boils. Then turn to small fire and boil for ½ hr.

When serving, take out the whole piece of ham, take off the bones and cut into small ¼-inch cubes and put back into the soup again.

Add salt if desired.

15.7. Ham and Celery Cabbage Soup

Same ham as Recipe No. 15.6
1 celery cabbage about 1 lb.
6 cups water, because the cabbage already has some water in it.

Prepare ham as in Recipe No. 15.6.

Cut cabbage into shreds (cut it across) or into ½-inch strips.

Put ham in the 6 cups of cold water and turn on big fire. When it boils, turn to low fire and cook for 20 min. Then add in the cabbage and cook together for 10 min.

Add salt if desired.

15.8. Winter Melon and Dried Shrimp Soup

2 oz. dried shrimps (sold in Chinatown)
7 cups water
1 lb. winter melon
1 t-sp. salt

Peel and cut the melons into slices of about ¼ inch thick and 1½ square inch area.

Put dried shrimps in a pot with the 7 cups of cold water. Heat until boiling. Then let it stand for ½ hr.

Then put the melon and salt in. Use low fire and cook for ½ hr. including the time to reheat the soup to boiling.

165

15.9. Celery Cabbage and Dried Shrimp Soup

2 oz. dried shrimps, see Recipe No. 15.8

1 lb. celery cabbage

6 cups of water (because the cabbage already has some water in it)

1 t-sp. salt

Put shrimps in the 6 cups of water and heat till it boils, then turn on low fire and cook for 20 min.

Cut cabbage into shreds or ½-inch strips and add into the soup with salt. Boil together for 10 min. more.

15.10. Celery Cabbage with Meat-Shred Soup

½ lb. pork chops (boneless!)	½ tb-sp cornstarch
1 lb. celery cabbage	1 t-sp. salt
1 tb-sp. soy sauce	7 cups water

Cut meat into shreds. Mix with the soy sauce and cornstarch. Heat the 7 cups of water to boiling.

Cut the celery cabbage into shreds. Add the cabbage and the salt into the boiling water and cook for 5 min. Then add in the seasoned meat and boil for 2 min. more.

15.11.A. Triple-Shred Soup

This is a famous leftover soup. We do not purposely make such kind of soup. But when we cook other dishes with these materials, we feel that this soup is coming.

Either leftover chicken soup, or ham soup (Smithfield, Virginia ham)

Winter bamboo shoots

White-cooked chicken meat

Boiled ham

Cut chicken, ham, and bamboo shoots into shreds and put in the soup. If you like, you can mix the chicken soup and ham soup to-gether. (But never use the juice from the canned bamboo.)

Since this is a leftover soup, the amount is indefinite and the ratio of ham, chicken, bamboo shoots is variable. Normally, it is about 1:1:1.

15.11.B. Triple-Flavor Soup

This soup is just as famous as the soup above. The only difference is that you cut the chicken meat, ham, and bamboo shoots into slices.

15.12. Fish-Slice Soup

1 lb. fillet of flounder or had-dock meat, or fillet of bass	1 tb-sp. cornstarch
	2 tb-sp. soy sauce
7 cups water	1 scallion or ½ small sweet
1 t-sp. salt	onion
1½ tb-sp. sherry	

Slice fish into 1-square-inch slices about ¼ inch thick. Mix with 1 tb-sp. sherry, 1 tb-sp. cornstarch, and 1 tb-sp. soy sauce.

Cut scallion into small sections ½ inch long, and put scallion, 1 t-sp. salt, ½ tb-sp. sherry, 1 tb-sp. soy sauce in 7 cups of boiling water. Heat till it boils again. Then add in the seasoned fish and boil for 2 min. more.

15.13. Sour-Hot Soup

This is also a very famous soup that sometimes will help you get rid of leftovers. But sometimes we also purposely make it with fresh materials. Whichever its origin, it is a most appetizing soup, if properly made, and is very helpful when one is not hungry but has to eat.

The eggs and characteristic seasoning exist in all kinds of Sour-Hot soup. As to the other things you can *ad lib;* they can be fish, meat, shrimps, bean curd, etc. Even the water itself can be replaced by chicken soup, meat soup, made from boiling meat bones, etc.

167

3 eggs

7 cups water or any soup

1 t-sp. salt

2 tb-sp. soy sauce

½ t-sp. taste powder (omit if you use soup instead of water)

2 tb-sp. cornstarch

3 tb-sp. vinegar

¼ t-sp. black pepper

½ lb. any other materials, chopped in small pieces

Mix salt, soy sauce, taste powder, and cornstarch with 1 cup cold water or soup. Then put it in 6 cups of boiling water or soup. Keep a low fire while doing the following.

Beat 3 eggs and pour very slowly into the soup. Keep stirring the soup while pouring the eggs. Then add in the vinegar and pepper and any other materials. If you have meat slices, prepare them as in Meat-Slice Recipes before adding into the soup.

15-14. Chicken- or Pork-Bone Soup

This is a base soup in which you can add many other things like eggs, *kaai-ts'oi*, celery cabbage, radishes, turnips, etc., in any desired amounts.

Put the bones in a heavy pot of water and, with small fire, cook for 4-5 hrs. It can be kept in the icebox for a week.

15.15. Abalone and Meat-Slice Soup

Few fresh abalones go to the market. Besides, canned abalone is more savory. That is why in China we cook mostly with canned abalone.

In America, most of the canned abalone is from Mexico. It does not appear often in ordinary American markets, but is to be had in Chinatown.

½ lb. same kind meat as in Recipe No. 15.1

Same seasoning as in Recipe No. 15.1

½ can abalone

5 cups water

1 t-sp. salt

Cut abalone into thin slices of about 1 square inch or shreds. Put the juice of canned abalone in a pot and add 5 cups water. Cook till it boils.

Prepare meat as in Recipe No. 15.1. When the soup boils add in the meat and the salt. When it boils again add in the abalone. Boil for 2 min.

15.16. Scallop and Radish Soup

3 bunches of radishes—about 30   7 cups water
    radishes   1 t-sp. salt
½ lb. fresh scallops

Peel the radishes. Wash the scallops and take off the small tough muscles on the side of each scallop. Leave them whole and put in a heavy pot with the radishes and the 7 cups of water. Start with low fire and cook for 10 min., then add salt and continue with low fire for 30 min. more.

II. BIG SOUPS

15.17. Bird's-Nest Soup

The Chinese name for the eating bird's nest is *yen-wo*, "swallow-nest." The swallows' nests that you find under your eaves, however, are not good to eat, as they are made of mud. The eating bird's nest is made by a special kind of seaside swallow which gathers the meat of small fish and makes it into a nest by mixing it with its saliva. It consists mostly of protein in a gelatinous state, but it is held to be potently nourishing according to Chinese tradition.

Bird's nest comes from "southern goods stores" in the form of dried transparent shallow cups, somewhat larger than a soup spoon. When "developed" by slow boiling, it separates into strips or shreds. There are two kinds of bird's nests, a hairy kind and a plain kind, both of the same general shape. A prevalent use of bird's nest is to make it into sweet dishes.

The piece-form bird's nest is extremely scarce in the Chinatowns in America. The kind you can buy come in boxes of dry, porous, brittle cakes made from bird's-nest powder ground from whole birds' nests. This is the kind used in making bird's nest soup in restaurants, a form of bird's nest which is also common in Canton.

Bird's nest has a rather faint, though very interesting, flavor. Good cooking of bird's nest lies in enhancing that flavor with the right kind of "seasoning to taste," such as with chicken.

Get:

½ box dry Bird's Nest	¼ lb. ham
4 cups cold water	2 t-sp. salt
6 cups chicken or pork meat soup	½ t-sp. taste powder (omit if
⅓ lb. chicken meat or pork meat	chicken soup is used)

Put the bird's nest in a heavy pot with the 4 cups of cold water. Cook over low fire for 1 hr. Then let it cool off. By this time all the water has gone into the bird's nest—that is, all the water that will go into it. Cut chicken or meat and the ham into shreds and put them in with the 6 cups of chicken or meat soup. Also add in the salt and taste powder. Cook till it boils. If it is not immediately served, put it in the icebox. Warm it before serving.

15.18. *Fu-yung* Bird's-Nest Soup

Cook the soup exactly the same way as in Recipe No. 15.17, with the addition of 2 or 3 egg whites, slightly beaten with a fork; put in the soup when it boils.

15.19. Clear Chicken Soup

One 5-7 lb. chicken (old hen pre-	1 scallion
ferred because it has more	2 tb-sp. sherry
flavor than young chicken)	2 t-sp. salt
2 quarts cold water	2 or 3 slices fresh ginger

Wash the chicken clean and put it in a heavy pot with the 2 quarts of cold water. Heat over big fire till it boils. Then add the scallion, salt, sherry, and ginger and turn to low fire to simmer for 2 hrs.

Warning: Successful clear-soup chicken in Clear Chicken Soup lies in keeping the soup clear. The main thing is to keep the fire low as soon as boiling starts, as continued brisk fire would make the chicken tough and the soup muddy.

Variation.—Add, during the last ½ hr. of cooking, about 2 lbs. of celery cabbage, cut across an inch apart, and 1 or more slices of (Virginia) ham.

For a Chinese menu, a good rounded-out dinner can be formed of this one dish, especially in this variation, with the possible addition of a couple of small stir-frying dishes.

For an American meal, where one would not know how to pinch meat off the whole immersed chicken with chopsticks effectively and neatly, the chicken may be taken out and placed in a plate. As the amount of salt is to make the soup taste just right, the meat tastes better when each morsel is dipped into soy sauce just before eating. The leftovers, the parts that have not been dipped, can keep for about a week. Better keep in soup, heat up to boiling temperature and cool before refrigerating.

15.20. Clear Duck Soup

This is duck soup.

> One 5-7 lb. duck
> 8 cups water
> ½ lb. Virginia ham—whole piece
> ⅓ can winter bamboo shoots ⎫
> 7-8 winter mushrooms ⎬ optional
> ⎭
> 1 scallion
> 1 tb-sp. salt

Wash duck and cut off the tail, including the oil sacs. Put duck in a heavy pot and boil over big fire. When it boils, skim the scum. Since duck is usually fatter than chicken, some of the fat may also be skimmed after it has been boiled out. Turn to low fire. Add in the whole piece of ham, sliced bamboo shoots, mushrooms, scallion (whole piece), and the 1 tb-sp. salt. Cook for 1½-3 hrs., depending on the condition of the duck. Test tenderness by pulling the bones.

As in the case of Clear Chicken Soup, you can add, during the last ½ hr. of cooking, 2 lbs. of celery cabbage, cut across into strips of 1 inch wide. Add more salt if desired. When serving, put the cabbage under the duck. Cut the ham into slices and put it, with the bamboo shoot slices and mushrooms, on top of the duck.

CHAPTER 16

POTS

The Chinese chafing pot with its contents serves very much the purpose that soup serves in a meal. Sometimes the chafing pot is the main dish in the meal and sometimes, coming after a few stir-fried dishes, it is one of the big dishes of the dinner. At a formal banquet, the serving of the chafing pot is a sign that the dinner is nearing its end.

In China there are two main types of chafing pot. The first type of chafing pot consists of a brass or pewter ·basin about 9 inches at its widest diameter, through the center bottom of which has been thrust a vertical, hollow brass or tin funnel, 7 inches tall, that tapers from 5 inches at the sealed bottom to 3 inches at the open top. About ⅓ of the way from the bottom up is a grate on which the burning charcoal is placed. The grate corresponds in position to the center bottom part of the basin intersected by the funnel. The charcoal lowered onto the grate through the open top heats the wall of the funnel next to the soup contained in the basin and in this way keeps the cooked food in a boiling state. A porcelain plate containing a little water is usually placed under the sealed bottom of the funnel to keep the chafing pot from burning the table. A small porcelain plate containing a little water can also be used to stifle the fire from above whenever you want the boiling to stop.

There are two ways of preparing the ingredients and the soup for this chafing pot. The first way is to cook everything in other pots, and then transfer them to the chafing pot; the burning charcoal is packed into that part of the funnel above the grate and fanned glowing red; and then the chafing pot with its contents is brought on to the table. The guests then help themselves to a bowlful of the ingredients and the soup. But don't burn your tongue!

The second way of preparing this type of chafing pot is to have only boiling water or some very good meat soup or chicken soup filling only half the basin. The pot is brought to the table with the soup boiling from the glowing charcoal. On the table are many little platefuls of all the other ingredients—both meats and vegetables—cut very thin and in small pieces. Now everyone around the table picks up what there is in front of him with his chopsticks and drops it into the boiling soup. After enough ingredients have gone in, the pot is covered with its special cover and allowed to come to a boil. As soon as the cover is removed, the guests may plunge in. It is all right to pick up what others have put in.

The second type of chafing pot consists of a very shallow but

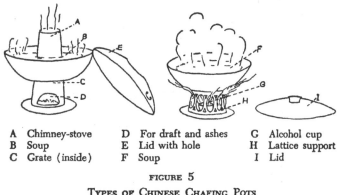

A Chimney-stove   D For draft and ashes   G Alcohol cup
B Soup   E Lid with hole   H Lattice support
C Grate (inside)   F Soup   I Lid

FIGURE 5
TYPES OF CHINESE CHAFING POTS

wide basin, holding from 8 to 10 cups of water. The basin is supported by a 5-inch wide and 3-inch long high hollow circular collar of brass, which in turn rests on a 6-inch brass plate. Fancy designs have been cut into the collar by cutting out ⅛-inch strips of brass. Resting on the brass plate that serves as the stand (under the basin and within the collar) is a cup which contains alcohol. The lighting of the alcohol will cause the fire not only to strike the bottom of the basin but also to escape through the latticework in the collar to heat up the sides of the basin. The flames coming through

174

the design take on a greenish color from the copper in the brass. The stand and the collar of the chafing pot are always placed on the table, and then the basin, with the water or the soup, is brought in and placed in position. Usually the water or the soup is first boiled in another pot and then poured into the basin; this will save a little time at the table. The other ingredients are all beautifully displayed in little plates around the chafing pot. Soon after the alcohol has been lit and as soon as the water or soup has started boiling, everyone must pitch in with chopsticks and fill the pot with both meat and vegetables, all finely sliced and in small pieces. Cover and bring the contents to boiling again. Then remove the cover and plunge in. A good eater beats a raw egg in his own bowl and spoons some of the boiling hot soup into the bowl over the egg. The egg may save you from burning your tongue.

Since it is very difficult in this country to get the centrally heated pots as described, you use as substitute a hot-plate electric stove and put a big pot on top of it, or better still use the old-style American chafing dish to do the cooking.

In Cantonese, chafing pots are called *ta-pin-lou,* which means to cook the slices from the side dishes on the table.

Some so-called pots are either large-bowl dishes or pots cooked over the kitchen range and brought to the table without any fire. Recipes Nos. 16.1 and 2 are real chafing pots. Nos. 16.3-5 are cooked in the kitchen.

16.1. Chrysanthemum Chafing Pot

Chrysanthemum chafing pot requires the second type of chafing pot, the wide flat basin with alcohol cup underneath. In America, you can use an electric stove underneath a large pot or basin.

First ingredients to go into the pot:

6-8 cups water
2 t-sp. salt
1 tb-sp. lard

Main ingredients for the pot and their preparation:

1 big head of white chrysanthemum flower—Take off the petals and wash them clean.

1 lb. celery cabbage—Wash and cut into shreds.

⅓ lb. peastarch noodles—Fry in deep oil for 1 min. (If you cannot get peastarch noodles in Chinatown you can substitute with ½ lb. very fine egg noodles. Prepare the noodles in the same way.)

¼ lb. spinach—Wash clean and leave whole.

½ lb. pork tenderloin—Cut into flying-thin slices. (Because the cooking time is short.)

White meat of 1 spring chicken of about 2-3 lbs.—Cut into flying-thin slices also. (Save the other parts of the chicken for other chicken dishes.)

½ lb. fresh shrimps—Take off the shells, peel off the dark gritty line along the back, and slice into two slices along the back.

If the shrimps are big, slice again into thinner slices.

¼ lb. chicken's, duck's, or pig's liver—Also cut into 3 flying-thin slices.

4 pig's kidneys—Wash the kidneys and take off the outer thin skin. Cut off as many flying-thin slices as you can until you reach the central dark and white part, which should be thrown away.

½ lb. raw oysters without shell—Wash clean.

2 tb-sp. sherry

1 tb-sp. cornstarch

2 tb-sp. water

Divide each ingredient into two parts and place each part in a small plate. In the case of the meat, the chicken, the liver, the shrimps, etc., arrange the slices in symmetrical designs.

Mix the sherry, cornstarch, and water together and put a little of the mixture on each of all the non-vegetables.

Ingredients for sauce to be used during the eating:

⅓ cup soy sauce or shrimp sauce

Sometimes a beaten raw egg with 1 t-sp. soy sauce for the bowl of each person.

The cooking and the eating: Place the 20 small dishes on the dining table. After the guests have been seated, bring on the electric stove (since the other cannot be had in America) and the pot which already has boiling water, lard and salt. These are placed in the center of the table. Everyone then uses his chopsticks and helps put all the vegetables and noodles in (but not the chrysanthemum). When the soup boils again, each person helps himself from the big pot into his own plate or bowl. Now the hostess puts in the chrysanthemum. She may then add salt, for soy sauce is never put into the big pot. Sometimes we break a whole raw egg into our bowl and then pour hot soup over it; sometimes we beat the egg in the bowl before pouring hot soup over it; and sometimes we like to poach a couple of raw eggs in the big pot itself. This last process is now popularly known as "depth-charging."

Chafing pots are usually served from November to March.

16.2. Colorful Variety Chafing Pot

For this dish we prefer the first type of chafing pot, the one with the funnel through the center of the cooking basin, but here in America, where that type of chafing pot is also not to be had, we can use an electric stove and a large pot on top.

In Chinese this is *shi-chin* (*sub-gum*) or "Ten Varieties," since some or all of the following things go into this pot. They are mostly pre-cooked.

(1) Celery cabbage—1 lb. Cut across into shreds
(2) and (3) Red-cooked chicken and meat
    (A) ½ of a 3-4 lb. chicken
    (B) 1½ lbs. meat   (D) 6 cups water
    (C) 6 tb-sp. soy sauce   (E) 2 t-sp. salt

Put everything in a pot. Heat over big fire till boiling, then simmer for 1 hr. If the chicken is not tender, boil it first and then add the meat and boil for 1 hr. more. Then take out the chicken and chop into enough pieces to go around. Take out the meat and cut into 1-inch cubes. Keep the gravy for further use in this recipe.

(4) Peastarch noodles—⅛ lb. Put into a pot of boiling water, heat again until boiling, then simmer for ½ hr. Let it stand in water before using.

(5) Egg wraplings—3 beaten eggs

> ¼ lb. ground meat
> 1 tb-sp. soy sauce
> ½ t-sp. lard or oil

Mix the ground meat with soy sauce. Rub the entire surface of a skillet with the ½ t-sp. lard or oil. Put 1 tb-sp. of beaten egg into the skillet, then tip the skillet around to make the egg form a small flat cake. Then put 1 t-sp. ground meat with soy sauce on the egg cake but slightly off center, fold over the egg into a semicircle like an apple turnover, and press around the edge. Then take it out. It is best to put in the meat and turnover before the egg cake is entirely cooked. Make altogether about 8 to 10 wraplings.

(6) Winter bamboo shoots—¼ can. Cut into slices.

(7) Uncooked Smithfield, Virginia ham—¼ lb. Cut into slices.

(8) Fried bean curd—1 pint. Cut into 1-inch cubes. Fry them in deep vegetable oil until brown.

(9) Fish balls—10 to 12. See Recipe No. 10.10 on how to prepare them.

(10) Trepang—1 lb. This is a common ingredient in Chinese cooking. If you cannot get it in Chinatown (hoi-sham), substitute with fresh scallops or canned abalone. Cut into slices.

These ten varieties are all placed in the pot in many layers. The order of the layers from the bottom up is as follows: cabbage shreds; fried bean curd; red-cooked chicken and meat; peastarch noodles;

egg wraplings; trepang (or scallops, or canned abalone); ham and bamboo shoots; and fish balls. Spread the ham slices and the bamboo slices by overlapping each slice a little. Then drop the fish balls around on the top of the chafing pot.

Pour in the gravy saved from the cooking of the red-cooked chicken and meat. Cook the whole pot in the kitchen over medium fire for ⅓ hr. Then bring the pot to the dining table and continue to heat over the electric stove. Help yourself from the pot. From time to time add a little water to the pot to keep it from burning or from getting too dry.

16.3. The First-Rank Pot

Although this is called a pot, nothing is cooked on the table. Everything is cooked in the kitchen, but the food is served on the table in one big pot or in a big serving bowl.

There are two kinds of First-Rank Pots, the Red First-Rank Pot and the White First-Rank Pot.

A. The Red First-Rank Pot:

1 chicken, about 3-4 lbs.	2 cups boiling water
1 duck, about 4-5 lbs.	1½ cups soy sauce
1 pork shoulder, about 4-5 lbs.	½ cup sherry
1 doz. hard-boiled eggs, shelled	3-4 slices fresh ginger
⅛ lb. dried winter mushrooms	(if you can get it)
(Get in Chinatown. Optional)	1 t-sp. salt
3 cups water	1 tb-sp. sugar

Put the whole shoulder into a big heavy pot with 3 cups of cold water. Heat over a big fire till it boils and then simmer for 1 hr. Then put in the whole chicken and the whole duck. (If the chicken and the duck are not tender, cook them with the shoulder from the very beginning. In that case, use 5 cups of water instead of 3.) Then add 2 cups boiling water and the soy sauce, sherry, ginger, and salt. Simmer again for ½ hr. Now put in the hard-boiled shelled eggs and the mushrooms and cook again for ½ hr. Then add in the

179

sugar and cook again for 10 min. more. Test by pulling at the bones of the chicken and duck: if they separate from the meat easily, they are done; if not, cook longer up to ½ hr.

If you serve the dish in a big serving bowl, put the shoulder, chicken, and duck in toward the center of the bowl and put the eggs around them. Then spread the mushrooms on top.

This dish can be kept in the icebox for almost a week.

B. The White First-Rank Pot:

This is a more soupy pot and there is no soy sauce used.

1 chicken, about 3-4 lbs.	3 lbs. celery cabbage, cut across into 1½-inch strips
1 duck, about 4-5 lbs.	
1 pork shoulder, about 4-5 lbs.	1 doz. hard-boiled and shelled eggs
3 cups cold water	
13 cups boiling water	⅛ lb. dried winter mushrooms or fresh mushrooms (optional)
1 tb-sp. salt	
½ lb. Virginia ham	
¼ can winter bamboo shoots, sliced (optional)	

Put the whole shoulder into a big heavy pot with 3 cups of cold water. Heat over big fire until it boils and then simmer for 1 hr. Then put in the whole chicken and the whole duck. (If the chicken and the duck are not tender, cook them with the shoulder from the very beginning. In that case, use 5 cups of water instead of 3.) Add the 13 cups of boiling water and simmer for another ½ hr. Then put in the salt, ham, bamboo-shoot slices, celery cabbage, hard-boiled and shelled eggs, and the mushrooms and cook together for another ½ hr., or longer, until the bones of the chicken or the duck separate from the meat easily.

Serve in the original pot or in a big serving bowl. Put the celery cabbage at the bottom, then put the shoulder, the duck, and the chicken in toward the center of the bowl, then the eggs around them. Slice the Virginia ham into thin slices and place them on top with the mushrooms and the bamboo-shoot slices. Finally pour in as much soup as possible. You can serve the extra soup in another bowl.

Serve with a small cup of soy sauce and a small dish of salt, for those who desire a saltier taste. The Chinese usually like the soup as it is. The white-cooked meat and vegetable are usually eaten by dipping in soy sauce first.

This dish can be kept in the icebox for several days.

16.4. Rinsed Lamb

About the making and eating of this famous pot, see Recipe No. 7.4.

16.5. Huichou Pot

This pot is a wonderful surprise for those "bad children" who do not like to eat rice but like to eat everything else, because this dish is a complete meal in itself and needs no extra rice to go with it. It is not found in many places in China outside of the Huichou region in southern Anhwei, where is also my home town of Shihtai.

We do not do any cooking at the table for the Huichou Pot, but have everything done in the kitchen. It is also served in one big heaping pot with everything in it. The following is a list of the ingredients and how they are prepared:

(1) and (2) Red-cooked chicken and meat.

3 lbs. of pork, the bacon-cut with the skin on, cut in 2-3 inch cubes. About ½ lb. for each person or 2 or 3 pieces each.

1 hen about 4-5 lbs. Chop into 12 pieces with the bones on.

6 cups water

1 cup soy sauce

Boil the meat and the chicken together in the 6 cups of water in a heavy pot until boiling, and then simmer for 2 hrs. Take out the chicken and the pork, and keep the juice for further use in this recipe.

(3) Taro—1 lb. Get in Chinatown. Peel it and cut into slices about ¼ inch thick. Put the taro in with the red-cooked

chicken and meat during the last ⅓ hr. of their cooking in the pot.

(4) Dried bamboo shoots—⅓ lb. Put in a pot with 5 cups water. Heat until boiling, then turn to low fire and boil 3 hrs. Then throw away the water and cut off the tough parts of the bamboo shoots.

(5) Fried bean curd—1 pint. Get it in already fried pieces in Chinatown. The big ones are triangular in shape. If they have only the small ones, cubical in shape, get 12. If these are not to be had fried, then get the ordinary kind and fry them at home yourself.

(6) Egg wraplings

| 4 beaten eggs | 1 tb-sp. soy sauce |
| ⅓ lb. ground meat | ⅓ t-sp. lard |

Mix the ground meat with the soy sauce. On the preparation of egg wraplings, follow directions given for egg wraplings under recipe for Variety Chafing Pot, Recipe No. 16.2.

(7) Celery cabbage—3 lbs. Cut across into 2-inch-long sections. Wash clean.

(8) Peastarch noodles—⅓ lb. Get in Chinatown. Scald in boiling water and soak for 1 hr. Do not boil.

Now put these ingredients all in layers in the large pot in the following order from the bottom to the top: the cabbage; dried bamboo shoots; taro; fried bean curd; chicken and meat; egg wraplings; and peastarch noodles.

Add 2 t-sp. salt and then pour in all the juice saved from the cooking of the red-cooked chicken and meat. Cover the pot and heat with big fire. When it boils, turn to low fire and cook for 1 hr. Serve in the pot.

16.6. Sandy-Pot Bean Curd

This is another of those pots that are not cooked on the dining table, but in the kitchen. Therefore you can serve it in a very big bowl.

Fresh bean curd—2 pints	¼ lb. mushrooms, cut each into
Meat—1 lb., cut into slices	four slices
9 cups cold water	1 t-sp. salt
4 tb-sp. soy sauce	1 t-sp. taste powder
1 package frozen peas	

Cut the bean curd into pieces of about 2 inches by 1¼ inches by ¼ inch. Put into a big heavy pot with 6 cups of water. Use big fire and boil for ½ hr. Then pour out and throw away the water.

Add in the soy sauce, meat slices, frozen peas, mushrooms, salt, taste powder, and the remaining three cups of water. Use big fire again and cook till boiling, then simmer for only 10 min. more. However, this dish can be kept on the stove over a low fire until ready to serve.

This dish alone and rice can make a complete meal.

In China, a special chafing pot made by mixing sand and cast iron and cast very thin is used to cook bean curd this way. Hence the name "Sandy-Pot Bean Curd."

C H A P T E R   1 7

SWEET THINGS

Everybody likes to have a sweet thing, if it is nice, and the Chinese are no exceptions. But you will never appreciate Chinese sweet things right unless you understand their place in Chinese life. There is no conception of "dessert" as the end part of lunch or dinner and there is no idea of "cereal" at a breakfast. It is true that we sometimes eat congee or thin boiled rice, at breakfast, but to put sugar and milk in it—eawk! No, sweet things have their places. They come at intervals for a change in a many-coursed dinner, or are eaten between meals to break up the monotony of not eating.

Sweet things may be divided roughly into four classes: 1. sweet dishes, 2. sweet *tien-hsin*, which is mostly pastry, 3. dried or preserved fruits or nuts, and 4. fresh fruits. A sweet dish is usually a make-up combination of things which is served as a course in a banquet, especially when it has a lot of liquid, and has to be eaten with a spoon, such as Orange Soup *Yüan-hsiao*. When it is in simple handy pieces, such as sesame-sprinkled hot biscuit with sugar stuffing, which you can eat with your hand and tea, it is *tien-hsin*. There is no sharp line between the two. For instance, Puree-of-Pea "Cakes" (Recipe No. 17.4) are just too messy to be eaten with hand and just too discrete to be eaten with a spoon and so are eaten with tiny Chinese dessert forks or with toothpicks. The recipes I am going to give below are mostly sweet dishes. I shall call them "dessert" for short when I forget what I said about their not being really desserts. As for sweet *tien-hsin*, there are so many kinds that it would take another book to tell about them, and I have to limit myself to a couple of recipes only. As for dried and fresh fruits, etc., you had better buy them in Chinatown than try to make them. For bread and pastry, see Chapter 20.

17.1. Eight-Jewel Rice Pudding

The Eight-Jewel Rice Pudding is a major Chinese dessert. Lovers of sweet things think it worth the time and trouble it takes to make it.

1 lb. good glutinous rice	½ cup sugar
2 plus 1 cups of water	Various honey-preserved fruits

Simmer the glutinous rice in 2 cups of water until the rice is slightly soft. Add the sugar with another cup of water and simmer for 15 more min. On the bottom of a large bowl, arrange honey-preserved fruits (in China dried fruits are used) of various colors to make a colorful pattern. Carefully pour the rice on top. (Sometimes puree of Chinese red beans or mashed Chinese white (flat) beans may be put between the preserved fruit and the rice. Cf. Recipes Nos. 17.4 and 17.5.) Rest the bowl on a steaming stand so that it will always be above water and steam for 3 hrs. in a large covered pot until the rice is very soft. Take the bowl out of the pot, hold the top of a large plate against the glutinous rice, invert both plate and bowl in one decisive movement. If successful, you can remove the bowl, and the pudding with the fruit design will come out on top. If not—well, you had better be! Serve hot.

This dessert may be kept in the refrigerator for many days and served after resteaming for more than an hour (to make sure that the pudding will be hot throughout).

17.2. Flowing Walnut Pudding

½ lb. walnut meat	⅔ cup rice flour
4 cups water	⅓ lb. brown sugar

Grind the walnut meat twice until it is very fine. Add 3 cups of boiling water and simmer for ½ hr. in a pot. With a piece of clean gauze, strain and discard the residue. Add the sugar, rice flour, and another 1 cup of water to the strained milk, and mix well. Heat to boiling while stirring constantly to avoid burning. Then simmer over very low fire for 3 min. Serve hot.

Any leftovers may be reheated before serving. However, extremely low fire has to be used to avoid burning at the bottom.

In some Chinese localities, people like this pudding so thin that it is almost a drink.

17.3. Almond Junket

In China, this dessert is made as follows: crush and grind dried almond to very fine. Boil with water and strain with a piece of cloth. The strained milk is mixed with agar agar, or gelatin, heated to boiling again, and then cooled to a jelly, which is cut into small pieces and served with cold sweetened water.

In this country, the dried almonds needed are not easily obtainable. The following recipe, however, may be conveniently used to get a dessert that looks and tastes very much like the real almond junket.

1 cup evaporated milk	1 small envelope plain
3 cups water	gelatin powder
5 tb-sp. sugar	3 t-sp. almond extract

Heat the evaporated milk, sugar, and water together to about 60-70 degrees Centigrade. Mix the gelatin powder with about 3 tb-sp. cold water and add to the hot liquid. Stir until the gelatin dissolves completely. Cool, add the almond extract, and put in refrigerator. After 3-4 hours, the whole thing will set into a jelly. Cut into rhombohedrons or any nice shape, add 1 cup of cold sweetened water and serve.

17.4. Puree-of-Peas Cake

½ lb. dried green peas (buy the skinned soup peas)
¾ cup sugar
2¼ cups water
2 tb-sp. cornstarch

Simmer the peas in 2 cups of water for 1½ hrs. Add in the sugar, followed by a mixture of the water and the cornstarch. Heat to boiling and stir. Cool in a tray, put into a refrigerator until it sets. Serve in 1-inch cubes.

17.5. Puree-of-Peas Pudding

½ lb. dried green peas
2 cups water

¼ cup sugar
2 tb-sp. lard

Simmer the peas with the water for 1½ hrs. By then the peas will have turned into a puree. Add in the sugar. Mix well.

Heat the lard in a skillet till hot. Add in the pureed peas, stir until the mixture becomes hot, and serve. (The Chinese like to serve sweet dishes hot instead of cold.)

(If the puree of peas has been left standing too long and has dried some, mix with a little water before frying with the lard. Otherwise it is very easily burned.)

17.6. Orange Soup with *Yüan-hsiao*

5 medium oranges, preferably Florida if in season
½ lb. glutinous rice flour (not ordinary rice flour or rice starch)
6½ cups water
½ cup sugar

Cut each orange into halves. With a sharp spoon take the pulps out (as you used to eat your orange at breakfast) and keep them in a bowl.

To make *yüan-hsiao,* knead the glutinous rice flour with ⅓ cup hot (not boiling) water. Then make into globules of about ⅜ inch in diameter. These are the *yüan-hsiao.* Boil 6 cups of water, put in the *yüan-hsiao* and continue boiling over big fire for 5 min. or until they turn very soft. Add in ½ cup sugar and the orange juice, heat to boiling again, and serve.

17.7. Steamed Jujube Cake

This dessert is very popular in southern Kiangsu.

- ½ lb. dried jujubes (a kind of date-like fruit with red skin, sometimes found in Chinatown under the name of *hung-tsou*)
- ½ lb. glutinous rice flour (Ordinary rice flour cannot be used because it turns hard when steamed).

Boil the jujubes for 1 hr. or long enough to remove the skin and the stones.

Knead the jujube meat with the glutinous rice flour. (If you prefer to put in some stuffing to make a pie out of the cake, refer to the recipe for *yüan-hsiao* with stuffing.)

Make the dough into any fancy forms of cakes by using biscuit molds. But they had better be as thick as biscuits. The size should be a little larger than a macaroon and smaller than a hot biscuit. (In China, wooden patterns specially designed for this purpose are used.) Shake the cakes out of the mold, gently of course, and lay them on steaming tiers with bamboo leaves or rush below (to avoid sticking) and steam for 5 min. over a big fire. The cakes should get very soft but keep their shapes.

CHAPTER 18

RICE

Rice is the main thing to eat in China, so much so that when we say *ch'ih-fan*, "eat rice," we mean to eat a meal. In the northern provinces, people eat much more wheat and other grain as their staple food, but to have white-grained rice to eat still connotes something very desirable. In some provinces, as we have seen, dry boiled rice is eaten at three meals a day.

There are two kinds of eating rice and a special kind of dessert rice. The last is a very glutinous kind of short-grained white opaque rice called *no-mi*, good for making Chinese desserts, either ground or boiled. (In Chinatown it's pronounced *"no-mai."*) Eating rice, or *hsien-mi* in Chinese, has more translucent grains. It has two kinds, a long-grained kind and an oval-grained kind. The first is easier to cook and is liked by more people. The second is more sticky— I call it "sticky" so as not to get it mixed up with the opaque kind of real glutinous rice—and harder to cook, because during cooking a sticky coating is formed over each grain, so that it is hard for any more water to go in. That is why sometimes in American cooking the first coating has to be washed away before continuing cooking. Steaming (see below) is also a good way to cook the oval-grained rice. In Japan, the usual eating rice is oval-grained.

The long-grained rice is much easier to cook. In China it is liked better than the oval-grained kind. In late years, such rice from Indo-China, known as Saigon rice, has been eaten in the coastal provinces, when rice cannot come from the interior. Due to poor inside transportation, inland rice often could not compete with the imported. In this country, the southern states have lately grown some very good long-grained rice and have supplied the eating rice of the Chinese restaurants. Good brands, from Texas, South

189

Carolina, Louisiana, etc., are sold in Chinatown or general markets.

There are two forms of rice as finished food, dry rice, and thin rice. Dry rice or rice proper is the usual main food of a meal and is made by boiling or steaming. Thin rice, called *chuk* in Cantonese, called *congee* by English-speaking people in the Orient, is made by boiling very little rice in a great deal of water. It is used in Kiangsu and Chekiang when it is very early in the morning, in Canton and America very late at night, in any place when it is very early or very late in one's life, or at any time when one does not feel hungry or strong enough to eat dry boiled rice.

18.1   Boiled Rice

Rice as *fan* can be boiled or steamed. Oval-grained rice had better be steamed, but either method can be used for either kind of grain. There is a great variation in personal preference as to the hardness or softness of rice desired. The rice in Chinese restaurants is much harder than is found in most parts of China. In any event, properly cooked rice should be dry and uniform in texture. Even the softest rice should have all moisture completely absorbed into each grain and not left between the grains. (This does not, of course, apply to congee.) Note the absence of salt in the recipes for plain rice.

(a) With long-grained rice
1 cup rice
1½-2 cups water (depending on softness desired)

Wash the rice and drain off water. Add 1½-2 cups clear water and boil over big fire while stirring occasionally to prevent sticking and burning. (Sticking causes burning.) Some add rice after boiling starts, but it makes no difference. Turn to very low fire after boiling for 5 min. or as soon as most of the visible water has been boiled off. Cover and cook for 20 min. or until a sample is soft and dry and gives no wet, shining appearance.

(b) With oval-grained rice

Same procedure as in (a) except for two things. One is that the water should be two cups instead of 2¾ for each cup of rice. The other is that after the first 15 minutes of simmering, the rice should be overturned with a ladle or a slice to help more uniform cooking, because the sticky coatings tend to keep the water from seeping through evenly. Put on lid and cook over low fire for 15 more min.

18.2. Steamed Rice: Changsha Style

This is dry-steamed rice and is commonly used in many places besides Changsha, capital of the rice-bowl province. Steamed rice usually has a loose, pleasant texture.

(a) With long-grained rice

        1 cup rice   2-3 cups water

Wash rice and drain off water. Add 2-3 cups of clear water and boil for 3 minutes of boiling time. Drain off the rice soup (which is often used as a drink served individually, like thin congee[1]). Put rice on steaming tier and steam for 30 min.

(b) With oval-grained rice

        1 cup rice   3-4 cups water

Wash rice and drain off water. Add 3-4 cups clear water and boil for 3 minutes of boiling time, stirring occasionally to prevent burning. Drain off rice soup and steam rice on steaming tier for 45 min.

18.3. Steamed Rice: Cantonese Style

This rice is steamed in a bowl instead of on a tier. With the same amount of rice and water, proceed as in the Dry-Steamed Rice in the preceding recipe. Boil for 5 min. Then, instead of steaming the rice on a tier, put the half-cooked rice in individual serving bowls

---

[1] This was my favorite drink when I lunched at school in Changsha, because all dishes in Changsha tasted so hot.—Rulan.

(but only ⅞ full to allow for expansion) and steam over medium fire for 1-1½ hours. Be sure to have enough steaming water, but don't let it get directly into the bowls.

18.4. White Congee

The best rice for congee is a kind of semi-glutinous fragrant rice grown in the Wusih region in lower Kiangsu Province. Failing that, ordinary oval-grained rice may be used.

> ⅓ cup rice   3-4 cups water
> A pinch of bicarbonate of soda (for quick softening)

Wash rice and drain off water. Put rice in 3 cups of clear water and bring to boil. Then simmer until whole thing becomes a nearly uniform mess like thin oatmeal. It is best eaten or sipped when so hot that you have to cool it by making a sipping noise as you shovel it over the edge of the bowl into your mouth with a pair of chopsticks. Most Americans and even Chinese who have sat at the same table with Americans cannot bring themselves to do this when other Americans are present. In that case, eat your congee with a spoon, as every baby does in China.

18.5. Egg Stirs Rice

The Chinese do not always cook just enough rice for one meal. There is usually a lot of leftover rice, which can be steamed or simmered again with a little water added and be as good as newly cooked, or better, if the first cooking was not thorough. One favorite way to use leftover rice is to stir-fry it with other materials, typically with eggs. Actually, we seldom boil rice afresh just for making Stirred Rice with various things, though, like the Triple-Shred Soup (Recipe No. 15.11.A), we often look forward to it while boiling fresh rice.

> 9 cups leftover boiled or   2 t-sp. salt
>   steamed rice   2 scallions chopped
> 8 eggs beaten   3 heaping tb-sp. lard

Steam the rice on a steaming tier over medium fire for 5 to 10 min., depending upon the softness of the rice you start with. If a tier or a double boiler with perforated inside bottom is not handy, simmer the rice with 1 cup of water for about 15 min. until the water is all evaporated or absorbed.

Mix the chopped scallion and 1 t-sp. salt in the beaten eggs.

Heat the lard in a skillet over big fire till hot and put in the eggs. Stir over continued big fire for ½ min. Then put in the rice that has just been boiled over and softened up and add 1 t-sp. salt. Stir evenly for 2 more min. The rice can be kept in the oven for a few minutes before serving.

Since there are eggs and fat, this form of rice is a complete meal without any accompanying dishes, especially if eaten with "Soup for the Gods" (Recipe No. 15.0) and a little relish, such as sauce-pickled cucumbers. It is a most convenient make-up meal for some-one who has missed a meal from getting up or coming home late. On Chinese trains "Flied Lice with Eggs" sells almost as fast as sandwiches on American trains.

18.6. Meat Shreds Stir Rice

Here is one of the few dishes in which beef is more commonly used than pork, though pork is not at all rare.

9 cups leftover boiled or steamed rice	2 tb-sp. soy sauce
	2 heaping tb-sp. lard
½ lb. beef or pork shreds	1 t-sp. salt

One or more of the following:

        3 onions shredded,
    or 3 sweet peppers, shredded,
    or 1 lb. celery cabbage,
    or 1 cup red-in-snow (cut out salt, if used)

Steam or simmer the rice as in the preceding recipe. Use 1 heap-ing tb-sp. of the lard and stir the rice in a skillet over big fire for 1-2 min. Take out the rice.

Mix the meat shreds with the soy sauce.

Heat the lard in a skillet over big fire till hot. Put in the meat shreds and stir for 1 min. Then put in the onions or one of the other alternatives, add in the salt, and stir for 2 min. Take out.

Put the rice on a serving plate. Then put the cooked meat shreds, etc., over the rice. This is also suitable for serving one person.

18.7. Variety Stirs Rice

Variety of the following kind is common in Canton.

9 cups leftover boiled or steamed rice	2 oz. almonds
2 tb-sp. raisins	2 oz. dried or ¼ lb. fresh shrimps
2 oz. Smithfield, Virginia ham, chopped	2-3 scallions, chopped
	2 heaping tb-sp. lard
2 oz. walnuts	2 tb-sp. soy sauce
	¼ t-sp. salt

Steam or simmer the rice as in Recipe No. 18.5.

Soak the walnuts and the almonds in enough boiling water to cover. Peel off skins when they can come off.

Heat shrimps in ¼ cup of water over big fire and stop as soon as it starts to boil. Pour soup away (for possible use in other dishes). If fresh shrimps are used, take off the shells and the dark gritty lines along the backs and cut each into four pieces.

Heat the lard over big fire in a skillet. If you use fresh shrimps, put into skillet and stir for 1 min. Then add the raisins, ham, nuts, and scallions, and stir for 1 min. more. Then add in the soy sauce, salt, and rice, and stir for 2 more min. If dried shrimps are used, the time for putting them into the skillet is the same as for the raisins, ham, etc., instead of 1 min. ahead.

This may be kept in the oven before serving.

C H A P T E R   1 9

NOODLES

In the northern provinces, wheat is eaten more than rice as the staple food. When it is eaten dry, it is in the form of *man-t'ou,* or steamed raised buns. When it is eaten wet, it is in the form of *mien,* or unraised noodles. In the central and southern provinces, noodles are occasionally eaten as the main food, as for instance at birthday parties, but usually as a between-meal refreshment.

There are noodles and noodles. They may be hand-swung, machine cut, regular-dried, or fine-dried. A good northern cook, or even a cooking maid, knows how to swing noodles by hand. *Hse* takes a roll of dough and swings it out by holding one end in each hand until it stretches to five or six feet long. *Hse* doubles it up and, holding the middle point, which now becomes one end, in one hand and the original two ends in the other, rolls the middle portion over a board with dry flour on it and swings out the same length (and half the thickness) as before. *Hse* doubles the two branches into four and repeats the same process until finally *hse* gets 32, 64, 128 . . . noodles, each five or six feet long, the number depending on how skillful the swinger is at swinging noodles and how thick or thin *hse* wants the noodles. The two thick ends are of course to be cut off. Swung-noodles, because of the stretching and the rolling, have a feel and texture that cut-noodles lack. Unfortunately noodle-swinging is a difficult art. What often happens is like this. You start swinging your dough. Before you reach 32, some of your noodles begin to break down on you. You get mad and make a mess of the dough. You start again, but don't dare go beyond 16. So you eat your door-bolt-thick noodles, which are nice, but more like bars of dough than noodles.

That's why most people eat cut noodles. You can roll dough into thin sheets and then cut them into noodles by hand, but machine-cut noodles are very common in China. They can be as thin as you like them. They may vary between about $\frac{1}{16}$ and $\frac{1}{8}$ inch.

Except in some very large Chinatowns in this country, fresh noodles, even machine-cut, are hard to get. So you have to depend mostly on dried noodles sold in packages. These can be got both in Chinatown and at any American market. American noodles are usually egg noodles. Some people prefer the purer wheat flavor of plain Chinese noodles, especially if good soup is used. The texture of plain noodles is also smoother.

A variety of dried noodles are the fine dried noodles, which are best in Fukien Province but very rare in this country. They are not unlike vermicelli, but are softer when boiled. They are round and white and slightly salted. When boiled they are very tender and easy to digest. That's why Fukien fine dried noodles, or *kua-mien* in Chinese, remind many people of the pleasures of being slightly sick.

The normal way of treating noodles is to boil them first. When they are further stir-fried with other things (sometimes partly browned), then it is *ch'ao-mien,* or *chow mein* in English. The common dry and brittle kind of chow mein found in restaurants in America is very little known in China. It is found in some places in Canton and Hongkong and mostly for foreigners to eat. When the American kind of *chow mein* meets stir-fried soft noodles in the same dish, then it is that famous American dish *"Chow Mein* with Noodles,"* a sign I have seen in Seattle, Washington, and Washington, D.C. Since *chow mein* already means "fried noodles," it proves my statement above that there are noodles and noodles.

Since regular dried noodles are the only kind easily obtained here, the recipes are given for this kind. If you should get any freshly cut noodles or by chance have learned to swing noodles, multiply the weight needed by two and decrease the boiling time to $\frac{2}{3}$ that given in the recipe.

The noodle recipes which we can conveniently use may be divided into soup noodles, pot noodles, hot-gravy noodles, cold-gravy noodles, and stirred noodles.

19.1. Soup Noodles

A bowl of soup noodles may serve as a whole meal if there is enough in a bowl or if they can be replenished after one bowl is finished. As a between-meal refreshment, one eats a relatively small amount. Soup noodles consist of (1) noodles, of course, (2) a soup, and usually (3) some garnishes or things that go with the noodles that give them the dish-name.

(1) **Noodles**—For a complete meal to serve six, take:

1 lb. dried noodles   5 cups water

Put in the noodles after the water starts boiling and boil for 10 min. for egg noodles and 20 min. for Chinese dried noodles. Pour off the water and rinse the noodles once with cold water.

(2) The soup may simply be the original soup of the garnishes or usually quite separate. In restaurants, "high soup" or the general stock from the common large pot in which meat and chicken have been boiled is often used. Soup for the Gods (Recipe No. 15.0) will make a good plain soup. A small pinch of taste-powder can always help out.

The two best-liked soups for soup noodles are Clear Chicken Soup (from Recipe No. 15.19) and the juice of Red-Cooked Meat (from Recipes Nos. 1.1., 1.2, etc.). When red-cooked juices are used, the soup should be $\frac{1}{3}$ juice and $\frac{2}{3}$ water. One of the most famous soup noodles is the Chinkiang White Soup Noodles in which the soup is from chicken bones boiled so long that the soup becomes milky white.

Almost any heavy soup is good, but light soups are usually uninteresting, such as winter melon soup, bean curd soup, sour-and-hot soup.

The *Yakko Mein* of Chinese restaurants in America is usually soup noodles with high soup of some degree of strength. *Yakko Mein*, or *i-ko mien*, means "an order of noodles."

(3) If there are garnishes, they give the noodles their name,

though *Yakko Mein* sometimes has a couple of slices of pork thrown in without adding any more to the name than "an order of." The following are some common names.

(a) With Celery Cabbage and Meat Shreds.—Follow all directions for Celery Cabbage and Meat Shreds Soup, Recipe No. 15.10. Except: Double the amount of each ingredient (to serve 6). Put the cooked and rinsed noodles in the hot soup before serving.

(b) With Ham and Chicken Shreds.—½ lb. Smithfield, Virginia ham boiled or steamed. 1 lb. clear-simmered chicken meat. 9 cups clear chicken soup.

Cut ham and chicken into shreds. Heat soup to boiling. Put the soaked and rinsed noodles in the hot soup and lay the ham and chicken shreds on top before serving.

(c) With Red-in-Snow.—If you have no appetite for supper, few things will make you feel happier inside than a bowl of Hot Soup Noodles with Red-in-Snow. To serve 6, use ½ lb. red-in-snow (salted mustard green) and water or diluted soup as in (b). Do not use soy sauce or salt. Fresh-water shrimp meat will enhance them greatly but ordinary (salt-water) shrimps are not so wonderful.

19.2. Pot Noodles

Pot noodles, or *Wo-min* in Cantonese, are glorified soup noodles served together in a big tureen, while ordinary soup noodles are usually served in individual bowls. The glorification consists in laying on top of the soup noodles ham slices, chicken slices, pork slices, fried fish tripe, shrimps, winter bamboo-shoot slices, *kaaits'oi* greens, mushroom slices, tender pea pods, etc., etc. Since only a little of a large number of things is used, it is not a very practical thing to make at home unless you happen to have some such leftovers. It is more of a restaurant food. The quality of the dish depends more upon how good a stock is used for the soup than the top glories. In its most complete form, it is called "Yangchow *Wo-Min*, Cantonese Style." [1]

---

[1] Cf. "Boston Baked Beans, New York Style."

19.3. Stirred Noodles

Stirred noodles are the real *ch'ao-mien* of China. We can't call this chow mein any more, since chow mein as an English term means the dry brittle kind of noodles so little known in China. Like soup noodles, stirred noodles get their dish names from the things that go with them.

The first part of cooking the noodles is similar to that of soup noodles. Use

1 lb. dried noodles   5 cups water   6 tb-sp. vegetable oil

Put the noodles in the water when it starts to boil. Boil for 10 min. for egg noodles or 20 min. for Chinese dried noodles. Then drain off the water and rinse once more with cold water.

Heat the vegetable oil in a big skillet over big fire. Divide the noodles into 6 portions. Roll up each portion like a shredded-wheat biscuit, and put it in the skillet. Fry till the outside is slightly browned but the inside still soft. Put in a serving pan and keep in the oven while preparing the accompaniment.

(a) With Meat Shreds:

        1 lb. pork chop shreds   2 heaping tb-sp. lard or
        ½ bunch celery   same amount of oil
        ½ lb. fresh shrimps   4 tb-sp. soy sauce
        ¼ lb. fresh mushrooms   1 t-sp. salt
        3-4 scallions or 1 onion   1 tb-sp. cornstarch
                        1 cup water

Cut the celery across obliquely into shreds 1 inch long. Cut mushrooms into slices of about ⅛ inch thick. Cut the scallions or onion into 1-inch-long shreds.

Shell the shrimps. Cut from the back into two slices. Then take out the dark gritty line at the back.

Heat the lard or oil in a skillet over big fire. When it is hot, put in the meat shreds and shrimps. Stir for 1 min. Then put in the mushrooms, celery, scallions or onion, soy sauce, and salt. Stir for 3 more min.

Mix the cornstarch with water. Put it also in the skillet and cook until the juice is translucent. Pour this on top of the noodles just before serving.

For the other accompaniments, the ingredients are the same as the above except that the meat and shrimps may be replaced by such materials as:

(b) Beef Shreds
(c) Chicken Shreds
(d) Ham Shreds
(e) Ten Varieties, which may be anything so long as they taste Chinese.

Stirred Noodles, because of their being richer than soup noodles, are often eaten in smaller quantities than full meals and are eaten with some other light soup, or in the case of between-meal refreshments, with tea. Some like to add vinegar to stirred noodles before eating.

19.4. Crossing-the-Bridge Noodles

The term "crossing-the-bridge" is not to suggest a suspension bridge hanging from noodles. The idea is rather that you are served with a dish of accompaniment which you pour on your portion of half-wet noodles. This pouring is the act of "crossing-the-bridge." The term is used in the Shanghai region. In the northern provinces, this dish is called "make-gravy noodles." "Crossing-the-bridge" noodles differ from soup noodles in that they have no drinking soup, and from stirred noodles in that they are not stir-fried after boiling. Instead of rinsing the noodles, just add 1 cup cold water at the end of boiling and take out the noodles.

A favorite form of "crossing-the-bridge" with many people is with crabs. Prepare the crab-meat as in Recipe No. 12.14. Serve the noodles and the crab-meat in separate dishes and let the person served enjoy the act of crossing the bridge with the crabs.

19.5. Cold-Mixed Noodles

Cold-mixing is always a pleasant thing to do in summer. The noodles are boiled as usual, then rinsed in cold water and kept in the icebox after the water has been drained off.

For the accompaniment, you can mix parts of any dish which is still good when cold. All dishes of pork or beef slices or shreds go well with cold noodles.

The dishes to be used are prepared as in their respective recipes, but be sure to use *vegetable oil* when it says "lard or vegetable oil," since lard freezes when cold.

Sometimes, we like to mix only with cool vegetables, as cucumber shreds, crushed radishes, etc., in addition to or instead of richer dishes.

Cold-mixed noodles are usually served unmixed so that each guest can cold-mix himself. Some like to mix in a lot of hot stuff in the cold mix-up.

19.6. Soy Jam Noodles

This is typical northern food. Many things go along with the noodles and the soy jam or hoisin sauce (item 10, p. 29).

(1) Noodles.—Boil as in previous recipes. Rinse with hot water after rinsing with cold water, if warm noodles are desired.

(2) Fried soy jam.—Use

     1½ lbs. pork meat

     ½ can *yünshi* soy jam (get in Chinatown)

     2 tb-sp. vegetable oil

Grind the pork meat. Heat the vegetable oil in a skillet over big fire until hot and put in the pork. Add in the soy jam soon after. Stir for 5 min. and take out. Put in a serving bowl.

(3) Other accompaniments.—

     1 small cucumber—Cut into thin shreds and serve in a plate.

> 1 bunch radishes—Also cut into shreds and serve in a plate
>
> ½ lb. raw pea sprouts—Wash very thoroughly and serve in a plate.
>
> ½ package frozen peas—Thaw out and serve in a plate.

Place all the accompaniments on the table with the bowl of soy jam. Serve each person with a bowl of noodles. Each will put in 1 tb-sp. soy jam for 1 bowl of noodles and also put in a little of each accompaniment. Mix well before eating.

How to Eat Noodles.—Noodles should not be wound on your chopsticks as you would wind spaghetti on a fork. It is also not good manners to put a great thick bunch of noodles into your mouth at one time. You can lift a dozen noodles or so with your chopsticks and shove the lifted part into your mouth and bite off, so that the remainder will ease back into your bowl. Instead of biting off, it is also all right to suck in the remainder, if not too long, and the accompanying noise is considered permissible and gives the right atmosphere to noodle-eating occasions. Be careful of course that the loose ends will not flip any of the juice onto your neighbor, especially when it is hot.

CHAPTER 20

PASTRY

If when I say "pastry" you have to think of the very sweet kind of French desserts, then you had better call it *tien-hsin*. But if you can remember that *tien-hsin* is usually plain or salty, is usually boiled or steamed, and sometimes eaten as the main part of a casual meal, then I will let you call it "pastry," which is easier for you to say.

In the widest sense, pastry includes breads, especially Steamed Bread (Recipe No. 20.1), which is one of the chief forms in which wheat-eating provinces eat wheat. For breakfast and for between-meal refreshments, there is more fancy work or stuffing. Two very common breakfast foods in China are sesame-sprinkled hot biscuits and puffed doughnuts. The making of these is so complicated that I have to leave their recipes to some other day. I shall content myself with some easy-to-make pastries. For sweet things, see Chapter 17.

20.1. Steamed Buns or *Man-t'ou*

While bread is baked in America, the Chinese eat baked wheat things, such as the sesame hot biscuit, only as breakfast things or light refreshments. The chief forms of wheat food in wheat-eating places are boiled or steamed instead of baked. Noodles are the chief boiled form and *man-t'ou* is the chief steamed form. To make *man-t'ou* we used to have to spend hours by the traditional method of raising the dough. But now, with the availability of fresh yeast, we need only to take:

3 heaping cups flour	1½ cups warm water from tap
1 tb-sp. sugar (optional)	1 cake or package fresh yeast

Melt the yeast (and sugar) in the warm water and pour in the flour, stirring (the Chinese use chopsticks) until the dough is formed

203

and does not stick too much to the mixing bowl. Spread some dry flour over a large chopping board and knead the dough on it for 3 or 4 min. Form a long shape and cut into 10 or 12 pieces. Make them round or whatever shape desired and place them 1 or 2 in. apart to allow expansion. Leave at room temperature for 40 min. or until they look well raised and feel light on the palm. Steam on a steaming tier over boiling water for 20 min. and the *man-t'ous* are done. If the tier has too large holes, a gauze placed over its bottom will give better support and make it easier to lift up the *man-t'ou* when done.

On Lotus Buns, see Rec. 9.9.

Variations: **Whole Wheat Buns** and **Wheat Germ Buns.** Even better tasting buns can be made by using 1¾ cups whole wheat flour (or wheat germ flour) and the other 1¼ cups white flour. With the mixed flours it is usually better to include the optional sugar. Two important differences are: (1) Lengthen the raising time to 1 hr., (2) the steaming time to 25 min.

Buns with the mixed flours taste so good that you don't feel the need of using butter or other enrichment and are thus easy on the calories.

Once properly steamed, all forms of *man-t'ou* and its variations can be refrigerated and re-steamed as needed, and will taste the same as if freshly made. A plastic bag will keep the *man-t'ou* from becoming dry.

20.2. Steamed Rolls and Fancy Rolls

When the dough is rolled, after being made flat, the result is often a roll. As everyday proletarian grain food, steamed bread as described above or simple one-fold rolls are eaten. For more elaborate dinners or as an incidental part of a meal, Fancy Rolls are really very simple to make, as you shall see below.

5 cups flour	1 t-sp. salt
2 cups lukewarm water	2 t-sp. vegetable oil
1 cake of fresh yeast	

Melt the yeast in the warm water and use it to knead the flour into dough as with Steamed Buns. Let stand and raise as before.

FIG. 6. FANCY ROLLS

When raised to about 4 times original size, divide dough into two halves and roll each half into a flat piece about 15 inches across. Use about 2 tb-sp. dusting flour to prevent sticking during rolling.

Rub half of the 1 t-sp. salt and of the 2 t-sp. vegetable oil on the surface of each piece and roll it up like a carpet before dancing. This operation will slightly lengthen the dough, so that the resulting long roll will now be about 18 inches. Cut it into 10 equal sections. Press one-third the way down on the middle of each section with a chopstick or the broad back of a chopping knife parallel with the original cutting. The result is a Fancy Roll dough.

Put aside for 10 min. and steam as with Steamed Buns.

Man-t'ou and Fancy Rolls make perfect complements to Red-Cooked Meat (Chapter 1).

20.3. Stuffed (Steamed) Buns or *Pao-tzŭ*

When *man-t'ou*, or Steamed Buns, is filled with stuffing, then it is *pao-tzŭ*. In some central dialects, the stuffed kind is also called *man-t'ou*, prefixed by the name of the stuffing. While the unstuffed bread serves often as the main part of a meal, accompanied by dishes, the stuffed kind is usually eaten at breakfast or as between-meal refreshments. The making of the bread part is the same as with *man-t'ou*.

Treat the flour as in Recipe No. 20.1. After the first raising, divide

205

the dough into 20 parts and roll them with a rolling pin into discs about 3 inches across.

There are many kinds of stuffing, salty or sweet.

A. Salty Stuffings.—

1 lb. ground pork chop, medium fineness	1 t-sp. sugar
	2 t-sp. salt
2 lb. celery cabbage	1 scallion chopped very fine
2 tb-sp. soy sauce	1 tb-sp. sesame oil or salad oil

Chop the celery cabbage very fine and squeeze most of its liquid off by straining hard in dry cloth.

Mix thoroughly the chopped pork, the chopped celery cabbage, and all the seasonings. This is cabbage-meat stuffing.

Variations.—Substitution of shrimp-meat for one-third of the meat; leaving out the celery cabbage, which will result in a smaller, harder, but more juicy stuffing; substitution of mutton for pork, with the addition of 3 slices of ginger chopped fine and addition of one more scallion.

Crab-meat, red-cooked meat, roast pork, chicken may also be used.

Vegetable stuffing may also be used. Spinach and leek are often used, in which case more sesame oil will be needed.

B. Sweet Stuffings.—

⅛ lb. walnut, ground fine

⅛ lb. almond, ground fine

⅛ lb. sesame seeds, roasted in a frying pan over medium fire for 1 or 2 min., ground or crushed

Some dozen kernels of melon seeds

½ cup sugar

1 tb-sp. lard

20 cubelets of fat pork, one in each *pao-tzŭ* (optional)

Mix the ground ingredients with the lard and divide into 20 stuffings.

A favorite form of sweet stuffing is puree of red beans, a kind of beans which tastes better and is harder to get than kidney beans. Mashed jujubes, made by boiling, skinning, and mashing dried jujubes, will make a good principal or partial stuffing. White or brown sugar alone will also make a good stuffing.

When your stuffing is ready, place one of the prepared pieces of dough on the palm of your left hand and put a portion, 1-2 tb-sp., of the stuffing in its center. With the fingers of your right hand, turn up the rim bit by bit to wrap around the stuffing, until only a small opening is left at top center. Close this top by pinching the edges together.

Steam the same way as with Recipe No. 20.1 for *man-t'ou.*

If both salty and sweet stuffings are used on the same day, it is usual to mark each sweet one with a red dot.

A form of Stuffed Bread famous in Chinkiang [1] is made with pork without the cabbage and wrapped in unraised dough. When fresh-water crab-meat is used as stuffing in this form of Stuffed Bread, then it is food for thought of home.

Leftover stuffed bread may be reheated by steaming or by shallow-frying. The latter tastes better but is too rich to serve as the main part of a meal, as the original steamed form can be.

20.4.A. New Year Dumplings or *Yüan-Hsiao*

Yüan-hsiao is a kind of boiled stuffed dumpling. The phrase really means the after-New-Year festival, occurring at full moon, or the fifteenth of the first month on the old calendar, when fancy lanterns are lit in homes and on the streets.

It seems funny how people everywhere like to eat time. In France, they eat *feeveoclock.* In Wenchow and Canton, they eat daybreak, they eat late-afternoon, and when not? And everywhere in China they eat the Festive Night *Yüan-hsiao.* We ordinarily tell children who like to have parties all the time, "You can't have Mid-

[1] No, my dear, my hometown Changchow makes better unraised *man-t'ou* than Chinkiang. I will never acquiesce when you call it Chinkiang *man-t'ou.* —Y. R. C.

Autumn every day and *yüan-hsiao* every night," but actually even grown-ups like the dumplings so well that they eat them all the year round. So you *can* have *yüan-hsiao* every night.[1]

Yüan-hsiao makes a good impromptu refreshment for drop-in callers not staying for a meal. It is also a favorite form of midnight snack, if you sleep well.

Yüan-hsiao differs from *pao-tzŭ* in several ways. A *yüan-hsiao* is made of rice flour instead of wheat flour. It always has sweet stuffing. It is boiled instead of steamed. Its shell is rolled on instead of wrapped on: in other words, you have your stuffing in place before you have anything to stuff it into.

For a typical recipe, use as shell:

1 lb. glutinous rice flour (ground from imported Mexican glutinous rice, sold in Chinatown as *no-mai-fan*[2])

For stuffing, use:

⅛ lb. walnut, ground fine
⅛ lb. almond, ground fine
⅛ lb. sesame, roasted in a pan over medium fire for 1 or 2 min. and ground or crushed
Some dozen kernels of watermelon seeds
½ cup sugar
1 tb-sp. lard

Mix the ground ingredients with the lard and roll the mixture into small balls, about ½ inch across.

Now for the rolling process, which used to fascinate us children as we watched the grown-ups do it and let saliva flow out of our open mouths. They took a shallow bamboo winnowing basket about 2 feet wide, but you take a large platter or a serving tray.

[1] The Mid-Autumn Moon Cake, by the way, can often be bought in Chinatown off season.

[2] When you go to Chinatown, be careful to say *fan* "flour" with a short *a* and a high rising tone. If you use a long *aa* and a low tone, it would mean "boiled rice."—Y. R. C.

Spread a layer of the dry glutinous rice flour to about ⅛-inch thick. Wet your stuffing balls by sprinkling enough water to wet them all around. Lay them on the tray of flour and shake the tray so as to have the flour stick to the sides of the stuffing. A skillful roller seems to move the tray in such a way that the balls roll on the flour by inertia, that is, by staying put when the tray shifts this way and that under them. But it is sometimes less work if you just tip the tray a little back and forth, so as to let the balls roll down grade. A beginner should practice over a table instead of over the floor.

When the layer of flour around the stuffing is so dry that no more flour will stick to it and the flour that you started with should be just about used up, then the Chinese way is simply to dip the whole winnowing basket into water. But since your tray will not drain, you do your second wetting of the balls by sprinkling. Then put on another layer of flour and roll as before. It takes four or five rollings to use up the 1 lb. of flour for the amount of stuffing given above, and then the *yüan-hsiao* is ready to boil. Do not wet after the last rolling, that is, until boiling.

Boil 6 cups of water. Drop the balls in after the boiling starts and boil for 5 min., counting from the time boiling starts again. The *yüan-hsiao* will then float to the surface. Now "drip water," which consists in adding 1 cup of cold water to the pot. This makes the skins hold. Boil for another 2 or 3 minutes. Serve in a bowl with some of the starchy soup. Two is too few, three is unlucky, so the minimum number to serve is four to a bowl. Any larger number is all right. Use of spoons is permissible.

20.4B. Soup Balls

Soup Balls or *T'ang-t'uan* does not mean any balls that are soup, such as billiard balls or eggs, but only kneaded rice flour with stuffing. A soup ball is very like *yüan-hsiao* and is often so-called, but differs from it in several ways. The flour is kneaded instead of rolled. Meat stuffing is used more often than sweet stuffing.

209

Finally, it is not particularly associated with a festival. For the skin, use:

½ lb. glutinous rice flour

¼ cup warm water. (The exact amount depends upon how dry or damp the flour is. Enough water should be used to make a soft dough.)

For the stuffing, use:

¼ lb. ground pork chop	1 scallion chopped very fine
2 tb-sp. soy sauce	1 tb-sp. cornstarch
½ t-sp. sugar	½ tb-sp. sesame oil or salad
¼ t-sp. sherry	oil

Mix the pork, soy sauce, sugar, sherry, scallion, cornstarch, and oil together.

Knead the flour with warm water into a dough and divide into 24 portions. Make them into hollow thimbles. Put 1 heaping t-sp. of the stuffing into each thimble, pinch the top together and roll the sealed thimble slightly so as to form a ball. Boil like *yüan-hsiao*. When you have boiled the balls until they float, then they are Boiled Balls. Serve hot. Use a spoon to receive the juice as you bite into each ball. The juice is too hot to get from the ball directly to the tongue and too good to spit out or to let leak into the soup, although it improves the soup.

As I said above, you can also use sweet stuffing. Do as with *yüan-hsiao*, Recipe No. 20.4. A, except that you knead instead of rolling.

20.4.C. Sweet-Olive *Yüan-hsiao*

Sweet-olive *Yüan-hsiao*, or unstuffed little *yüan-hsiao*, is only about half the size, that is, about ⅛ the volume, of stuffed or regular *yüan-hsiao*. It is simply a lot of glutinous rice flour globules boiled as a hot dessert. It is so called because sweet olive, or *Osmanthus fragrans*, is the usual flavoring used. Sweet olive is a tree with tiny four-petaled yellow or light-yellow flowers with a scent not quite like vanilla or lilac because it is richer and warmer. Actually this dessert may be boiled with any sweet flavor. It is of course very easy to make it with orange pulp in this country after you have got your glutinous rice flour.

20.5A. Soup *Hun-t'un* or Ramblings

I translate the Chinese name[1] *hun-t'un* as "Ramblings" since they differ from the ordinary neat-edged wraplings by having fluffy or rambling edges like the tails of a goldfish.

Get:

60-70 sheets of wrapper or *hun-t'un* skin (The Cantonese words for that sound like "One-Ton Pay.")

1 lb. ground pork chop

4 tb-sp. soy sauce

1 tb-sp. sesame oil or salad oil

½ t-sp. salt

12 cups water

½ t-sp. taste powder, unless stock is used for water

1 scallion chopped

Mix the meat with (only) 2 tb-sp. of the soy sauce, the oil, salt, and scallion. Put ½ t-sp. of the stuffing on the center of each skin. Gather and pinch lightly where it meets again after wrapping around the meat, leaving the edges to ramble freely.

Boil 6 cups of water over big fire and put the ramblings to boil for 1 min., counting from the second boiling.

Have 6 other cups of boiling water ready and put in 2 tb-sp. soy sauce and ½ t-sp. taste powder to make the receiving soup.

Take out the boiled ramblings with a leaking ladle and put into the soup. Serve in individual bowls.

20.5B. Cocktail *Hun-t'un*

1 lb. *hun-t'un* skin	½ t-sp. taste powder
1 lb. ground pork chop, not too lean	(monosodium glutamate)
	1 t-sp. salt
3 tb-sp. soy sauce	2 bunches spinach
1 t-sp. sugar	

[1] The same spoken word *hun²-t'un²*, written differently (this is *hun²-t'un*), means in fact the nebulous state of confusion when the world began.—Y. R. C.

Put spinach in boiling water and boil for 2 min., change to cold water, then squeeze out water. Chop into small pieces. Mix the soy sauce, salt, and sugar with the meat. After ½ hr., mix the spinach with the meat. This is the stuffing.

Into each piece of *hun-t'un* skin, put 1 t-sp. of the stuffing. Fold one end of skin over the opposite end and press lightly to close the skin all around the stuffing. Then join the other two ends in the reverse direction, with a dab of water to stick. This is a *hun-t'un* ready to fry. After having made enough of the uncooked *hun-t'un* for use, fry in deep oil (not too hot) until lightly brown on both sides, which should take about 5 min. If not to be used immediately, then put in warm oven. To warm over from cold, put in 300°F oven for 10 min.

If you live far from a Chinatown or a co-op where they sell *hun-t'un* skin ("One-Ton Pay"), buy a good supply and store in deep freeze, where it will keep for at least six months.

20.5C. Sweet-Sour Fried *Hun-t'un*

Same ingredients as Recipe No. 20.5B, but omit spinach and halve the salt to ¼ t-sp., also halve the size of stuffing in each *hun-t'un* to ½ t-sp., since no spinach is used. Fry and drain off oil as before.

To make the sweet and sour sauce, use:

2 tb-sp. soy sauce	2 tb-sp. vinegar
3 tb-sp. sugar	1 tb-sp. cornstarch

Mix cornstarch in 3 tb-sp. water. Boil rest of ingredients with another 3 tb-sp. water. Then pour in the cornstarch water and reboil until translucent, which will make a tasty dipping sauce, good either cold or hot.

20.6A. *Chiao-tzŭ* or Wraplings

Chiao-tzŭ means corner-things. It is like ravioli, but has two corners instead of four. The essential idea is a small round piece of dough wrapped around some stuffing so as to form a half-pie. Wraplings are usually cooked by boiling and are often the main food of a meal in the northern provinces. To make a meal of typical northern wrapling, use:

6 cups flour   3 cups water

Knead into even dough, using dusting flour on the kneading board to prevent sticking. Divide into 60 equal parts. This sounds harder than it is. Since it is much easier to judge length than volume, you make the dough into bars of about equal thickness and cut the total lengths into equal parts. Work each piece with your fingers into a lens-shaped or lentil-shaped cake, then roll it flat with a rolling pin to about 3½ inches in diameter by about ⅛ in. thick. This is the wraplet or wrapling skin.

Many kinds of stuffing are used in wraplings, though sweet stuffing is rather rare. In full-meal wraplings, the stuffing should not be too rich or too strongly flavored. Chopped meat and celery cabbage is the most typical stuffing. To match the amount of dough given above, use:

- 1½ lbs. pork, medium fatness or rather thin, ground medium fine
- 3 lbs. celery cabbage, ground through medium meat-grinder and *drained of juice*
- 6 tb-sp. soy sauce
- 1 tb-sp. salt
- 3 tb-sp. vegetable oil

Mix meat, vegetable, and seasoning to form a uniform stuffing.

Take one of the wraplings and make six folds on half of the circle so that it puckers up into a hollow on one side. Using a pair of chopsticks or the back of a spoon, put 2 t-sp. of the stuffing into the hollow. Fold the straight half of the wrapling over the puckered half and pinch so as to weld-seal the dough all along the edges. There is your wrapling ready to cook. (See Figure 7.) You can, if you like, hold a flat wrapling and put on the stuffing first, and then make the two kinds of folding process afterward, which is sometimes faster. A fancy job is to make an S-shaped edge by puckering up one quadrant, instead of half-circle, and reversing the straight and puckered sides for the remaining part. The edge is often dentilated, especially to indicate a different stuffing when different kinds are boiled in the same pot. When celery cabbage and Chinese leek are both used, the former is usually wrapped with the plain edge and the latter with dentilated edge. Children who

FIG. 7. A WRAPLING

make themselves useful in the kitchen by generally getting in your way usually make wraplings by just folding one edge over the other over the stuffing and wonder why it won't stand up.

To boil the wraplings, boil a gallon of water over big fire and put in all the wraplings after boiling starts. This will stop the boiling for a while. After boiling starts again, pour in 2 cups of cold water and turn to medium fire. After the third boiling, pour in 2 more cups of cold water. This process is known as dripping the water, which gives holding strength to the wraplings. The wraplings are to be taken out right after the third dripping. The whole boiling process takes about 10 min.

Serve dry with leaking ladles and serve the starchy soup in individual bowls. Some like to dip-eat the wraplings in vinegar, some in soy sauce, some just eat them plain. The soup is very good, especially if some of the wraplings got accidentally broken during boiling, as they often do. With wraplings as a full meal, no other dish is needed, although salted "little dishes" may be used as relish.

If you have any leftovers, you should separate them before putting them in the icebox. They are good when shallow-fried the next morning and eaten with tea or congee (Recipe No. 18.4).

Variations.—There are variations and variations, the former having to do with the wraplet and the latter with the stuffing. Variations in both ways come mostly from the fact that wraplings make meals in the North but light refreshments in the South. Thus, in

214

one style commonest in Kiangsu, in the region around Shanghai, hot-dough is used and the wraplings are steamed. The finished pastry looks shiny and slightly translucent instead of white and opaque and is more chewy. Southern style also has thinner wraplings and bigger stuffing, and shrimp-egg soy sauce is often used to enhance the flavor. In this region, wraplings are often served in the soup, sometimes with soy sauce added in the soup. Another variation is in the use of rice flour instead of wheat flour. This is common in Canton and in American-Chinese restaurants. Then they are called *fan-kwo*, "(rice) flour-fruit." On the use of eggs as the wrapling, see Recipe No. 16.2.

Variations in stuffing are many. In the northern provinces mutton wraplings are a favorite. Chopped scallion and ginger to "defish" the sheep make a fine flavor. In the South, straight meat stuffing is often preferred, since there is no objection to having it rich if it is not the chief thing to eat. Fennel leaf, good for coughing, often takes the place of celery cabbage. Very thin Chinese leek, *Allium odorum,* is specially liked by many and calls for fancy trimmings on each wrapling to mark it off from the plain ones.

20.6B. Pot Stickers or *Kuo-t'ier*

Pot Stickers, a favorite Northern food, are simply Wraplings grilled on a griller. The skins and the stuffing are made in the same way. As a variation, the skin may be made by rolling the dough into large sheets about $\frac{1}{16}$ inch thick, or thinner, and cutting out round pieces with a cookie cutter about 3½ inches in diameter. Then wrap in the stuffing as in Fig. 7. With a little stretching you form wraplings about ¾-in. wide by 4-in. long.

Preheat your electric griller to 350°F, with 2 tb-sp. salad oil over it. Lay the formed wraplings in close contact with each other, so that with a 9-by-14-in. griller you can grill about 30 pot stickers at one time. Grill for 5 min., with lid on. Open the lid and brush the tops with a wetted pastry brush and grill 5 min. more. Turn up temperature to 400°F for an additional 10 min. or until bottoms are brown and slightly crisp. Serve by transferring the pot stickers with a spatula. If it is desired to serve in the griller, turn off heat before the 10 min. is up, since the griller will retain the heat for a few minutes.

Though pot stickers are so called, they should not stick so hard to the bottom as to break when spaded up. If they do, more oil should have been used to start with. Instead of an electric griller, a large grilling pan over the kitchen fire will also do, in which case you will have to experiment with your stove to have the time and temperatures right.

Pot stickers are a typical Northern-style food and are found in some Northern Chinese restaurants in New York and San Francisco under the name of *kuo-t'ier*, which means literally "pot sticker." Leftovers can be regrilled, especially if underdone the first time.

20.6C. Hotdough Wraplings

Same ingredients as No. 20.6A, except that you (1) use very, very hot water to mix the dough, so that the result will be more chewy and velvety, and (2) instead of cabbage to go with the meat, use mushrooms (preferably the dried and developed kind), bamboo shoots, fresh small shrimps, to be ground with the meat.

Place wraplings on steaming tier (you can use the upper perforated partition of a steak grilling set, minus the dripping pan) and steam over brisk fire with lid closed for 15 min. In picking up the wraplings from the tier, be sure not to break the skins. Better lift with a pair of chopsticks, bite and suck, but don't burn your tongue!

This is a Southern refreshment, to eat for pleasure, whereas regular wraplings (20.6A) are a Northern food, to eat at regular meals, and therefore with less fancy condiments.

20.7. Spring Rolls

Spring Rolls are so called because they are eaten during the old-style New Year days, which are nearer springtime than the new-style New Year. They are not steamed raised rolls, but fried unraised stuffed rolls of very thin dough. The skin or wrapling is like that of Ramblings, except bigger. In China, it is made flying-thin from baking thin paste of a certain starch, which makes a crisper and lighter food than with flour. Here in Chinatown, it is the same sheet of wheat dough as for Rambling skins, only cut to 8 by 8 instead of 4 by 4 inches.

16 sheets of Spring Roll skin
1 lb. pork (chop) shreds (less commonly beef shreds)
½ lb. fresh shrimps chopped
3 scallions cut into shreds
1 lb. pea sprouts
2 tb-sp. soy sauce
1 t-sp. sugar
1 t-sp. salt
3 heaping tb-sp. lard
Enough vegetable oil for deep frying

Wash the pea sprouts.

Heat the lard in a skillet over big fire and stir-fry the meat shreds and the shrimps for 1 min. Add scallions and pea sprouts and stir for 2 more min., adding sauce, sugar and salt toward the end.

Take out and divide into 16 portions. Place each portion on a sheet of the Spring Roll skin and fold up slantwise like a Chinese package. (See Fig. 4, p. 95 for diagram and description.) Only do not tuck in the last corner. Just roll over and paste it on with a little water. The frying will make it stay put.

Heat the deep-frying oil over medium fire, turn to low if it has a tendency to smoke. Deep-fry the rolls for 6 min. Turn each so as to have each side immersed, since the upper side tends to float outside of the oil. The rolls are done when they are golden brown. They can be left warm in the oven before serving.

20.8. Fried Scallion Cakes

4 cups flour
2 cups water
1 bunch scallions, chopped fine

Knead the flour and water into a soft dough and then divide into 6 portions. Roll each portion with a rolling pin into a cake of about 1 foot in diameter. Spread

2 tb-sp. chopped scallion
1 tb-sp. lard or vegetable oil
¼ t-sp. salt

over each cake. Roll up each cake (as you would roll up a carpet)

215

and then twist into a standing spiral, like a fattened water-heater. With the rolling pin, flatten the spiral from top down into a cake of about ½ foot in diameter.

Melt 1 tb-sp. of lard or vegetable oil in a deep frying pan. Put in the cake, apply cover, and fry for 2 min. on each side over a medium fire. Turn to a low fire and fry for 3 more min. on each side (that is, 10 min. altogether for each cake) until the outside of the cake has turned light brown, while the inside is still soft. Cut each into six pieces as you do a pie and serve hot.

Fried scallion cake, when properly made, at once takes away that hungry feeling. Sometimes one cake with soup makes a good hearty meal. Millet congee, if you can get millet, is even better than soup.

20.9. Doilies (Wheat Tortillas)

"Doilies" is the name given by Americans in Peiping to the very thin wheat cakes which are usually eaten with the famous Peiping Roast Duck. Being baked from unraised dough, they are even more like doilies than American pancakes are. The Chinese name is *pao-ping* which simply means "thin cake." The use of doilies is by no means limited to Red-Cooked Duck. (See Chapter 9.) One often makes a meal out of doilies just like steamed bread or steamed rolls. There are certain dishes that commonly go with doilies, but I shall tell you how to make the doilies first.

To make the doilies properly, use:

> 3 cups flour
> 1½ cups water just under boiling hot
> 3 tb-sp. vegetable oil

Mix the hot water with the flour. This makes what we call hot-dough, which is more translucent and chewy after cooking than cold-dough. Divide the dough into 24 pieces. Make each into a flat cake about 2 inches in diameter. Wet one side of a cake with some of the vegetable oil. Lay another cake on top of it and roll the two together with a rolling pin so as to form a double doily of about

6 inches in diameter. Do the same with the other pieces, and you will have 12 double doilies.

Heat a heavy pancake pan (griddle) over low fire and bake each side of the doilies for 3 min. under cover, opening the lid of course when you turn it over. The done doilies should be piled on a hot plate and covered with a piece of cloth. Sometimes you can let the top doily act as the covering cloth. It is not bad manners to take from under the top doily if it is so understood at the table.

Three things usually go with doilies to make a complete meal, Pea Sprouts Stir Meat Shreds (Recipe No. 3.3), Stirred Eggs (Recipe No. 13.1), and plain congee (Recipe No. 18.4). Instead of rice congee, you can also substitute millet congee or Soup for the Gods (Recipe No. 15.0).

Serve the doilies and the dishes on the table, but the congee in individual bowls. The doilies may be eaten two together, but it is more elegant to take a single sheet at a time, and it is very easy to separate the double doilies in two on account of the layer of oil between them. Take some of the eggs and some of the meat shreds and pea sprouts and arrange them in a row in the center of the doily. Have the smooth wet inside face up if you use a single sheet. If you have not put too much stuff on the doily, you can now roll it up and fold up one end and bite at the other end length by length until you finish the whole doily with its juicy contents. With practice, this can be done gracefully without letting the juice trickle down your wrist.

A fairly acceptable substitute is wheat (not corn!) tortillas.

20.10. Egg Rolls

Egg Rolls are not an egg dish, but a kind of "dot-heart" pastry.

Same filling, prepared the same way, as in Spring Rolls (Recipe No. 20.7), except that the skin is made of eggs, as follows:

Beat 6 eggs with ⅔ cup flour and 1 cup water. Use a 10-inch pan, slightly greased, and make thin pancakes, heated on one side only.

Wrap and fry as with Spring Rolls, but cut up into shorter sections before serving, if desired. (We don't cut up Spring Rolls.)

CHAPTER 21

MEALS AND MENUS

Now that you have already learned how to cook in Chinese, it is easy to learn how to eat in Chinese. From the Introduction, you already know something about the meal systems in China. I shall now describe to you some typical meals in detail, and then conclude with some sample meals which you can fit in with eating conditions in this country. When a food used is already described in one of the recipes, I shall refer to it by number and name without further description.

21.1. Breakfasts.—In some provinces, such as Hunan, when breakfast is just another dinner, it need not be described specially. Breakfast as breakfast is cultivated much in the Canton region and the Shanghai region, which calls itself "the South," the place where the *North China Daily News* used to be published. The simplest light breakfast has congee (Recipe No. 18.4) as its main food served in individual bowls and the usual accompaniments are four small shallow dishes of minor dishes. A typical good menu consists of:

    (1) Salted Peanuts
    (2) 100-Year Preserved Duck's Eggs with Soy Sauce
    (3) Salted Radishes
    (4) Soy-Pickled Cucumbers

Since these are salty, only a very small amount of each is eaten with each bowl of congee. This is all that you get at a regulation breakfast at no extra charge in boarding places, hotels, etc. It can be quite filling for a while. Three bowls of hot congee gives you a feeling of full realization that the world is good. But in order to make this feeling last the rest of the morning, it is usually necessary to add more solid things at extra charge. Besides eggs in various forms, more or less hard, pastry is most commonly eaten to make a breakfast more solid. Stuffed Buns (Recipe No. 20.3) and Ramblings (Recipe No. 20.5) are very common. The only widely eaten baked food in China, the sesame-sprinkled hot biscuit, is a typical breakfast pastry, as is also the puffed doughnut.

A modification of the home breakfast is the tea house breakfast. There you start the day with tea, just plain green tea with nothing else. Then you order some pastry to eat with the tea, but very often you order soup foods, like noodles (Recipe Nos. 19.1 and 19.4) or ramblings (Recipe No. 20.5).

21.2. Refreshments.—Between-meal refreshments or teas or midnight snacks form one class of eating occasion where sweet things or pastry are often eaten. Noodles, fried or boiled, are also common. A refreshment is usually more casual and is often eaten away from the table, while a breakfast, though it may have nothing but congee and minor dishes, is eaten at the table. Plain congee and eggs are usually not eaten as a refreshment in this sense.

Because of the two-meal system in the Canton region, as we have noted in the Introduction, the midday tea and the midnight snack have grown into important meals, but they retain their informal character in excluding rice and dishes. No matter how much you eat—sometimes you eat more than at regular meals—the foods are less organized and consist of various forms of sweet things and pastry or noodles. At a noonday tea in a Cantonese restaurant, each guest is asked what kind of tea is desired, whether Dragon Well, or Chrysanthemum, or what. Then dishes of *tim-sam* (Cantonese for *tien-hsin*), each containing four pieces, are placed before you. You eat what you like and are charged for by the piece. Very often you top it off with some Stirred Noodles (Recipe No. 19.3), or, if you are in America, you can order *chow mein*. Soup Noodle (Recipe No. 19.1) is even a better finale, as we often like to end a tea with soup. (See Introduction.)

Seasoned congee or *chuk* is famous among Cantonese midnight snacks. If the waiter cannot understand *chuk* as you pronounce it, see if it is more intelligible if you say the word "joke" with a jerk, a sort of quick, high and clipped-off "joke." Into plain congee are put slices of ginger, Chinese parsley, salt, bits of squid, Chinese greens, and other colorful things. The famous variety known as *yü-shaang-chuk*, "fish-raw congee" uses raw fish slices instead of meat as the main thing. The congee is served boiling hot and the fish slices are put in to cook in your bowl. They are done in less than one minute of immersing. After the fish slices are cooked, you often drop a raw egg into the congee to enrich it when you break it around. A few drops of soy sauce after that and your supper is ready to sip.

I have so far described refreshments without giving any typical complete menus, since they do not have such clear structures but may be eaten in any way in any order in tea houses. At home you cannot, of course, make one or two of a lot of different things, and you usually snatch one snack at a time.

21.3. Regular Meals.—There is no difference between lunch and dinner or dinner and supper in most places. You just have noon-meal and evening-meal, or early meal and late meal. A typical meal consists of four meat-dishes, two vegetable dishes, one light soup, and dry boiled rice, serving eight. If there are fewer people, you decrease the amount rather than the variety. If there are more people, you may increase the variety to six or eight, but not many more except at a formal dinner. When you travel alone and order a Chinese meal on a train or in a hotel, a guest meal will consist of a meat dish, a vegetable dish, and a soup, plus the usual rice, but we consider that a very dull way of eating. As soon as you have two people eating together, we should like to have four dishes to make a square meal. As a menu for a typical family meal, one may have, say:

Red-cooked Meat with Turnips	(Recipe No. 1.3)
Stirred Shrimps	(Recipe No. 11.13)
Cabbage	(Recipe No. 14.2)
Cold-Mixed Cucumbers	(Recipe No. 14.15)
Bean Curd and Meat-Slice Soup	(Recipe No. 15.4)

There is no point in working out the menus from breakfast Sunday morning through supper Saturday night for a typical week. The chief idea is that you should aim at a balance between heavy and light dishes, between vegetables and non-vegetables, between fish and non-fish. As said in the Introduction, all dishes are served on the table at about the same time and you eat from any of them at any time throughout the meal. There are five dishes or bowls of food besides your individual rice. But there are no courses at a family meal.

A regular family meal has no dessert.

21.4. Informal Invitation Dinner.—When you just have a couple of friends to dine informally at home or at a restaurant for small eats, there is usually a wine-drinking first part before the dinner proper, when rice is served. The first part may be no more than a few small cold dishes, not unlike the *hors d'oeuvres* of American dinners, followed by big dishes, or it may start with a few medium-sized stir-fried dishes followed by less heavy dishes and rice to finish up. This sort of informal dinner has therefore at least two courses or stages. When there are stir-fried dishes, the best way to eat them is of course one course at a time, when each is at its best. Here are two examples of informal dinners:

A. First course of 4 hors d'oeuvres:

(1) Chinkiang Fresh Salted Pork	(Recipe No. 5.4)
(2) (Hand-Torn) Smoked Carp	(Recipe No. 10.12)
(3) Cold-Mixed Celery	(Recipe No. 14.10)
(4) Cold-Mixed Spinach with Dried Shrimps	(Recipe No. 14.4)

Main course of First-Rank Pot (Recipe No. 16.3) and the usual rice.

B. Stirred Shelled Shrimps	(Recipe No. 11.1)
Stirred Mushrooms	(Recipe No. 14.12)
Stirred Squids	(Recipe No. 12.5)
Red-Cooked Chicken	(Recipe No. 8.1)
Celery Cabbage and Lion's Head	(Recipe No. 4.3)
Ham and Winter Melon Soup	(Recipe No. 15.6)

In menu B, if wine is used, the first three dishes should be served in succession before the big dishes so as to prolong the drinking time and have the stir-fried things eaten at their best. If it is a no-wine dinner, all dishes may be served at the same time or at different times according to convenience.

21.5. Banquets.—A banquet or formal dinner must have so many dries, so many sweets, so many fries, so many meats. For if it is formal, it must have form. I now give you two examples of Chinese banquets from nuts to soup.

A. Elaborate Banquet. To serve 10-12.

Four Fruits:	Tangerines, grapes, pears, sliced lotus stems
Four Dries:	Melon seeds, peanuts, fried almonds, fried walnuts
Four Sweets:	Preserved *hai-t'ang* (midget crab apples); hawthorn jelly; preserved kumquats; candied green plums
Four Cold Cuts	100-year-old eggs in soy sauce Ham slices Pot-stewed duck, cold cut (Recipe No. 9.5) White-cut chicken (Recipe No. 8.18)

The 16 dishes should all be arranged on the table before the guests sit down. As soon as they do, the four dishes of fruits are taken away from them. They will have a chance at them later. Hence the dinner really starts with nuts, which is just to help out the conversation before real eating starts with the cold cuts.

Four Stir-fries served in succession:

Stirred Scallops	(Recipe No. 12.7)
Stirred Shelled Shrimps	(Recipe No. 11.1)
Pot-stewed Duck	(Recipe No. 9.5)
Chicken Globules Oyster Sauce	(Recipe No. 8.7)

Four Large Affairs:

  (1) Red-Cooked Shark's Fin   (Recipe No. 12.13)

As I told you, when this dish comes on the table, all the guests will say, "*Ai, T'ai fei-shih lê!*" "Oh, you shouldn't have put yourself to so much trouble!"

  (2) Bird's Nest Soup   (Recipe No. 15.17)
  (3) Sweet-Sour Fish   (Recipe No. 10.4)
  (4) Arhat's Fast   (Recipe No. 14.28)

Four *Tien-hsin:* two sweet and two salty:

Eight-Jewel Rice (Recipe No. 17.1)
Orange Gruel   (Recipe No. 17.6, less the *yüan-hsiao* part)
Soup Wraplings (Recipe No. 20.6, Var.)
Spring Rolls   (Recipe No. 20.7)

Four Heavies:

  (1) Sand-Pot Bean Curd   (Recipe No. 16.6)
  (2) Red-Cooked Shoulder   (Recipe No. 1.1)
  (3) Clear-Simmered Chicken   (Recipe No. 15.19)
  (4) Ham and Celery Cabbage Soup (Recipe No. 15.7)

Alternating with the four heavies, may come a Chrysanthemum Pot (Recipe No. 16.1), if it is in season, or some other pot. At this time, wine, often accompanied by games of finger-guessing, will be concluded and it is time to serve Rice (Recipe No. 18.1), sometimes also Fancy Rolls (Recipe No. 20.2). If you are not still hungry now, or if you do wish for something very light, rice congee (Recipe No. 18.4) or millet congee is served. But many like to end a dinner with 4 tb-sp. of clear soup.

It naturally takes experience to prepare such a dinner right, but it also takes much experience to eat such a dinner so as to get the most out of it.

One trick to remember. If you ever undertake to prepare such a dinner, be sure that all the quantities specified in the recipes should be reduced to one third.

B. Medium Grade Banquet. To serve 10-12.

Four Combination Cold Dishes. These are dishes which consist of two different halves:

(1) Cold (canned) Abalone Slices;
    Cold-Mixed Celery   (Recipe No. 14.10)
(2) Ham Slices;
    Cold-Mixed Cucumbers   (Recipe No. 14.15)
(3) White Cut Chicken;   (Recipe No. 8.18)
    Cold Radishes (Recipe No. 14.16, minus sugar & vinegar)
(4) Splashed Shrimps;   (Recipe No. 11.13)
    Cold-Mixed Spinach   (Recipe No. 14.4)

Four Hot Fries:

(1) *Fu-yung* Chicken Slices   (Recipe No. 8.9)
(2) Mushrooms Stir Meat Slices   (Recipe No. 2.2)
(3) Tile-piece Fish   (Recipe No. 10.5)
(4) Stirred Shelled Shrimps   (Recipe No. 11.1)

Four Heavies:

(1) Clear-Steamed Fish   (Recipe No. 10.2)
(2) Eight-Jewel Duck   (Recipe No. 9.4)
(3) Red-Cooked Lion's Head   (Recipe No. 4.3,
                                       Var.)
(4) Ham and Winter Melon Soup   (Recipe No. 15.6)

The Four Heavies may come on the table at the same time when wine stops and rice starts, or possibly the fish will come up first while some of the guests may still have to finish their finger guessing games, where the loser of two out of three plays has to dry his cup. In any case, the host will ask everyone to refill his cup and dry it while he tells the waiter with the bowls of rice just a minute, please.

At a Cantonese-style banquet, four rather simple but savory small dishes, such as salt-fish, stirred *kaai-laan* green, etc., are served instead of or in addition to the Four Heavies. They are good rice-senders-down when you have had enough of the heavy things.

21.6. Special Eating Parties.—There are a number of special eating parties in China, at which we chiefly eat just one thing and everything else is secondary. You can compare them with the New England Clambake or a Hawaiian *luau,* where you eat a whole hog roasted underground.

(a) Rinsed Lamb (Recipe No. 7.4) makes one of such special parties.

(b) The Huichou Pot (Recipe No. 16.5) is usually such a very large affair that you can eat little else if you have that, so that when you have a party with that pot, you just invite your friends to a Huichou Pot.

(c) Eating (Peiping) Roast Duck is another such occasion. There are a few small *hors d'oeuvres* or a few small hot fries, but the shiny Roast Duck served centrally in slices is the main thing you come out for. It is usually eaten with sweet (salty) flour jam and fresh scallion. The grain food is Doilies (Recipe No. 20.9), with which you wrap up the duck. At a certain stage, the frame of the duck is removed to make soup with celery cabbage and to make flavor for Steamed Eggs (Recipe No. 13.6).

(d) Eating Doilies as an occasion consists of Doilies with the usual Stirred Eggs and Pea Sprouts Stir Meat Shreds (Recipe Nos. 13.1 and 3.3) and millet congee.

(e) Wrapping Wraplings (Recipe No. 20.6) is so called because relatives or friends often co-operate in making the hundreds of wraplings necessary for making a full meal of them. Instead of saying: "I invite you to a picnic; bring your own lunch," we say: "I invite you to eating *chiao-tzŭ;* wrap your own wraplings." Actually we call the occasion either Wrapping Wraplings or Eating Wraplings, whether the guests help in the kitchen or not. The hostess usually protests when they offer to.

(f) Crab Parties are for many the favorite form of eating parties. Though often called Plain Boiled Crabs, they are really steamed rather than boiled. Each guest is served a dish of Chinkiang vinegar with minced ginger, with optional soy sauce. The steamed crabs are served whole and each guest eats them in great detail one by one, accompanied by wine or spirit. Six large crabs eaten in about sixty minutes form an average serving. Some restaurants give special tools, nutcrackers and hammers, etc., for eating crabs, but your teeth and fingers are the chief means of eating. The satisfaction you can get out of a meal of crabs depends upon how messy you are willing to get. You really must make a mess of it to make a meal of it.

According to old traditional Chinese medicine, the crab is one of those things which are supposed to have a "cold nature" and has to be supplemented by a cup of hot drink of brown sugar and ginger. Whatever the truth is, it certainly gives a nice contrasting taste after the crabs. Another popular theory is that crabs will crawl in your stomach, so that the more crabs you eat the hungrier you get. It is therefore customary to serve some light lunch or refreshments or even a full meal immediately after a crab party. Because no fat or starchy food is eaten with the crabs, the stomach with crabs in it does usually feel like having something more mealy to stay it. So a crab party usually turns out to be a sort of overgrown *hors d'oeuvres*.

(g) I must not leave the special eating parties without mentioning watermelon parties. As I told you before, we do not eat dessert, and fruit is not part of breakfast or any other meal. When we eat watermelon, we just eat watermelon. A family group or a few friends may gather of a summer afternoon and eat a couple of watermelons. You roll up your sleeves and wash your fingers. But if you forget to wash your fingers, you do it anyway as you eat.

21.7. American Style Meals.—I have been telling you how we do eat in China. Now how can you eat Chinese meals in America? To this question, two types of answers have been given. One common answer is found in certain conventionalized American-Chinese dishes, such as *chow mein* and what not, which Americans understand are what the Chinese eat and which the Chinese understand are what Americans like. They get firmly established as institutions or cultural types, very interesting to think of and often good to eat. The other answer also comes from American-Chinese restaurants. Because it is more difficult to change your ways of eating than the things to eat, Chinese dishes are served in the American way. The

most extreme case is the serving of frankly American meals in
Chinese restaurants, where sometimes the only thing Chinese about
it is the name of the restaurant, "Tom Lee's," or perhaps the motto
in the Chinese "Fortune Cake" dessert predicting "All men are
brothers." The kind of Chinese food that is most convenient for you
to order or to make yourself is a meal in American form with just
one main dish of Chinese cooking. This is in fact what I had in
mind when I wrote the recipes from Chapter 1 to Chapter 15, and
this is why the amounts of material given are for serving the dish
as the one main course for six persons. If you eat in pure Chinese
style, with several dishes at one meal, the quantities in all the recipes
should of course be reduced proportionately. Besides the main Chinese dish, you can have American food, such as apple pie and coffee,
which you find served even in Chinese restaurants in Chinatown
patronized chiefly by the Chinese.

The next step you may take in eating in Chinese may be to have
all food Chinese but served and eaten within the framework of an
American meal. In China, especially when there are foreign guests
not used to Chinese ways of eating, this is sometimes practiced and
is called "Chinese meal foreign eaten." Each guest is served individually and there is no common dish or dishes you eat directly
out of. A menu at such a meal may be something like this:

Bird's Nest Soup with Chicken Shreds	(Recipe No. 15.17)
Phoenix-Tail Fried Shrimps	(Recipe No. 11.6)
Pineapple Fish	(Recipe No. 10.6)
Paper-Wrapped Chicken	(Recipe No. 8.16)
Red-Cooked Egg Plant	(Recipe No. 14.21)
Eight-Jewel Duck	(Recipe No. 9.4)
Almond Junket	(Recipe No. 17.3)
Almond Cakes	
Dragon Well Green Tea	
Preserved Kumquats, Litchi Nuts, etc.	

So you start with soup, a succession of medium dishes and one
main dish, and the dessert and drink and nuts, thus reversing the
normal Chinese order, which is from nuts to soup.

There are several reasons why "Chinese meal foreign eaten" has never become popular in China. In the first place, stir-fried dishes get cold and have no pep when divided into small portions. Then you have no choice as to when to await, and when to avoid, and when you do get ready to attack, you are given only this portion and no more. Much food is wasted in this way. But the greatest difficulty is that you do not feel natural when you eat Chinese food in American. You feel you are missing something essential. You do not feel that you are eating a meal. It is not *ch'ih-fan*. Now when I say "you" I mean "we" of course. So far as *you* are concerned, I would recommend first concentrating on preparing one dish or so in your usual scheme of meals and then try occasionally community eating as a lark. When you know how to shovel rice or congee gracefully over the edge of your bowl and leave a clean bowl at the end of your meal, then you are doing better than even some American old-timers in China, and we will feel that you belong.

21.8. Buffet Parties.—As I cook more and more and as I entertain more and more, I am more and more convinced of the adaptability of Chinese food to "the American way of life." It might seem that the informality of a streamlined American buffet party would be quite contrary to the spirit of a 16-course Chinese banquet. It is. But then few Chinese have anything to do with 16-course banquets. In informal entertaining, when there are more guests than can be seated at one table, the same set of dishes are served in suitable portions to two or more square tables. If there are more guests, you need only have more tables and more quantity of the same dishes in the kitchen.

Now it is only a short step from this kind of a party to a buffet party. Instead of having the main supplies in the kitchen, you lay them on the "buffet" (actually your dining table, of course). Instead of being served pieces you do not want, you serve yourself with pieces you do.

For buffet menus, I would suggest two cold and two hot for 4-dish menus and three cold and three hot for 6-dish menus. For the hot dishes there should be one stir-fried and one slow-cooked dish, or if there are three hot dishes, either one plus two or two plus one.

As is the case with other forms of eating, the total color scheme is also something a thoughtful hostess wants to consider. With Chinese dishes, especially, it is easy to lapse into a general drabbish brown and one should remember to enliven the table with enough white, green, or red.

Sample menus for Chinese buffet parties:

A. Four-dish menu.

(1) Cold Mixed Spinach (dried shrimps optional)	(Recipe No. 14.4)
(2) Red-Cooked Chicken	(Recipe No. 8.1A)
(3) Celery Stirs Meat Shreds	(Recipe No. 3.1)
(4) Tea Eggs or Pot-Stewed Eggs	(Recipe No. 13.7 or 8.20 supplem.)

B. Six-dish menu.

(1) Red-Cooked Meat (in small pieces) with Yellow Turnips	(Recipe No. 1.3 or 6.3)
(2) Stirred Shelled Shrimps	(Recipe No. 11.1 A or B)
(3) Sweet Peppers Stir Meat Shreds (Use pork or beef according as first dish uses beef or pork.)	(Recipe No. 3.8)
(4) Cold Mixed Spinach (dried shrimps optional)	(Recipe No. 14.4)
(5) Sweet-Sour Cabbage	(Recipe No. 14.2C)
(6) Salt-Water Duck	(Recipe No. 9.8)

In both menus it is well to leave the stir-fried dishes until the guests have started their rounds. This, incidentally, solves one of the dilemmas I have often faced when I have to both cook and entertain. You must by now have noticed several places where I have insisted on the importance of prompt eating of stir-fried dishes. With the informality of comings and goings of hosts and guests around the buffet, the hostess can slip away and stir-fry a couple of dishes to catch the guests just finishing their first round or coming for the second round. Thus the stir-fried dishes will be shown at the best advantage, hot from the pan. The beauty of it is that your absence won't be so conspicuous, because while you are walking to and from the table, everybody else will also be walking to and from the table, all of which makes the party gay.

21.9. Cocktail Recipes.—Any savory, salty dish that is not too filling will go well with cocktails, as often mentioned in the various chapters. For convenient reference, here is a list of recipes which can be so used:

5.1, 5.3, 5.4, 5.11	11.6, 11.7, 11.13
6.1, 6.10, 6.17	13.7
7.2	14.12, 14.16
8.20, 8.25	20.5B
9.8	22.2, 22.4, 22.5
10.9, 10.11, 10.12	

In addition, pressed bean curd and 100-year-old eggs go particularly well with drink. They are not in the recipes, as they can be bought ready to eat from the Chinese stores. The 100-year-old eggs—actually they "ripen" in 100 days—are good with some diced ginger and soy sauce.

Light as most of these goodies are, Recipes Nos. 6.17, Beef Emit-Silk (on toast), and 20.5B, Fried One-Ton, do offer some staying power, if you have to miss dinner to catch a Chinese opera or a concert. In that case, come back for a midnight congee.

CHAPTER 22

SOYBEAN FOODS

The soybean is the most versatile of all Chinese food materials, perhaps of all food materials. I have often referred to soy(bean) sauce and bean curd in the preceding recipes. Now I must take up the soybean more fully. I shall however not describe the manufacturing of the soy sauce, as it has to be done on a factory scale and it is generally available anyway.

Under various disguises the soybean is used in vegetarian restaurants, often under Buddhist auspices, to produce sumptuous dinners, featuring "sliced chicken breast," "roast duck," "baked ham," that not only fool the eye, but also the tongue, almost. But, as always, I want to concentrate on the important, everyday things and de-emphasize the fancy and elaborate. Dishes with bean curd are cheap and easy to prepare. Those who can afford fancy dishes can combine it with meat, etc., but just plain cabbage and bean curd connotes home sweet home.

The soybean is sometimes used whole, but mostly used in crushed form, from which come bean curd and soybean milk. In China, in Japan, in American Chinatowns, and nowadays in some co-ops, bean curd is made on a large scale and people buy it in stores instead of making it themselves and the milk is usually obtainable in health-food stores. With the advent of the electric blender as a common household gadget, grinding soybeans is no longer an adventure and it is now possible and worthwhile to make your own fresh bean curd for the small family that tastes better and costs next to nothing. For gypsum powder (calcium sulphate), you may have to go to a druggist or chemical supplies store, as the general markets do not carry it. The work involved will be most rewarding, even if you do have access to stores where bean curd is sold.

Equipment Needed.—(1) Electric blender. (2) Form for setting, for which you can fashion a thin, wooden box to hold about 5 quarts, with perforated bottom and a loosely fitting cover, so that it will sink into the box under slight pressure. (3) Large piece of coarse cotton, not smaller than 2 x 2 ft. square. (4) Several pieces of thin cotton or muslin to line the form.

Ingredients.—

> 2 lbs. dry soybeans
> 5 qts. water
> 2 tb-sp. gypsum

Grinding and Straining.—Wash and soak beans in lukewarm water overnight, using enough water for the beans to expand and still stay immersed. Drain water and rinse beans. Blend about 1 cup of beans to 2 cups of water at a time, *or less if motor tends to slow down or get stuck!* Blend for 5 min. Pour the puree into a large pot and repeat process until all the beans are used up. If any of the 5 quarts of water remains, add it to the pot.

Strain the puree over a large bowl through the 2 x 2-ft. cloth by gathering the edges well in one hand and squeeze the bulge with the other. This can be done more easily by dividing the puree in two installments, or having two people, one to hold the edges and one to squeeze. The operation is done when the residue reaches a pasty consistency or when the operators are tired. For those indefatigable souls who wish to extract as much as possible, they can pour another quart of water into the pasty residue, mix well and squeeze *that* through the cloth again. The liquid is Bean Milk, the residue is Bean Lees. Both are good.

Heating and Setting.—Bring to a boil ⅘ of the bean milk, stirring to prevent burning. Remove from fire and mix in the remaining ⅕. After about 5 min., the liquid will be at about the right temperature for setting. It is not critical, but has to be about right or it won't set.

Dissolve the gypsum in 1 cup of water, straining out any coarse impurities. Pour solution into the bean milk and stir well, then let stand to set, which will take about 20 min. Sprinkle a few drops of water over the top. If they do not sink, but remain as puddles on top, then the bean has curded into bean curd—almost.

Forming.–Line the wooden box with the thick cloth or muslin, making it good and flat over all the five surfaces and leave enough edges to flap over the top. Fill this with the now clotty near-curd and fold the edges of the cloth over. Place the lid on top with some weights (such as glasses of water). Since the lid fits very loosely and the bottom is perforated, the weight will force out the water and compress the material to a firmer state. The process may be hastened by pressing on the top with your hands for the first four or five minutes. After 30 min., more or less, depending upon whether you want it firm or soft, the bean curd is formed. Lift out whole thing gently by the edges of the cloth. Cut into convenient pieces and store on refrigeration, in enough clear water to cover, until ready to cook. Don't panic if you lift it out too soon and everything falls to pieces. Just dump the whole thing back into the form and press again. When it is finally formed, nobody will see or taste any difference.

Bean Curd Recipes.–Dishes with bean curd have already been described in Recipes Nos. 14.29 through 14.36. Following are recipes for some special soybean foods.

22.1. Soybean Milk

For making soybean milk to use as such, vary the preceding procedure as follows:

(1) Proportion of beans to water should be:

1 lb. soybeans   4 qts. water

(2) Blend for 3 min. (instead of 5 min.).
(3) Heat the whole liquid (instead of part of it).

The remaining procedure, the soaking and the squeezing, is the same as for making bean curd.

The resulting concentrate is to be diluted 3 to 1 before use. The Chinese like it hot, with a little sugar added. Other flavors may be added if you like, but it will mask the fine flavor of the bean. Some take off the skinny top formed on boiling because it is fat. Others,

HOW TO COOK AND EAT IN CHINESE

especially children, fight for it. But there is not much fat in it and
it is not animal fat anyway.

22.2. Soybean Lees

When you grind something for the juice, the leftovers to be thrown
away are the dregs and the leftovers you want to keep are the lees.
When you grind and strain soybeans to make soybean milk, the leftovers are lees, because they are good. For the best lees, grind 3 min.
(instead of 5 min.).

lees from 2 lbs. soybeans	1 t-sp. taste powder
2 cups soy sauce	16 tb-sp. salad oil
2 tb-sp. sugar	

Divide proportionally all ingredients into two or three portions if
your pan is not large enough. Heat the oil over moderate fire and
stir in the lees, followed by the seasoning, for 4 or 5 min. When the
whole amount has been stirred in, put in a baking pan and bake
for 4 hrs. at 250°F, turning it over every half hour or so, breaking
up the large clots, if any. It is done when dry and loose, but overdone
if brittle and hard.

Bean lees are good to make sandwiches, to go with congee (thin
rice), oatmeal, or with cocktails.

22.3. Frozen Bean Curd

Frozen bean curd is a favorite food in China because it not only
tastes better, but also has an interesting texture. The reason is that
when bean curd is frozen and thawed out it becomes porous, so that
juice gets into, instead of just around, the bean curd. Before the
days of the deep freeze, you had to wait for winter to freeze bean
curd. Now you just put it in the freezing compartment and the next
morning you can thaw it out, with hot water if you are in a hurry,
to make whatever you do with ordinary bean curd in Recipes
Nos. 14.29, 14.30, 14.33 or such basic red-cooking recipes as No. 1.2
Red-Cooked Meat and No. 10.1 Red-Cooked Fish.

22.4. Soy Sauce Beans

This is soybeans baked in soy sauce, but don't call it "baked beans," since it does not mean that at all. Use:

1 lb. soybeans	2 tb-sp. sugar
8 tb-sp. soy sauce (sic!)	5 cups water

Soak beans in lukewarm water overnight and pour off water. Then boil the beans with the sauce, sugar, and 5 cups of (cold) water over brisk fire. When it boils, turn down to smallest simmering fire (avoiding draft that might blow it out!) and boil 3 hrs., turning over a little every ½ hr. until all juice is absorbed. (Add ½ cup hot water if it dries before end of 3 hrs.)

Transfer contents to baking tray and bake at 250°F low fire, turning over every ½ hr. For eating now, bake 1 hr.; for keeping longer, bake 1½ hrs. and put in airtight jar, which will make a nice gift. If you go to a tea, picnic, or cocktail party with it, the hostess may take out some of it and share it back with you.

Variation.—A little after halfway during the boiling, add in (canned) bamboo shoots (since you can't get them fresh here), cut into slices and proceed as before, whence the Chinese name *sun-tour*, "bambooshoot beans."

22.5. Preserved Soybeans

Preserved soybeans are made in winter, when meat and other preserves are made, hence the name. Take:

2 lbs. soybeans	optional:
8 tb-sp. salt	4 t-sp. hot chili powder or
15 slices ginger, or 2 t-sp. ginger powder	1 small bag hot red pepper

Wash beans, change to lukewarm water and soak overnight. The water should be about twice the depth to allow for expansion. Next morning change to cold water, again to twice the depth of beans, and bring to boil over brisk fire, watching so as not to spill the beans or the water. Simmer for 4 hrs.

Drain off juice and keep on refrigeration for later use. Prepare a large paper box and line it with plenty of excelsior (straw is used in China). Put the cooked beans in a cloth bag and place it in the excelsior in the box and place the box in the warmest place in the house for 24 hrs. or more until beans become sticky. Top of a radiator (with insulating piece) or near, but not over, a hot-air vent will be good.

Dice the ginger and break the hot pepper, if used, in two. Take out the beans from the bag and mix with the seasoning and leave for 6 hrs. Mix the now seasoned beans with the original bean juice and divide in several medium-small jars, say, pint size, and keep in the cooler for 5 days. Now you can eat them raw, since they are already cooked, or lightly shallow-fry them, which will make them keep longer.

This is a rich tasting relish for tea or cocktails or a garnish for other dishes like meat slices, etc. The Chinese miss this food when they come to America and you will surprise them by having it.

CHAPTER 23

CHINESE DIET AS DIET

I have often said that the Chinese don't need to diet, because the Chinese diet is practically already diet. The Chinese eat more vegetables than animal food. Of vegetable foods more greens and less starchy things are used than in America. And of course sweets do not form a regular part of meals and some Chinese rarely eat sweets anyway. As for fats, they are more important as a medium for cooking than as eating material and the excess fat in dishes is usually removed when it has served its function as heater, binder, etc. This is true of meats and poultry cooked in their own fat as well as of deep-frying and stir-frying things. Thus, without conscious planning, perhaps out of centuries of dietary experience, eating in Chinese naturally has a relatively small intake of calories and a correspondingly larger proportion of minerals, vitamins, and bulk. If the average amount of animal protein tends to be low, it is made up partly by the wide use of soybean foods, as we have just described in the preceding chapter. Theorizing apart, it has been my own experience that whenever I am on a straight American diet, as when I travel, I gain weight, while if I eat at home, with one American meal and two Chinese meals a day, I drop back to normal, and this has happened to me time and again.

"Diet and like it," I might almost say, as a slogan for promoting Chinese cooking. But speaking seriously, as a physician, I must say that specific and sometimes very strict regimes may be necessary for persons with such special conditions as will require medical supervision. On the other hand, with many people who take to reducing as a fad or for hypochondriac reasons, it were far better for them to eat a varied diet in moderation and be physically active, which is what I do when I am at home. Calories do count, but it is not the only thing that counts in health.

228i

In the following pages I shall: (I) first go over some general methods by which Chinese foods usually are or can be prepared as "health foods"; then (II) make specific applications to the recipes in the preceding chapters; and finally (III) present some new recipes which are not only interesting diet dishes, but interesting dishes period, exclamation.

I. COOKING FROM A DIETETIC POINT OF VIEW

A. Stir-Fried Dishes.—The virtue of stir-frying lies mainly in its quick, high-temperature cooking, which leaves taste and color fresh and the nourishment least affected. The oil itself lends a little texture, but is not an important part of the food as such. Therefore "it isn't done" in Chinese eating to pour the oily juice on the rice—unless one is really so poor as to need the grease.

B. Salads.—Chinese salads usually have a little sprinkling of sesame oil to lend flavor (the Chinese variety has more flavor than the Italian), and used much more sparingly than salad oil is used in American salads. Salad dressing, too, is never used on rice.

C. Boiled Dishes.—In the boiled dishes, as described in the recipes, no oil is added, and flavor is sometimes enhanced by adding various forms of dried plants, dried shrimps, dried scallops, etc. If chicken, pork, ham, etc. or their bones are long-boiled for soup, the little fat that comes off them may be removed. When very clear soup is called for, excess fat may be removed by pulling a sheet of absorbent paper over the top when the soup is still warm.

D. Red-Cooked Dishes.—Red-cooked poultry and meats tend to be fat, as the juice is more concentrated. To remove excessive fat, boil the main piece with all seasonings until half-done. Put on refrigeration to get fat to congeal on the top. Remove the now tangible fat and finish the cooking. If any vegetable such as celery cabbage, carrots, turnips, etc. are to be cooked together, they should be added *after* the excess fat has been removed.

E. Dishes with Vegetable Oils.—While research workers are still writing and rewriting their last chapter on the subject of vegetable versus animal fat, those who wish to play safe can substitute cotton, corn, or safflower oil for lard. Peanut oil and oil from the seeds of some Chinese greens, such as certain varieties of *bock choy*, tend to smoke in stir-frying, and certain coagulating oils such as Crisco are not suitable for most Chinese dishes. I find that in most of my recipes where lard is called for, vegetable oil will taste just as good.

F. Salt in Chinese Diet.—Although sugar is used sparingly in Chinese cooking, salt is often used liberally in the so-called small dishes or relishes. Because cooked dishes form the main bulk of American meals and rice is only a side dish, I have already reduced the amount of salting in all the recipes from the usual amount for Chinese, who normally eat rice as the main dish and other cooked dishes as side dishes, so to speak (see p. 23). For those whose condition will require specially low sodium intake, the amount of salt and/or soy sauce should of course be further reduced.

II. APPLICATIONS TO RECIPES

Applying now the general methods just described, let us see what we can do with the recipes in the preceding chapters. The paragraphs below are numbered by the chapters to which they refer.

1–8. Red-Cooked Meats and Chicken.—As described above, fats can be removed by cooling the cooked meats, etc. and taking off the frozen fat or, for small amounts floating on top of soups, by pulling over the top a piece of absorbent paper. For meat and chicken recipes which call for frying in oil, change it to boiling in water over brisk fire for 5 min. This applies to Recipes Nos. 1.2; 5.2, 5.3, 5.6; 6.1, 6.2; 7.1, 7.2; 8.1, and 8.2. It goes without saying that if as much fat as possible is removed while cutting the raw materials, it will simplify matters.

9. Ducks.—Recipes Nos. 9.1 and 9.8 can be treated as with meats and chicken, except that being fatter, ducks should be placed in the refrigerator to get the fat well frozen. Since we often put in vegetables to be boiled with ducks, don't forget to take out the fat *before* putting in the vegetables.

10. Fish.—For fish recipes calling for pre-frying, such as Nos. 10.1, 10.4, and 10.6, the frying can be changed to quick boiling for

10, 15, or 20 min., depending upon the size of the fish or the pieces, in which case there is of course no need to rub flour over the fish. Some of the recipes, e.g. Nos. 10.2 and 10.3, already call for steaming, but omit the net-fat around the shad in No. 10.2 and omit the lard in No. 10.3. In No. 10.11 change frying to boiling, which some like even better. In all cases add 50 per cent more cooking wine as originally called for to strengthen the defishing. Fish dishes without frying should be eaten as soon as done.

13. Eggs.–In Recipes Nos. 13.3 and 13.6 the ground meat should be either very lean or, in the case of No. 13.6, some people prefer it without meat.[1] Recipe No. 13.4, Thin-Flowing Eggs, is of course good only with a lot of fat and so cannot be made into a good low-calorie dish. Recipe No. 13.7, Tea Eggs, on the other hand, is what we call "light," as eggs go.

14. Vegetables.–In the stirred vegetables, vegetable oil can be used instead of lard, as called for in Recipes Nos. 14.1, 14.3, and 14.5. In the other recipes vegetable oil has already been specified or given as an alternative to lard. Remember that the use of oil with vegetables is for quick cooking to preserve the freshness of color and nutriment. You are not supposed to pour oily juice over your rice, unless times are so hard, as they sometimes are, that you actually need the calories. On boiling instead of stir-frying vegetables, see Recipes Nos. 23.3A & B.

15. Soups.–Of the "Simple Soups" in Chapter 15, Recipes Nos. 15.0, 15.8, 15.9, 15.11, 15.12, 15.13, and 15.16 have little or no fat anyway. In the meat-slice and ham soups, Nos. 15.1–5, 15.6, 15.14, and 15.15, the meat slices can be cut lean before cooking, but the ham should be cooked with the fat, to be removed afterwards, as with the big soups.

For the "Big Soups," Recipes Nos. 15.17–20, which are themselves main dishes, they should be cooked and refrigerated before adding vegetable garnishes. After removing the fat, then put in whatever vegetable is called for and cook again. For removing fat completely, see above about use of absorbent paper.

[1] I always object to having odds and ends in my custard.–Y. R. C.

III. SPECIAL RECIPES

Here are some new recipes and special modifications of old recipes other than simple omission of fat.

23.1. Plunging Recipes

Plunging quickly into boiling soup is easier than frying or stir-frying and is of course less greasy, and the quick cooking preserves the taste. Green vegetables such as spinach and watercress can also be added for balance of taste and color as well as nutrition.

23.1A. Plunged Shrimp Cakes

1 lb. fresh shrimps	2 more tb-sp. water
2 eggs	½ t-sp. salt
4 tb-sp. cooking wine	1 t-sp. sugar
or equiv. sherry	1 tb-sp. cornstarch
4 tb-sp. water	2 scallions cut fine

Shell and clean the shrimps. Divide the left-hand column of ingredients (shrimps, eggs, wine and water) approximately in halves and blend each half in blender for 2 min. Combine the halves, add the rest of the ingredients (water, salt, sugar, cornstarch, and scallion) and mix together by hand. Boil 5 cups of water and plunge in one by one the shrimp cakes formed by scooping from the mixture with a round tablespoon. To prevent sticking, the spoon should be dipped momentarily into the boiling water before scooping the shrimp. When the cakes float to the top, turn to low fire and they are done in two minutes. If ½ lb. of pork is mixed with the shrimp, the boiling time should be a couple of minutes longer.

23.1B. Shrimp Cakes Soup

Make plunged shrimp cakes as above, but boil 3 min. longer. In addition, put in the water:

1 tb-sp. soy sauce	½ t-sp. taste powder
1 t-sp. salt	

23.1C. Plunged Fish Cakes

This is really a variation of Recipe No. 10.10, Soup Fish Cakes, which was for fresh-water fish, with a lot of small bones that needed a lot of scraping and fussing. In the present recipe we use sea fish, such as rock cod, sea bass, sole, or butterfish and since these do not have many small bones, their flesh can be put through the blender as with shrimp. Otherwise proceed as in Recipe No. 10.10.

23.2. Meeting Recipes

The meeting of one thing with another has been described in some recipes as in Nos. 6.9, 12.1, and 12.12, which need a certain amount of oil to be good. Here we shall consider a form of meeting consisting of first plunging and then, instead of serving with liquid, meeting the sauces or garnishes with the main ingredient out of the soup.

23.2A. Meeting Shrimp Cakes or Fish Cakes

Plunge shrimp cakes or fish cakes as in No. 23.1B or C. Take out when done. Put 1 t-sp. cornstarch and 1 tb-sp. soy sauce in 1 cup of the original water and mix into a translucent sauce, to pour over the cakes, adding canned small mushrooms for garnish, if desired.

23.2B. Sweet-Sour Shrimp or Fish Cakes

Plunge the shrimp or fish cakes as in Recipe No. 23.1A or C. Make sauce as below:

3 or 4 tb-sp. sugar	1 tb-sp. cornstarch
2 tb-sp. vinegar	10 tb-sp. water
2 tb-sp. soy sauce	1 scallion cut fine

Boil the sugar, vinegar, soy sauce and half of the water. Then mix the cornstarch with the rest of the water and add in the boiling sauce, throwing in the scallion last, and the sauce will be ready to pour over the shrimp or fish cakes.

As a variation, garnish with canned small mushrooms, litchi, or longan, or with fresh sweet pepper, strawberries, peaches, pears, etc., which will add to both taste and color. Except for strawberries, garnish should be put in the boiling sauce for a brief moment. If canned fruit is used, a cup of the juice may be used to substitute for 1 cup of water and 3 tb-sp. of sugar.

23.3A. Boiled Vegetables

1 lb. cabbage, bock choy, celery   ½ t-sp. salt
   cabbage, or *kaai-ts'oi*   2 cups water

Cut vegetable into 1-in. pieces and put in the water and salt. Bring to a quick boil and simmer until juice is neither too much nor dried up. Cabbage or bock choy takes about 20 min. and celery cabbage or *kaai-ts'oi* about 15 min. Because *kaai-ts'oi* is slightly bitter, add 1 t-sp. sugar, unless you like the bitterness, as some do. If you prefer the vegetable soft, simmer longer, with closed lid.

23.3B. Sweet-Sour Vegetables

For this, use cabbage or celery cabbage. Boil, with salt as in 23.3A, but for only 10 min. When it is nearly done, mix and add:

2 tb-sp. sugar   2 tb-sp. vinegar
1 tb-sp. soy sauce   1 tb-sp. cornstarch

and it is done when the juice is translucent.

23.4. Foil-Wrapped Recipes

In Recipe No. 8.16 I described the Paper-Wrapped Chicken. Now, instead of wrapping in paper and frying in oil, you get just as good results, or even better, by using aluminum foil and baking in the oven. With this method, you can use beef, lamb, pork, as well as chicken. Foil-wrapped foods, if not baked right away, can be kept in deep freeze, in which case increase baking time by 2 min.

23.4A. Foil-Wrapped Beef

For beef, use tenderloin, rump steak, or chuck roast. Following recipe is in terms of seasonings per lb.

1 lb. beef   1 tb-sp. cooking wine
1 t-sp. sugar   1 tb-sp. cornstarch
3 tb-sp. soy sauce or   2 scallions
1 tb-sp. soy sauce plus   enough coriander leaves for 2 or
1 hpg tb-sp. *hoisin* sauce   3 leaves in each package

Cut beef against the grain into ⅛-in. slices or thinner. Cut scallions into 1-in. sections, halving the bulbs if too thick. Mix all seasonings and divide evenly the meat and seasonings and scallions and coriander and spread on squares of aluminum foil. The meat should be only one layer thick. Since, however, thin meat slices tend to curl, one layer is really equivalent to more than one thickness of the meat. With foil-wrapping, it is not necessary to make many small packets. A convenient size will be 12-in. squares. Usually 4 to 6 packages can be made out of 1 lb. of meat and served individually. Wrap as you do with Paper-Wrapped Chicken (see Fig. 4, p. 95). Be sure to have the seams right side up all the time, so that the juice won't come out. An alternative is to use a pie dish for bottom and foil only for the top, but all-foil wrapping gives evener heating contact.

Preheat oven to 450°F. Warn your guests that the pièces de résistance are coming in six minutes, for that is the exact length of time the meat has to be in the oven to come out just right. The packages, still right side up, I hope, should be opened at the table and both the meat and all the juice can be poured over your bowl of rice, or eaten as is—it's hot!

As variations, use lamb or pork, the latter to be baked 2 min. longer.

23.4B. Foil-Wrapped Chicken

The best parts to use are breast and upper leg. Note that the baking time of 6 min. is longer than the frying time for paper.

In all these recipes, the texture will be neither like roast, nor like fried, neither like boiled, nor like baked. In fact it does not taste like something that has come out of the oven.[1]

[1] You mean out of this world!—Y. R. C.

NOTE ON TEA

Tea[1] is the most common form of beverage in China. Anyone who can afford it—and tea is cheap if you do not insist on quality—drinks tea instead of water. You offer tea, plain, whenever a caller comes to the house or even to your office. Business or government offices usually have a constant supply of hot tea just like drinking fountains in American offices. An institution which unfortunately is slowly being crowded out by modern life is the tea house, where people gather to chat, to discuss business, to settle disputes,[2] to listen to dramatic storytellers, or, as the greatest of Chinese pastimes, just to kill time. You can get difficult-to-eat things, like melon seeds, or thirst-producing things, like salted peanuts, to make you want to drink more and more of the tea as the waiter makes his round to pour more and more water onto the same leaves. In general, we do not serve tea at meals. We drink tea so much of the time that we have to give it a rest two or three times a day.

There are two main varieties of tea, green tea and black tea (called "red tea" in Chinese). The two do not come from different varieties of the tea plant, but are the results of different methods of preparation of the leaves. Green tea is made from quicker drying and fewer stages of handling, such as rolling and fermenting, than black tea. Because green tea looks and tastes nearer the original

[1] The word tea was borrowed from the Chinese, originally pronounced *da* or *dya*. In modern Mandarin it is pronounced *ch'a*, with a rising pitch. When you order tea in an American restaurant, where Cantonese is spoken, you have to use a low falling pitch in saying *ch'a*. A wrong intonation on *ch'a* will make the waiter think you can't use chopsticks and want a fork.—Y. R. C.

[2] The phrase *shang ch'a-kua'r* ("go to the tea house") has in addition to the literal meaning, the special sense of "having a dispute arbitrated at a tea house."—Y. R. C.

229

condition of the plant, only good and tender leaves are generally used for making green tea. Hence the popular idea that green tea is superior to the black. As a matter of fact, the best black tea, such as that of Keemun or of P'u-êrh of Yunnan or *t'ieh-kuan-yin* of Fukien, is just as good as the best green tea or better.

The simplest way to make tea is the best. Just pour boiling hot water over the leaves, and you have tea. After drinking the tea, leaving a small residue, you can pour in more boiling water to make a second or third infusion. It is probably news to most Americans that with good China tea, the second infusion is sometimes better than the first for green tea, and always better for black tea. When you order tea in American restaurants, you probably drink a full portion of the coloring matter and some tea, while the best part of the tea is thrown away. The very fastidious tea drinkers in China often throw away a quick first infusion and only drink the second.

Tea may be made in cups or pots. At parties and in the tea houses, each person usually has an individual covered cup, with leaves in each cup. The cover serves to keep the leaves from your lips as you drink the tea. For making the black tea of P'u-êrh or the *t'ieh-kuan-yin* ("The Iron Avalokiteçvara") of Fukien, actual boiling for a few seconds will help. Except in restaurants which have been under the Western influence, Fukien and eastern Kwangtung are the only places where tea comes to the dinner table. It is served very strong in small wine cups, just like wine. In offices and some homes, the teapot is kept warm in wadded mufflers (with just the nozzle showing) or over a slow-glowing ball of charcoal dust, buried in ashes, placed under the pot. In my school days, to pour myself a cup of this nice-tasting black tea was considered sufficient excuse for leaving my desk.

In normal times, it is easy to get tea from any part of China. Green tea from Lungching ("Dragon Well" of Hangchow) is so well known that the name gets loosely used to mean any high-grade green tea. The green tea of southern Anhwei is among the best in China, but the black tea of Keemun, of the same region, overshadows the green tea, since it forms a large bulk of the China tea which is used in this country.

230

Like the black tea from India, Ceylon, Java, or Sumatra, which forms the greater part of the tea Americans drink, Keemun tea can be used successfully with sugar and lemon or cream. But it is just as good when taken straight. For my part, the best tea is tea. It is only tea lacking in self-confidence that has to be made to seem good through borrowed fragrance. Thus jasmine tea of Peiping seldoms fails to please, though connoisseurs enjoy it with disdain. Litchi tea, with its faintly sweet flavor, is a good starter for Americans to take tea the Chinese way, without sugar, and is widely served in American Chinese restaurants.

I shall not mention any quantities in connection with tea-making, as it can vary a great deal. Suffice it to say that in the Chinese way, do not use so much tea (leaves), make the water hotter (by having your cup or pot hot beforehand), steep it longer, and no sugar or lemon, please. If you insist, here is

Recipe T.

1 t-sp. tea $\pm$ any desired amount
1 cup boiling water

Pour water over tea.

Leftovers, steeped in more hot water, are often better than the original.

INDEX

NOTE: Numbers in parentheses are the recipe numbers.

INDEX

INDEX

INDEX

242

INDEX

248

CPSIA information can be obtained
at www.ICGtesting.com
Printed in the USA
BVHW091753150722
642228BV00003B/111